Revelatory
AI
Self-Driving Cars

Practical Advances in
Artificial Intelligence and Machine Learning

Dr. Lance B. Eliot, MBA, PhD

Disclaimer: This book is presented solely for educational and entertainment purposes. The author and publisher are not offering it as legal, accounting, or other professional services advice. The author and publisher make no representations or warranties of any kind and assume no liabilities of any kind with respect to the accuracy or completeness of the contents and specifically disclaim any implied warranties of merchantability or fitness of use for a particular purpose. Neither the author nor the publisher shall be held liable or responsible to any person or entity with respect to any loss or incidental or consequential damages caused, or alleged to have been caused, directly or indirectly, by the information or programs contained herein. Every company is different and the advice and strategies contained herein may not be suitable for your situation.

DEDICATION

To my incredible daughter, Lauren, and my incredible son, Michael.

Forest fortuna adiuvat (from the Latin; good fortune favors the brave).

CONTENTS

i

ACKNOWLEDGMENTS

I have been the beneficiary of advice and counsel by many friends, colleagues, family, investors, and many others. I want to thank everyone that has aided me throughout my career. I write from the heart and the head, having experienced first-hand what it means to have others around you that support you during the good times and the tough times.

To Warren Bennis, one of my doctoral advisors and ultimately a colleague, I offer my deepest thanks and appreciation, especially for his calm and insightful wisdom and support.

To Mark Stevens and his generous efforts toward funding and supporting the USC Stevens Center for Innovation.

To Lloyd Greif and the USC Lloyd Greif Center for Entrepreneurial Studies for their ongoing encouragement of founders and entrepreneurs.

To Peter Drucker, William Wang, Aaron Levie, Peter Kim, Jon Kraft, Cindy Crawford, Jenny Ming, Steve Milligan, Chis Underwood, Frank Gehry, Buzz Aldrin, Steve Forbes, Bill Thompson, Dave Dillon, Alan Fuerstman, Larry Ellison, Jim Sinegal, John Sperling, Mark Stevenson, Anand Nallathambi, Thomas Barrack, Jr., and many other innovators and leaders that I have met and gained mightily from doing so.

Thanks to Ed Trainor, Kevin Anderson, James Hickey, Wendell Jones, Ken Harris, DuWayne Peterson, Mike Brown, Jim Thornton, Abhi Beniwal, Al Biland, John Nomura, Eliot Weinman, John Desmond, and many others for their unwavering support during my career.

And most of all thanks as always to Lauren and Michael, for their ongoing support and for having seen me writing and heard much of this material during the many months involved in writing it. To their patience and willingness to listen.

Dr. Lance B. Eliot

INTRODUCTION

This is a book that provides the newest innovations and the latest Artificial Intelligence (AI) advances about the emerging nature of AI-based autonomous self-driving driverless cars. Via recent advances in Artificial Intelligence (AI) and Machine Learning (ML), we are nearing the day when vehicles can control themselves and will not require and nor rely upon human intervention to perform their driving tasks (or, that <u>allow</u> for human intervention, but only *require* human intervention in very limited ways).

Similar to my other related books, which I describe in a moment and list the chapters in the Appendix A of this book, I am particularly focused on those advances that pertain to self-driving cars. The phrase "autonomous vehicles" is often used to refer to any kind of vehicle, whether it is ground-based or in the air or sea, and whether it is a cargo hauling trailer truck or a conventional passenger car. Though the aspects described in this book are certainly applicable to all kinds of autonomous vehicles, I am focused more so here on cars.

For this book, I am going to borrow my introduction from those companion books, since it does a good job of laying out the landscape of self-driving cars and my overall viewpoints on the topic.

INTRODUCTION TO SELF-DRIVING CARS

This is a book about self-driving cars. Someday in the future, we'll all have self-driving cars and this book will perhaps seem antiquated, but right now, we are at the forefront of the self-driving car wave. Daily news bombards us with flashes of new announcements by one car maker or another and leaves the impression that within the next few weeks or maybe months that the self-driving car will be here. A casual non-technical reader would assume from these news flashes that in we must be on the cusp of a true self-driving car.

We are still quite a distance from having a true self-driving car. A true self-driving car is akin to a moonshot. In the same manner that getting us to the moon was an incredible feat, likewise, is achieving a true self-driving car. Anybody that suggests or even brashly states that the true self-driving car is nearly here should be viewed with great skepticism. Indeed, you'll see that I often tend to use the word "hogwash" or "crock" when I assess much of the decidedly *fake news* about self-driving cars.

Indeed, I've been writing a popular blog post about self-driving cars and hitting hard on those that try to wave their hands and pretend that we are on the imminent verge of true self-driving cars. For many years, I've been known as the AI Insider. Besides writing about AI, I also develop AI software. I do what I describe. It also gives me insights into what others that are doing AI are really doing versus what it is said they are doing.

Many faithful readers had asked me to pull together my insightful short essays and put them into another book, which you are now holding.

For those of you that have been reading my essays over the years, this collection not only puts them together into one handy package, I also updated the essays and added new material. For those of you that are new to the topic of self-driving cars and AI, I hope you find these essays approachable and informative. I also tend to have a writing style with a bit of a voice, and so you'll see that I am times have a wry sense of humor and poke at conformity.

As a former professor and founder of an AI research lab, I for many years wrote in the formal language of academic writing. I published in referred journals and served as an editor for several AI journals. This writing here is not of the nature, and I have adopted a different and more informal style for these essays. That being said, I also do mention from time-to-time more rigorous material on AI and encourage you all to dig into those deeper and more formal materials if so interested.

For those of you that are reading this book and have a penchant for writing code, you might consider taking a look at the open-source code available for self-driving cars. This is a handy place to start learning how to develop AI for self-driving cars. There are also many new educational courses spring forth. There is a growing body of those wanting to learn about and develop self-driving cars, and a growing body of colleges, labs, and other avenues by which you can learn about self-driving cars.

This book will provide a foundation of aspects that I think will get you ready for those kinds of more advanced training opportunities. If you've already taken those classes, you'll likely find these essays especially interesting as they offer a perspective that I am betting few other instructors or faculty offered to you. These are challenging essays that ask you to think beyond the conventional about self-driving cars.

THE MOTHER OF ALL AI PROJECTS

In June 2017, Apple CEO Tim Cook came out and finally admitted that Apple has been working on a self-driving car. As you'll see in my essays, Apple was enmeshed in secrecy about their self-driving car efforts. We have only been able to read the tea leaves and guess at what Apple has been up to. The notion of an iCar has been floating for quite a while, and self-driving engineers and researchers have been signing tight-lipped Non-Disclosure Agreements (NDA's) to work on projects at Apple that were as shrouded in mystery as any military invasion plans might be.

Tim Cook said something that many others in the Artificial Intelligence (AI) field have been saying, namely, the creation of a self-driving car has got to be the mother of all AI projects. In other words, it is in fact a tremendous moonshot for AI. If a self-driving car can be crafted and the AI works as we hope, it means that we have made incredible strides with AI and that therefore it opens many other worlds of potential breakthrough accomplishments that AI can solve.

Is this hyperbole? Am I just trying to make AI seem like a miracle worker and so provide self-aggrandizing statements for those of us writing the AI software for self-driving cars? No, it is not hyperbole. Developing a true self-driving car is really, really, really hard to do. Let me take a moment to explain why. As a side note, I realize that the Apple CEO is known for at times uttering hyperbole, and he had previously said for example that the year 2012 was "the mother of all years," and he had said that the release of iOS 10 was "the mother of all releases" – all of which does suggest he likes to use the handy "mother of" expression. But, I assure you, in terms of true self-driving cars, he has hit the nail on the head. For sure.

When you think about a moonshot and how we got to the moon, there are some identifiable characteristics and those same aspects can be applied to creating a true self-driving car. You'll notice that I keep putting the word "true" in front of the self-driving car expression. I do so because as per my essay about the various levels of self-driving cars, there are some self-driving cars that are only somewhat of a self-driving car. The somewhat versions are ones that require a human driver to be ready to intervene. In my view, that's not a true self-driving car. A true self-driving car is one that requires no human driver intervention at all. It is a car that can entirely undertake via automation the driving task without any human driver needed. This is the essence of what is known as a Level 5 self-driving car. We are currently at the Level 2 and Level 3 mark, and not yet at Level 5.

Getting to the moon involved aspects such as having big stretch goals, incremental progress, experimentation, innovation, and so on. Let's review how this applied to the moonshot of the bygone era, and how it applies to the self-driving car moonshot of today.

Big Stretch Goal

Trying to take a human and deliver the human to the moon, and bring them back, safely, was an extremely large stretch goal at the time. No one knew whether it could be done. The technology wasn't available yet. The cost was huge. The determination would need to be fierce. Etc. To reach a Level 5 self-driving car is going to be the same. It is a big stretch goal. We can readily get to the Level 3, and we are able to see the Level 4 just up ahead, but a Level 5 is still an unknown as to if it is doable. It should eventually be doable and in the same way that we thought we'd eventually get to the moon, but when it will occur is a different story.

Incremental Progress

Getting to the moon did not happen overnight in one fell swoop. It took years and years of incremental progress to get there. Likewise, for self-driving cars. Google has famously been striving to get to the Level 5, and pretty much been willing to forgo dealing with the intervening levels, but most of the other self-driving car makers are doing the incremental route. Let's get a good Level 2 and a somewhat Level 3 going. Then, let's improve the Level 3 and get a somewhat Level 4 going. Then, let's improve the Level 4 and finally arrive at a Level 5. This seems to be the prevalent way that we are going to achieve the true self-driving car.

Experimentation

You likely know that there were various experiments involved in perfecting the approach and technology to get to the moon. As per making incremental progress, we first tried to see if we could get a rocket to go into space and safety return, then put a monkey in there, then with a human, then we went all the way to the moon but didn't land, and finally we arrived at the mission that actually landed on the moon.

Self-driving cars are the same way. We are doing simulations of self-driving cars. We do testing of self-driving cars on private land under controlled situations.

We do testing of self-driving cars on public roadways, often having to meet regulatory requirements including for example having an engineer or equivalent in the car to take over the controls if needed. And so on. Experiments big and small are needed to figure out what works and what doesn't.

Innovation

There are already some advances in AI that are allowing us to progress toward self-driving cars. We are going to need even more advances. Innovation in all aspects of technology are going to be required to achieve a true self-driving car. By no means do we already have everything in-hand that we need to get there. Expect new inventions and new approaches, new algorithms, etc.

Setbacks

Most of the pundits are avoiding talking about potential setbacks in the progress toward self-driving cars. Getting to the moon involved many setbacks, some of which you never have heard of and were buried at the time so as to not dampen enthusiasm and funding for getting to the moon. A recurring theme in many of my included essays is that there are going to be setbacks as we try to arrive at a true self-driving car. Take a deep breath and be ready. I just hope the setbacks don't completely stop progress. I am sure that it will cause progress to alter in a manner that we've not yet seen in the self-driving car field. I liken the self-driving car of today to the excitement everyone had for Uber when it first got going. Today, we have a different view of Uber and with each passing day there are more regulations to the ride sharing business and more concerns raised. The darling child only stays a darling until finally that child acts up. It will happen the same with self-driving cars.

SELF-DRIVING CARS CHALLENGES

But what exactly makes things so hard to have a true self-driving car, you might be asking. You have seen cruise control for years and years. You've lately seen cars that can do parallel parking. You've seen YouTube videos of Tesla drivers that put their hands out the window as their car zooms along the highway, and seen to therefore be in a self-driving car. Aren't we just needing to put a few more sensors onto a car and then we'll have in-hand a true self-driving car? Nope.

Consider for a moment the nature of the driving task. We don't just let anyone at any age drive a car. Worldwide, most countries won't license a driver until the age of 18, though many do allow a learner's permit at the age of 15 or 16. Some suggest that a younger age would be physically too small to reach the controls of the car. Though this might be the case, we could easily adjust the controls to allow for younger aged and thus smaller stature. It's not their physical size that matters. It's their cognitive development that matters.

To drive a car, you need to be able to reason about the car, what the car can and cannot do. You need to know how to operate the car. You need to know about how other cars on the road drive. You need to know what is allowed in driving such as speed limits and driving within marked lanes. You need to be able to react to situations and be able to avoid getting into accidents. You need to ascertain when to hit your brakes, when to steer clear of a pedestrian, and how to keep from ramming that motorcyclist that just cut you off.

Many of us had taken courses on driving. We studied about driving and took driver training. We had to take a test and pass it to be able to drive. The point being that though most adults take the driving task for granted, and we often "mindlessly" drive our cars, there is a significant amount of cognitive effort that goes into driving a car. After a while, it becomes second nature. You don't especially think about how you drive, you just do it. But, if you watch a novice driver, say a teenager learning to drive, you suddenly realize that there is a lot more complexity to it than we seem to realize.

Furthermore, driving is a very serious task. I recall when my daughter and son first learned to drive. They are both very conscientious people. They wanted to make sure that whatever they did, they did well, and that they did not harm anyone. Every day, when you get into a car, it is probably around 4,000 pounds of hefty metal and plastics (about two tons), and it is a lethal weapon. Think about it. You drive down the street in an object that weighs two tons and with the engine it can accelerate and ram into anything you want to hit. The damage a car can inflict is very scary. Both my children were surprised that they were being given the right to maneuver this monster of a beast that could cause tremendous harm entirely by merely letting go of the steering wheel for a moment or taking your eyes off the road.

In fact, in the United States alone there are about 40,000 deaths per year by auto accidents, which is more than 100 per day. Given that there are about 263 million cars in the United States, I am actually more amazed that the number of fatalities is not a lot higher.

During my morning commute, I look at all the thousands of cars on the freeway around me, and I think that if all of them decided to go zombie and drive in a crazy maniac way, there would be many people dead. Somehow, incredibly, each day, most people drive relatively safely. To me, that's a miracle right there. Getting millions and millions of people to be safe and sane when behind the wheel of a two-ton mobile object, it's a feat that we as a society should admire with pride.

So, hopefully you are in agreement that the driving task requires a great deal of cognition. You don't' need to be especially smart to drive a car, and we've done quite a bit to make car driving viable for even the average dolt. There isn't an IQ test that you need to take to drive a car. If you can read and write, and pass a test, you pretty much can legally drive a car. There are of course some that drive a car and are not legally permitted to do so, plus there are private areas such as farms where drivers are young, but for public roadways in the United States, you can be generally of average intelligence (or less) and be able to legally drive.

This though makes it seem like the cognitive effort must not be much. If the cognitive effort was truly hard, wouldn't we only have Einstein's that could drive a car? We have made sure to keep the driving task as simple as we can, by making the controls easy and relatively standardized, and by having roads that are relatively standardized, and so on. It is as though Disneyland has put their Autopia into the real-world, by us all as a society agreeing that roads will be a certain way, and we'll all abide by the various rules of driving.

A modest cognitive task by a human is still something that stymies AI. You certainly know that AI has been able to beat chess players and be good at other kinds of games. This type of narrow cognition is not what car driving is about. Car driving is much wider. It requires knowledge about the world, which a chess playing AI system does not need to know. The cognitive aspects of driving are on the one hand seemingly simple, but at the same time require layer upon layer of knowledge about cars, people, roads, rules, and a myriad of other "common sense" aspects. We don't have any AI systems today that have that same kind of breadth and depth of awareness and knowledge.

As revealed in my essays, the self-driving car of today is using trickery to do particular tasks. It is all very narrow in operation. Plus, it currently assumes that a human driver is ready to intervene. It is like a child that we have taught to stack blocks, but we are needed to be right there in case the child stacks them too high and they begin to fall over.

AI of today is brittle, it is narrow, and it does not approach the cognitive abilities of humans. This is why the true self-driving car is somewhere out in the future.

Another aspect to the driving task is that it is not solely a mind exercise. You do need to use your senses to drive. You use your eyes as vision sensors to see the road ahead. You vision capability is like a streaming video, which your brain needs to continually analyze as you drive. Where is the road? Is there a pedestrian in the way? Is there another car ahead of you? Your senses are relying a flood of info to your brain. Self-driving cars are trying to do the same, by using cameras, radar, ultrasound, and lasers. This is an attempt at mimicking how humans have senses and sensory apparatus.

Thus, the driving task is mental and physical. You use your senses, you use your arms and legs to manipulate the controls of the car, and you use your brain to assess the sensory info and direct your limbs to act upon the controls of the car. This all happens instantly. If you've ever perhaps gotten something in your eye and only had one eye available to drive with, you suddenly realize how dependent upon vision you are. If you have a broken foot with a cast, you suddenly realize how hard it is to control the brake pedal and the accelerator. If you've taken medication and your brain is maybe sluggish, you suddenly realize how much mental strain is required to drive a car.

An AI system that plays chess only needs to be focused on playing chess. The physical aspects aren't important because usually a human moves the chess pieces or the chessboard is shown on an electronic display. Using AI for a more life-and-death task such as analyzing MRI images of patients, this again does not require physical capabilities and instead is done by examining images of bits.

Driving a car is a true life-and-death task. It is a use of AI that can easily and at any moment produce death. For those colleagues of mine that are developing this AI, as am I, we need to keep in mind the somber aspects of this. We are producing software that will have in its virtual hands the lives of the occupants of the car, and the lives of those in other nearby cars, and the lives of nearby pedestrians, etc. Chess is not usually a life-or-death matter.

Driving is all around us. Cars are everywhere. Most of today's AI applications involve only a small number of people. Or, they are behind the scenes and we as humans have other recourse if the AI messes up. AI that is driving a car at 80 miles per hour on a highway had better not mess up. The consequences are grave.

Multiply this by the number of cars, if we could put magically self-driving into every car in the USA, we'd have AI running in the 263 million cars. That's a lot of AI spread around. This is AI on a massive scale that we are not doing today and that offers both promise and potential peril.

There are some that want AI for self-driving cars because they envision a world without any car accidents. They envision a world in which there is no car congestion and all cars cooperate with each other. These are wonderful utopian visions.

They are also very misleading. The adoption of self-driving cars is going to be incremental and not overnight. We cannot economically just junk all existing cars. Nor are we going to be able to affordably retrofit existing cars. It is more likely that self-driving cars will be built into new cars and that over many years of gradual replacement of existing cars that we'll see the mix of self-driving cars become substantial in the real-world.

In these essays, I have tried to offer technological insights without being overly technical in my description, and also blended the business, societal, and economic aspects too. Technologists need to consider the non-technological impacts of what they do. Non-technologists should be aware of what is being developed.

We all need to work together to collectively be prepared for the enormous disruption and transformative aspects of true self-driving cars.

WHAT THIS BOOK PROVIDES

What does this book provide to you? It introduces many of the key elements about self-driving cars and does so with an AI based perspective. I weave together technical and non-technical aspects, readily going from being concerned about the cognitive capabilities of the driving task and how the technology is embodying this into self-driving cars, and in the next breath I discuss the societal and economic aspects.

They are all intertwined because that's the way reality is. You cannot separate out the technology per se, and instead must consider it within the milieu of what is being invented and innovated, and do so with a mindset towards the contemporary mores and culture that shape what we are doing and what we hope to do.

WHY THIS BOOK

I wrote this book to try and bring to the public view many aspects about self-driving cars that nobody seems to be discussing.

For business leaders that are either involved in making self-driving cars or that are going to leverage self-driving cars, I hope that this book will enlighten you as to the risks involved and ways in which you should be strategizing about how to deal with those risks.

For entrepreneurs, startups and other businesses that want to enter into the self-driving car market that is emerging, I hope this book sparks your interest in doing so, and provides some sense of what might be prudent to pursue.

For researchers that study self-driving cars, I hope this book spurs your interest in the risks and safety issues of self-driving cars, and also nudges you toward conducting research on those aspects.

For students in computer science or related disciplines, I hope this book will provide you with interesting and new ideas and material, for which you might conduct research or provide some career direction insights for you.

For AI companies and high-tech companies pursuing self-driving cars, this book will hopefully broaden your view beyond just the mere coding and development needed to make self-driving cars.

For all readers, I hope that you will find the material in this book to be stimulating. Some of it will be repetitive of things you already know. But I am pretty sure that you'll also find various eureka moments whereby you'll discover a new technique or approach that you had not earlier thought of. I am also betting that there will be material that forces you to rethink some of your current practices.

I am not saying you will suddenly have an epiphany and change what you are doing. I do think though that you will reconsider or perhaps revisit what you are doing.

For anyone choosing to use this book for teaching purposes, please take a look at my suggestions for doing so, as described in the Appendix. I have found the material handy in courses that I have taught, and likewise other faculty have told me that they have found the material handy, in some cases as extended readings and in other instances as a core part of their course (depending on the nature of the class).

In my writing for this book, I have tried carefully to blend both the practitioner and the academic styles of writing.

It is not as abstract as is typical academic journal writing, but at the same time offers depth by going into the nuances and trade-offs of various practices.

The word "deep" is in vogue today, meaning getting deeply into a subject or topic, and so is the word "unpack" which means to tease out the underlying aspects of a subject or topic. I have sought to offer material that addresses an issue or topic by going relatively deeply into it and make sure that it is well unpacked.

In any book about AI, it is difficult to use our everyday words without having some of them be misinterpreted. Specifically, it is easy to anthropomorphize AI. When I say that an AI system "knows" something, I do not want you to construe that the AI system has sentience and "knows" in the same way that humans do. They aren't that way, as yet. I have tried to use quotes around such words from time-to-time to emphasize that the words I am using should not be misinterpreted to ascribe true human intelligence to the AI systems that we know of today. If I used quotes around all such words, the book would be very difficult to read, and so I am doing so judiciously. Please keep that in mind as you read the material, thanks.

Some of the material is time-based in terms of covering underway activities, and though some of it might decay, nonetheless I believe you'll find the material useful and informative.

COMPANION BOOKS BY DR. ELIOT

1. **"Introduction to Driverless Self-Driving Cars"** by Dr. Lance Eliot
2. **"Innovation and Thought Leadership on Self-Driving Driverless Cars"**
3. **"Advances in AI and Autonomous Vehicles: Cybernetic Self-Driving Cars"**
4. **"Self-Driving Cars: The Mother of All AI Projects"** by Dr. Lance Eliot
5. **"New Advances in AI Autonomous Driverless Self-Driving Cars"**
6. **"AV Driverless Self-Driving Cars & AI"** by Dr. Lance Eliot and Michael B. Eliot
7. **"Transformative Artificial Intelligence Driverless Self-Driving Cars"**
8. **"Disruptive Artificial Intelligence and Driverless Self-Driving Cars"**
9. "State-of-the-Art AI Driverless Self-Driving Cars" by Dr. Lance Eliot
10. "Top Trends in AI Self-Driving Cars" by Dr. Lance Eliot
11. **"AI Innovations and Self-Driving Cars"** by Dr. Lance Eliot
12. **"Crucial Advances for AI Driverless Cars"** by Dr. Lance Eliot
13. **"Sociotechnical Insights and AI Driverless Cars"** by Dr. Lance Eliot.
14. **"Pioneering Advances for AI Driverless Cars"** by Dr. Lance Eliot
15. **"Leading Edge Trends for AI Driverless Cars"** by Dr. Lance Eliot
16. **"The Cutting Edge of AI Autonomous Cars"** by Dr. Lance Eliot
17. **"The Next Wave of AI Self-Driving Cars"** by Dr. Lance Eliot
18. **"Revolutionary Innovations of AI Driverless Cars"** by Dr. Lance Eliot
19. **"AI Self-Driving Cars Breakthroughs"** by Dr. Lance Eliot
20. **"Trailblazing Trends for AI Self-Driving Cars"** by Dr. Lance Eliot
21. **"Ingenious Strides for AI Driverless Cars"** by Dr. Lance Eliot
22. **"AI Self-Driving Cars Inventiveness"** by Dr. Lance Eliot
23. **"Visionary Secrets of AI Driverless Cars"** by Dr. Lance Eliot
24. **"Spearheading AI Self-Driving Cars"** by Dr. Lance Eliot
25. **"Spurring AI Self-Driving Cars"** by Dr. Lance Eliot
26. **"Avant-Garde AI Driverless Cars"** by Dr. Lance Eliot
27. **"AI Self-Driving Cars Evolvement"** by Dr. Lance Eliot
28. **"AI Driverless Cars Chrysalis"** by Dr. Lance Eliot
29. **"Boosting AI Autonomous Cars"** by Dr. Lance Eliot
30. **"AI Self-Driving Cars Trendsetting"** by Dr. Lance Eliot
31. **"AI Autonomous Cars Forefront"** by Dr. Lance Eliot
32. **"AI Autonomous Cars Emergence"** by Dr. Lance Eliot
33. **"AI Autonomous Cars Progress"** by Dr. Lance Eliot
34. **"AI Self-Driving Cars Prognosis"** by Dr. Lance Eliot
35. **"AI Self-Driving Cars Momentum"** by Dr. Lance Eliot
36. **"AI Self-Driving Cars Headway"** by Dr. Lance Eliot
37. **"AI Self-Driving Cars Vicissitude"** by Dr. Lance Eliot
38. **"AI Self-Driving Cars Autonomy"** by Dr. Lance Eliot
39. **"AI Driverless Cars Transmutation"** by Dr. Lance Eliot
40. **"AI Driverless Cars Potentiality"** by Dr. Lance Eliot
41. **"AI Driverless Cars Realities"** by Dr. Lance Eliot
42. **"AI Self-Driving Cars Materiality"** by Dr. Lance Eliot
43. **"AI Self-Driving Cars Accordance"** by Dr. Lance Eliot
44. **"AI Self-Driving Cars Equanimity"** by Dr. Lance Eliot
45. **"AI Self-Driving Cars Divulgement"** by Dr. Lance Eliot
46. **"AI Self-Driving Cars Consonance"** by Dr. Lance Eliot
47. **"Revelatory AI Self-Driving Cars"** by Dr. Lance Eliot

These books are available on Amazon and at other major global booksellers.

CHAPTER 1

ELIOT FRAMEWORK FOR AI SELF-DRIVING CARS

This chapter is a core foundational aspect for understanding AI self-driving cars and I have used this same chapter in several of my other books to introduce the reader to essential elements of this field. Once you've read this chapter, you'll be prepared to read the rest of the material since the foundational essence of the components of autonomous AI driverless self-driving cars will have been established for you.

When I give presentations about self-driving cars and teach classes on the topic, I have found it helpful to provide a framework around which the various key elements of self-driving cars can be understood and organized (see diagram at the end of this chapter). The framework needs to be simple enough to convey the overarching elements, but at the same time not so simple that it belies the true complexity of self-driving cars. As such, I am going to describe the framework here and try to offer in a thousand words (or more!) what the framework diagram itself intends to portray.

The core elements on the diagram are numbered for ease of reference. The numbering does not suggest any kind of prioritization of the elements. Each element is crucial. Each element has a purpose, and otherwise would not be included in the framework. For some self-driving cars, a particular element might be more important or somehow distinguished in comparison to other self-driving cars.

You could even use the framework to rate a particular self-driving car, doing so by gauging how well it performs in each of the elements of the framework. I will describe each of the elements, one at a time. After doing so, I'll discuss aspects that illustrate how the elements interact and perform during the overall effort of a self-driving car.

At the AI Self-Driving Car Institute, we use the framework to keep track of what we are working on, and how we are developing software that fills in what is needed to achieve Level 5 self-driving cars.

D-01: Sensor Capture

Let's start with the one element that often gets the most attention in the press about self-driving cars, namely, the sensory devices for a self-driving car.

On the framework, the box labeled as D-01 indicates "Sensor Capture" and refers to the processes of the self-driving car that involve collecting data from the myriad of sensors that are used for a self-driving car. The types of devices typically involved are listed, such as the use of mono cameras, stereo cameras, LIDAR devices, radar systems, ultrasonic devices, GPS, IMU, and so on.

These devices are tasked with obtaining data about the status of the self-driving car and the world around it. Some of the devices are continually providing updates, while others of the devices await an indication by the self-driving car that the device is supposed to collect data. The data might be first transformed in some fashion by the device itself, or it might instead be fed directly into the sensor capture as raw data. At that point, it might be up to the sensor capture processes to do transformations on the data. This all varies depending upon the nature of the devices being used and how the devices were designed and developed.

D-02: Sensor Fusion

Imagine that your eyeballs receive visual images, your nose receives odors, your ears receive sounds, and in essence each of your distinct sensory devices is getting some form of input. The input befits the nature of the device. Likewise, for a self-driving car, the cameras provide visual images, the radar returns radar reflections, and so on. Each device provides the data as befits what the device does.

At some point, using the analogy to humans, you need to merge together what your eyes see, what your nose smells, what your ears hear, and piece it all together into a larger sense of what the world is all about and what is happening around you. Sensor fusion is the action of taking the singular aspects from each of the devices and putting them together into a larger puzzle.

Sensor fusion is a tough task. There are some devices that might not be working at the time of the sensor capture. Or, there might some devices that are unable to report well what they have detected. Again, using a human analogy, suppose you are in a dark room and so your eyes cannot see much. At that point, you might need to rely more so on your ears and what you hear. The same is true for a self-driving car. If the cameras are obscured due to snow and sleet, it might be that the radar can provide a greater indication of what the external conditions consist of.

In the case of a self-driving car, there can be a plethora of such sensory devices. Each is reporting what it can. Each might have its difficulties. Each might have its limitations, such as how far ahead it can detect an object. All of these limitations need to be considered during the sensor fusion task.

D-03: Virtual World Model

For humans, we presumably keep in our minds a model of the world around us when we are driving a car. In your mind, you know that the car is going at say 60 miles per hour and that you are on a freeway.

You have a model in your mind that your car is surrounded by other cars, and that there are lanes to the freeway. Your model is not only based on what you can see, hear, etc., but also what you know about the nature of the world. You know that at any moment that car ahead of you can smash on its brakes, or the car behind you can ram into your car, or that the truck in the next lane might swerve into your lane.

The AI of the self-driving car needs to have a virtual world model, which it then keeps updated with whatever it is receiving from the sensor fusion, which received its input from the sensor capture.

D-04: System Action Plan

By having a virtual world model, the AI of the self-driving car is able to keep track of where the car is and what is happening around the car. In addition, the AI needs to determine what to do next. Should the self-driving car hit its brakes? Should the self-driving car stay in its lane or swerve into the lane to the left? Should the self-driving car accelerate or slow down?

A system action plan needs to be prepared by the AI of the self-driving car. The action plan specifies what actions should be taken. The actions need to pertain to the status of the virtual world model. Plus, the actions need to be realizable.

This realizability means that the AI cannot just assert that the self-driving car should suddenly sprout wings and fly. Instead, the AI must be bound by whatever the self-driving car can actually do, such as coming to a halt in a distance of X feet at a speed of Y miles per hour, rather than perhaps asserting that the self-driving car come to a halt in 0 feet as though it could instantaneously come to a stop while it is in motion.

D-05: Controls Activation

The system action plan is implemented by activating the controls of the car to act according to what the plan stipulates.

This might mean that the accelerator control is commanded to increase the speed of the car. Or, the steering control is commanded to turn the steering wheel 30 degrees to the left or right.

One question arises as to whether or not the controls respond as they are commanded to do. In other words, suppose the AI has commanded the accelerator to increase, but for some reason it does not do so. Or, maybe it tries to do so, but the speed of the car does not increase.

The controls activation feeds back into the virtual world model, and simultaneously the virtual world model is getting updated from the sensors, the sensor capture, and the sensor fusion. This allows the AI to ascertain what has taken place as a result of the controls being commanded to take some kind of action.

By the way, please keep in mind that though the diagram seems to have a linear progression to it, the reality is that these are all aspects of the self-driving car that are happening in parallel and simultaneously. The sensors are capturing data, meanwhile the sensor fusion is taking place, meanwhile the virtual model is being updated, meanwhile the system action plan is being formulated and reformulated, meanwhile the controls are being activated.

This is the same as a human being that is driving a car. They are eyeballing the road, meanwhile they are fusing in their mind the sights, sounds, etc., meanwhile their mind is updating their model of the world around them, meanwhile they are formulating an action plan of what to do, and meanwhile they are pushing their foot onto the pedals and steering the car. In the normal course of driving a car, you are doing all of these at once. I mention this so that when you look at the diagram, you will think of the boxes as processes that are all happening at the same time, and not as though only one happens and then the next.

They are shown diagrammatically in a simplistic manner to help comprehend what is taking place. You though should also realize that they are working in parallel and simultaneous with each other. This is a tough aspect in that the inter-element communications involve latency and other aspects that must be taken into account. There can be delays in one element updating and then sharing its latest status with other elements.

D-06: Automobile & CAN

Contemporary cars use various automotive electronics and a Controller Area Network (CAN) to serve as the components that underlie the driving aspects of a car.

There are Electronic Control Units (ECU's) which control subsystems of the car, such as the engine, the brakes, the doors, the windows, and so on.

The elements D-01, D-02, D-03, D-04, D-05 are layered on top of the D-06, and must be aware of the nature of what the D-06 is able to do and not do.

D-07: In-Car Commands

Humans are going to be occupants in self-driving cars. In a Level 5 self-driving car, there must be some form of communication that takes place between the humans and the self-driving car. For example, I go into a self-driving car and tell it that I want to be driven over to Disneyland, and along the way I want to stop at In-and-Out Burger. The self-driving car now parses what I've said and tries to then establish a means to carry out my wishes.

In-car commands can happen at any time during a driving journey. Though my example was about an in-car command when I first got into my self-driving car, it could be that while the self-driving car is carrying out the journey that I change my mind. Perhaps after getting stuck in traffic, I tell the self-driving car to forget about getting the burgers and just head straight over to the theme park. The self-driving car needs to be alert to in-car commands throughout the journey.

D-08: V2X Communications

We will ultimately have self-driving cars communicating with each other, doing so via V2V (Vehicle-to-Vehicle) communications. We will also have self-driving cars that communicate with the roadways and other aspects of the transportation infrastructure, doing so via V2I (Vehicle-to-Infrastructure).

The variety of ways in which a self-driving car will be communicating with other cars and infrastructure is being called V2X, whereby the letter X means whatever else we identify as something that a car should or would want to communicate with.

The V2X communications will be taking place simultaneous with everything else on the diagram, and those other elements will need to incorporate whatever it gleans from those V2X communications.

D-09: Deep Learning

The use of Deep Learning permeates all other aspects of the self-driving car. The AI of the self-driving car will be using deep learning to do a better job at the systems action plan, and at the control's activation, and at the sensor fusion, and so on.

Currently, the use of artificial neural networks is the most prevalent form of deep learning. Based on large swaths of data, the neural networks attempt to "learn" from the data and therefore direct the efforts of the self-driving car accordingly.

D-10: Tactical AI

Tactical AI is the element of dealing with the moment-to-moment driving of the self-driving car. Is the self-driving car staying in its lane of the freeway? Is the car responding appropriately to the controls commands? Are the sensory devices working?

For human drivers, the tactical equivalent can be seen when you watch a novice driver such as a teenager that is first driving. They are focused on the mechanics of the driving task, keeping their eye on the road while also trying to properly control the car.

D-11: Strategic AI

The Strategic AI aspects of a self-driving car are dealing with the larger picture of what the self-driving car is trying to do. If I had asked that the self-driving car take me to Disneyland, there is an overall journey map that needs to be kept and maintained.

There is an interaction between the Strategic AI and the Tactical AI. The Strategic AI is wanting to keep on the mission of the driving, while the Tactical AI is focused on the particulars underway in the driving effort.

If the Tactical AI seems to wander away from the overarching mission, the Strategic AI wants to see why and get things back on track. If the Tactical AI realizes that there is something amiss on the self-driving car, it needs to alert the Strategic AI accordingly and have an adjustment to the overarching mission that is underway.

D-12: Self-Aware AI

Very few of the self-driving cars being developed are including a Self-Aware AI element, which we at the Cybernetic Self-Driving Car Institute believe is crucial to Level 5 self-driving cars.

The Self-Aware AI element is intended to watch over itself, in the sense that the AI is making sure that the AI is working as intended. Suppose you had a human driving a car, and they were starting to drive erratically. Hopefully, their own self-awareness would make them realize they themselves are driving poorly, such as perhaps starting to fall asleep after having been driving for hours on end. If you had a passenger in the car, they might be able to alert the driver if the driver is starting to do something amiss.

This is exactly what the Self-Aware AI element tries to do, it becomes the overseer of the AI, and tries to detect when the AI has become faulty or confused, and then find ways to overcome the issue.

D-13: Economic

The economic aspects of a self-driving car are not per se a technology aspect of a self-driving car, but the economics do indeed impact the nature of a self-driving car. For example, the cost of outfitting a self-driving car with every kind of possible sensory device is prohibitive, and so choices need to be made about which devices are used. And, for those sensory devices chosen, whether they would have a full set of features or a more limited set of features.

We are going to have self-driving cars that are at the low-end of a consumer cost point, and others at the high-end of a consumer cost point. You cannot expect that the self-driving car at the low-end is going to be as robust as the one at the high-end.

I realize that many of the self-driving car pundits are acting as though all self-driving cars will be the same, but they won't be. Just like anything else, we are going to have self-driving cars that have a range of capabilities. Some will be better than others. Some will be safer than others. This is the way of the real-world, and so we need to be thinking about the economics aspects when considering the nature of self-driving cars.

D-14: Societal

This component encompasses the societal aspects of AI which also impacts the technology of self-driving cars. For example, the famous Trolley Problem involves what choices should a self-driving car make when faced with life-and-death matters. If the self-driving car is about to either hit a child standing in the roadway, or instead ram into a tree at the side of the road and possibly kill the humans in the self-driving car, which choice should be made?

We need to keep in mind the societal aspects will underlie the AI of the self-driving car. Whether we are aware of it explicitly or not, the AI will have embedded into it various societal assumptions.

D-15: Innovation

I included the notion of innovation into the framework because we can anticipate that whatever a self-driving car consists of, it will continue to be innovated over time. The self-driving cars coming out in the next several years will undoubtedly be different and less innovative than the versions that come out in ten years hence, and so on.

Framework Overall

For those of you that want to learn about self-driving cars, you can potentially pick a particular element and become specialized in that aspect. Some engineers are focusing on the sensory devices. Some engineers focus on the controls activation. And so on. There are specialties in each of the elements.

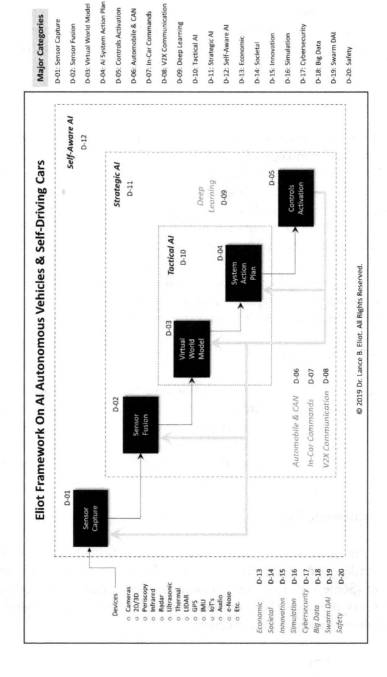

Eliot Framework On AI Autonomous Vehicles & Self-Driving Cars

Major Categories

D-01: Sensor Capture
D-02: Sensor Fusion
D-03: Virtual World Model
D-04: AI System Action Plan
D-05: Controls Activation
D-06: Automobile & CAN
D-07: In-Car Commands
D-08: V2X Communication
D-09: Deep Learning
D-10: Tactical AI
D-11: Strategic AI
D-12: Self-Aware AI
D-13: Economic
D-14: Societal
D-15: Innovation
D-16: Simulation
D-17: Cybersecurity
D-18: Big Data
D-19: Swarm DAI
D-20: Safety

Self-Aware AI
D-12

Strategic AI
D-11

Deep
Learning
D-09

Tactical AI
D-10

D-05
Controls
Activation

D-04
System
Action
Plan

D-03
Virtual
World
Model

D-02
Sensor
Fusion

D-01
Sensor
Capture

Devices
o Cameras
o 2D/3D
o Periscopy
o Infrared
o Radar
o Ultrasonic
o Thermal
o LIDAR
o GPS
o IMU
o IoTs
o Audio
o e-Nose
o Etc.

Automobile & CAN   D-06
In-Car Commands   D-07
V2X Communication   D-08

Economic   D-13
Societal   D-14
Innovation   D-15
Simulation   D-16
Cybersecurity   D-17
Big Data   D-18
Swarm DAI   D-19
Safety   D-20

CHAPTER 2

CONGESTION-FREE PIPEDREAM AND SELF-DRIVING CARS

I was on my way to give a talk in downtown Los Angeles and encountered the usual and exasperating late afternoon traffic on the infamous 405 freeway.

Our traffic snarls are legendary and yet this particular day it seemed even worse than normal (how is that possible?). I figured that I'd use my familiarity with the local terrain to find a means around the congestion, but when I got off the freeway to do so there were equally frustrating clogs on the local streets. I then swung back onto the freeway and slogged forward until finally reaching downtown, which of course also had streets that were painfully full and maddeningly jammed up.

My travel time was about 2 and ½ hours and the total distance driven was about 40 miles. Don't even try to convert that into my average speed since it will only cause me even greater agony and consternation. Obviously, things were a lot slower than the capability of my modern-day conventional automobile. I sometimes wonder if the car gets angry that it can't be let loose to fire-up its horsepower, maybe like a caged horse that cannot sprint with the wind.

My talk was about the future of self-driving driverless autonomous cars.

Since the attendees had all pretty much also endured the congested roads while getting to the venue, they were waiting eagerly to hear how great things will be once we have driverless cars. There are pundits that keep touting the aspect that there will never be congested traffic ever again. Via self-driving cars, we'll all be traveling in congestion-free heaven, and as a passenger in an autonomous car you'll feel the exhilaration of moving at top speeds nearly all the time.

Imagine that you won't suffer in stop-and-go traffic anymore. Though you won't be driving the car, since true autonomous cars won't need and won't presumably have a provision for any human driving, especially the vaunted Level 5, you'll certainly still be aware of the pace of the self-driving car and would likely be chagrined if the state-of-the-art vehicle was not smoothly proceeding on your journey.

With some hesitation and trepidation, I opened the talk by pointing out that the likelihood of congestion-free driving due to the advent of self-driving cars is not very promising, and at best if it were to occur, it will be well beyond the upcoming future.

The crowd looked quite dejected about this prediction.

Why wouldn't autonomous cars bring us to the congestion-free nirvana?

Let's unpack the matter and see what reality holds in store for us.

Factors Impacting Driverless Cars On-The-Roads

There are various experiments that have been done on special closed tracks or proving grounds trying to gauge whether AI driven autonomous cars can maneuver in a fashion that will avert traffic snarls. If you had exclusively self-driving cars, they indeed would seem to be able to drive in a smoother manner than humans do, generally being able to maintain a proper distance between cars and adjusting quickly to the ebb and flow of the cars ahead of them.

In some cases, these experiments are done with the added benefit of V2V (vehicle-to-vehicle) electronic communications taking place among the driverless cars. This might be akin to equipping human drivers with walkie talkies or smartphones to group chat while driving, letting other nearby drivers know what they are doing at the wheel of the car.

For self-driving cars, V2V is likely even better utilized than if it was humans trying to converse with each other, since humans might be delayed in verbalizing their actions, humans might mistakenly utter one thing and do something else, and the time required to orally describe your efforts is many times more time consuming than would be the bits-and-bytes communications among AI systems in the self-driving cars.

Though some put V2V onto a pedestal for driverless car efforts, I'll just mention that it is not entirely as divine as might be assumed. With any kind of technology, there can be errors, glitches, transmission delays, and other snafus that occur with such real-time electronic communiques. There is also the concern that driverless cars might get swamped by V2V messages, zillions being broadcast all at once, and the AI might not readily be able to discern important ones from idle messages, plus there is the chance too of cyber security breeches messing with V2V aspects. Etc.

I'm not saying that V2V is not going to be a handy and vital element, it will be, and just want to make sure that we all realize that reality will still be in existence and the blemishes and qualms also need to be baked into what is possible versus what is likely.

In any case, the proving grounds experiments are often undertaken as though the world will be a different place when the advent of driverless cars arises. Let's see if we can agree on one crucial proposition, namely that we're going to have a mixing of human driven cars and autonomous AI-driven cars, which will last for quite a while.

In the United States alone, there are around 250 million conventional cars. Economically it is not feasible to wave a magic wand and suddenly toss away those conventional cars and replace them with driverless cars, nor do I see much hope in trying to convert those conventional cars into autonomous cars (some have been working on kits to do so, but this doesn't seem like a viable avenue, I would assert).

Mixing Of Traffic With Human Drivers And AI-Drivers

I know many AI developers that are irked that society won't just get rid of human drivers and let autonomous cars take over our roadways.

It would be a whole lot easier to develop the AI systems for driving if the AI didn't need to contend with human driver foibles. Plus, humans are not likely to be able to adequately do V2V with AI-driven cars, at least not in the same way that the AI-to-AI of homogenous driverless cars would be able to do. Therefore, there are at least two strikes against human drivers, they tend to be gnarly and uncivil in their driving, and they wouldn't tend to be very good V2V cooperators.

If you buy into my point that we are going to have a mixture of human-driven cars and of AI-driven cars, doing so for an extended period of time, many years to come, some suggest that maybe we can divide our roads into those that take the driverless cars and other roads that take human-driven cars (with the possibility too of allowing the driverless cars to go into the human-driven cars lanes, but ban the human drivers from getting into the self-driving cars "only" lanes).

There are unfortunately stumbling blocks about trying to divide up the roads in this manner.

One is the logistics aspects of converting roads into those that permit only one type or the other. It is not physical and architecturally so easily undertaken. The cost too to do these conversions would be relatively high, and some might question whether it is a worthwhile cost for society to bear, just to allow driverless cars to proceed at a presumably faster pace.

Another perspective is that perhaps human driven cars could only be on our roadways at certain times of the day or days of the week. Maybe you can drive your car on Tuesday and Thursdays during midday, but not the rest of the week, which is reserved solely for self-driving cars. Upon giving this notion some thought, I believe you'd reject it nearly outright as not especially practical and the pushback by the public would be substantial, one would think.

Yet another idea involves charging a fee, similar to what today is being called congestion pricing, meaning that if you are using a car on certain roads at certain points in time, you'll need to pay a special fee to do so.

This would presumably discourage traffic at those times and get people to somehow spread out when they need to travel. Such a fee could be applied to say human-driven cars and not driverless cars, acting as a discouragement of human drivers and an encouragement of using autonomous cars.

In the case of driverless cars, some are referring to this as a kind of zombie-car tax, wherein the zombie is a driverless car that has no human driver (I'm guessing the AI-driving systems might get offended at being repugnantly referred to as a brainless zombie, ha!).

Some critics worry that any kind of division or subdividing might cause unintended adverse consequences leading to other strife or societal repercussions. Suppose only the wealthy could afford driverless cars and an entire set aside of the roads was now being used more so by the well-to-do and essentially denied to those that aren't rich. It could become a fairness issue.

City planners have been discussing whether to make downtown areas become autonomous car zones, meaning that any car entering into a boundary area of downtown could only use a driverless car within those downtown streets. Again, not an easy way to solve the problem. If you work in downtown and are driving your own car to work, does this mean that you now need to find a place outside of downtown to park your car, and then take a ridesharing driverless car to your office? That doesn't' seem to make much sense in terms of the use of cars and getting around.

Okay, so we're seemingly back to the conundrum that we'll have a mixing of human driven cars and AI-driven autonomous cars, and that the mix likely suggests that we're not going to have streamlined traffic.

As an aside, I realize and acknowledge that those supportive of mass transit are irked by this entire discussion and debate, since they would say stop using cars as the dominant mode of travel. Get out of those darned cars, whether human driven or AI-driven, and use mass transit instead. Thus, problem solved. Well, it's certainly a worthy idea, but for the moment let's continue the everyday usage-of-cars deliberation and revisit mass transit in a future discussion.

Mixing And Congestion

Some hope that human drivers might become more tolerant and civil drivers if they were surrounded by driverless cars.

If an autonomous car next to them is providing the proper driving distance of some number of car lengths to the car ahead of it, maybe human drivers will do the same. I'm not holding my breath on that one. So far, human drivers are more likely to exploit the civility of a driverless car, jumping into the gap that was intended by the AI as a safer driving measure, rather than respecting the purity of such driving approaches.

The other side of the coin is that some suggest we need to make the AI be a tougher, meaner, and more realistic driver, mimicking the antics of human drivers.

Well, there is some merit to the idea, but it certainly would not seem to solve the traffic congestion problem. Presumably, you'd worsen traffic congestion by having more and more cars all playing the same kinds of tricks on each other, regardless of human driven or AI-driven. In a twist on this notion, it could be suggested that the AI self-driving cars might so intimidate human drivers that either human drivers will shape-up to be more civil at driving or they will toss in the towel and switch over to driverless cars (a bit of controversy there).

You might try to argue that the advent of autonomous cars will give rise to expanded use of ridesharing, which seems to make sense. Maybe that will dispense with congestion.

Curiously, some studies of ridesharing in downtown areas tend to show that ridesharing can actually make congestion worse, rather than better. This partially seems to be due to the aspect that the ridesharing cars need to drop-off and pick-up passengers, often doing so at places of the streets that causes blockage or traffic snarls. Also, ridesharing doesn't necessarily seem to be getting people out of their own cars, plus it seems that whereas people might have walked or taken a bus for short downtown hops they instead are using ridesharing.

CHAPTER 3

DEMOLITION DERBY OF
SELF-DRIVING CARS

I recently went to my local county fair and did all the usual things that one does at such events, including eating cotton candy, going on the whirly rides, and of course watching the annual demolition derby.

Demolition derbies were first popularized in the 1960s and 1970s and became what some people consider an actual sport, a motorsport, consisting of drivers competing to see which of them can last the longest in an automotive war of attrition. Typically involving at least a half dozen cars, the drivers overtly attempt to ram into the other cars, hoping to stop the other cars from continuing to participate. The last car able to drive in the arena is the winner.

There's nothing seemingly more satisfying than hearing the crunch and grind of metal against metal as the cars bash and smash into each other. In addition to the final winner of this gladiator style rampage, there are oftentimes trophies for the "Best in Show" and also a "Mad Dog" award for the driver that was the most aggressive and crazily brazen during the automotive battle.

Some would say this is barbaric. Maybe it should be outlawed, some suggest.

The drivers are certainly faced with danger, though there are various ways that the risks are somewhat mitigated.

Usually, the cars are stripped of their glass windows and other potent debris, and various alterations might be made to protect the gasoline tank from readily exploding (along with permitting only a minimum amount of gasoline in the tank itself during the skirmish). Drivers wear a fire-protective suit and helmet. Rules of engagement usually state that it is not allowed to ram the drivers side door, a restriction intended to reduce the chances of injury to the driver.

I'm not saying that those precautions make the demolition derby into a risk-free occasion. The odds of something untoward befalling a driver is still quite real.

Why do we get a thrill from watching a demolition derby?

Here's some potential reasons:

- **The excitement of seeing cars getting bashed up.** We all know that in real life you can't just smash your car and so there is certainly a thrill of being able to watch it happen and do so without having to worry about your car insurance or other such facets.

- **Due to the possibility that the drivers will get hurt.** I don't think most attendees necessarily are purposely hoping that the drivers will get injured, though admittedly the idea sits in the back of their minds that there is human danger involved and this seems to heighten the tension and titillation involved.

- **Revenge against cars.** Maybe you are jaded and feel unjustly beholden to cars, since they in a sense are our masters, more than we seem to be their master. If that's the case, seeing them take a bruising would be sweetly satisfying and a just revenge.

- **Innate gladiator spirit.** You might ask a similar question as to why the Romans watched the gladiators in the coliseum, perhaps as humans we all have an innate spirit that spurs us toward spectacle and mayhem.

- **Since it is a sport.** Okay, believe it or not, some people do earnestly consider demolition derbies to be a genuine sport and they keep track of stats on the drivers and their cars. As such, these devoted fans would say there is no justification or explanation needed, just as there is no explanation needed to go watch a baseball game, a football game, and so on.

Here's a question to ponder, what will become of the vaunted demolition derby once we have true self-driving driverless cars?

Let's unpack the matter.

Advent Of Self-Driving Cars

Assuming that we eventually will have true self-driving driverless cars, ones that are driven entirely by AI and there is no human driver involved, you need to consider whether our attitudes towards cars will change.

Some argue that we will feel less sentimental towards our cars. Perhaps we will no longer associate any kind of emotional bonding with cars and will see them as all interchangeable "robots" that merely ensure that we can get from point A to point B.

Others suggest that we might actually become closer to our cars due to the AI providing a type of personality and beckoning us to use self-driving cars. Imagine that each time you go for a ride the car itself remembers you and chats with you pleasantly, asking about your day and taking care of the driving task obediently for you.

In any case, what about demolition derbies, will we still have them?

Maybe we will.

There are these possible combinations of how such derbies might be undertaken:
- Only self-driving cars in the derby (with no passengers)
- Self-driving cars in the derby and passengers allowed
- Mix of self-driving cars and human driven cars in the derby
- Only human driven cars in the derby

I'll discuss each of these combinations and explain the nuances involved.

By the way, I don't consider a remote-controlled car to be the same as a self-driving car.

I mention this facet because you could even today setup a bunch of cars that would have remote controls, allowing humans sitting around the arena to control the otherwise empty cars. That's the kind of approach you often see at the battle bot competitions. I'm not addressing that possibility herein because it doesn't fit to the theme of truly autonomous self-driving driverless cars.

Only Self-Driving Cars In A Derby

The most novel approach involves having only self-driving cars undertake a demolition derby.

This is essentially an AI versus AI contest.

Do keep in mind that today's demolition derbies do involve a modicum of strategy.

The derby competing human drivers in current times tend to have a battle plan, aiming to say disable a particular car that they think has the best driver in it, or perhaps they want to knock out of the competition the lesser capable drivers. In short, it isn't necessarily all randomness and chaos, and instead the drivers are trying to take whatever shrewd actions they can to maximize their own chances of winning the derby.

As such, the AI of a self-driving car might likewise need to be boosted with a capability of being able to be "smart" about how to compete during a demolition derby.

Furthermore, if you are a believer that the AI systems of driverless cars are going to be imbued with a "no illegal driving" dictum, the AI would need to be recoded to allow for it to ram its self-driving car into other cars (an act that would otherwise presumably be illegal on normal roadways).

A variant of the self-driving cars aspect is whether human passengers could potentially ride inside the smashing and bashing cars.

You might find the idea horrific that people would ride inside the driverless car while it is trying to ram into the other cars, but I'd bet that people will want to take a chance and go along for the ride. You could have professional "passengers" that become celebrities for their antics while riding inside a battling self-driving car (imagine the YouTube channels!), or you could have everyday folks that want the thrill of the matter.

The human passengers might not have any input into the driving task and be there simply as added weight.

I suppose the passengers could also be interacting with the AI, trying to offer suggestions of what to do, though if the humans do so, keep in mind that I'm emphasizing that the AI can already fully drive the car on its own. As such, the human rider offering ideas can be disregarded by the AI or given whatever consideration it wants to undertake.

This does bring up though a somewhat thorny topic.

If humans do go for a ride during a self-driving car demolition derby, you might argue that this is a violation of a so-called "Laws of Robotics" (attributed often to Issac Asimov), namely that AI is supposed to never try and intentionally harm humans.

Whether such a rule actually exists or not, the AI would either need to be coded to allow the endangerment of humans or at least not already care about whether it does so or not.

Another twist involves the potential interaction among the AI systems of the various self-driving cars engaged in the demolition derby.

We are aiming to have self-driving cars that use V2V (vehicle-to-vehicle) electronic communication, enabling the AI systems to share with each other about the roadway conditions. For example, a self-driving car up ahead of your self-driving car detects that there is debris on the freeway, perhaps a fallen sofa that came off the back of a truck, and via V2V cautions your self-driving car.

During a demolition derby, would the V2V be allowed or would it be shutoff?

Most of today's demolition derbies have a rule that the human drivers cannot try to gang-up on other drivers. Instead, each driver is supposed to be performing solo and not intentionally getting other drivers to work in unison. Admittedly, this does sometimes happen anyway, in the spur of the moment, but nonetheless it is usually frowned upon.

The organizer of a self-driving car demolition derby would have to establish various rules, including permitting or banning the use of V2V during the contest.

Would you care which of the AI self-driving cars wins at a demolition derby?

For the contest that lacks any human passengers, I guess you could become uncaring about which of the self-driving cars prevails. If your perspective is that all AI self-driving cars are pretty much the same, merely unfeeling robots of a kind, it doesn't then seem to matter which ones happens to win the derby.

I somehow doubt though that people would take such a view.

I'd bet that inevitably there would be wagering or at least cheering for one of the self-driving cars over another. Maybe the blue painted one versus the red painted one. Maybe the larger self-driving car over the smaller self-driving car. I think that us humans would find some reason to get excited for and have an allegiance for one of the self-driving cars over another. Human nature.

Other Variants Of The Demolition Derbies

In a highly spirited display of mankind versus machine, you could mix together the self-driving driverless cars with human driven cars at a demolition derby.

Assuming that the rules prevented any kind of ganging up, it would imply that each human driver was on their own and each AI system was on its own.

Would you be rooting for the human drivers, or would you be rooting for the AI systems?

Anyone that thought the AI was overrated would undoubtedly be cheering for the human drivers. For those that relish the high-tech innovation of AI, they would be clamoring for the self-driving cars to prevail.

Yet another variation would be to have a demolition derby with no self-driving cars at all and instead be entirely a human driven contest.

Wait a second, you might say, isn't that what happens today?

Yes, but in the future, let's assume that gradually we do away with human driving, and eventually reach a point that driving is almost always done via self-driving driverless cars. Some argue that we won't ever give up the desire to drive and thus we won't allow ourselves to become so dependent upon AI driving systems.

In whatever way things turn out, if humans driving a car does become a rarity, perhaps the demolition derby will be the only place that you'll be able to see humans driving a car.

A twist upon this twist is that suppose the demolition derby is not about demolition, and instead has the human drivers showing that they can drive in a straight line, they can do parallel parking, etc.

In essence, after we've all become deskilled at driving, we might find it as exciting to see humans be able to drive in even civil manners, let alone in destructive ways.

None of us will likely be alive once that day arrives, since it is a far away future and who knows what things will be like by then.

Conclusion

A high-tech person might right away point out that you couldn't presumably have self-driving cars participate in a demolition derby because the AI depends upon sensitive sensors such as cameras, radar units, LIDAR, ultrasonic devices, and the like.

Those electronic devices would likely get punched out right away and therefore the self-driving car would nearly immediately be blinded, either than flailing around aimlessly and chaotically, or having to come to a halt as though the car itself was disabled.

I assure you that those sensors could be relocated to areas of the self-driving car that would be relatively protective of the devices. Plus, the sensors could be the specially hardened versions that you might see used on a military vehicle.

In short, I don't believe that the sensors aspects would be a problem per se, nor would the on-board computer processors and memory be an issue (all of which could be protected).

If there is money to be made via undertaking demolition derbies with self-driving cars, I guarantee you that it can be done.

Another argument would be whether the cost of self-driving cars might be so high that it would not be feasible to have them get ruined in a demolition derby setting.

Well, again, this is readily solved, namely by how much you would charge for people to watch the demolition derby. If enough people want to see it, and at a premium price, it really wouldn't matter how costly the self-driving cars are.

The more beguiling question might be whether we should use self-driving cars in demolition derbies.

CHAPTER 4
AI INTELLIGENCE EXPLOSION
AND
SELF-DRIVING CARS

Sometimes you kick-off a process and in a domino-like manner, it gets going, and going, and going, seemingly feeding off itself and rapidly agitating in an almost unstoppable manner.

Those popular YouTube videos of pouring chemicals into a beaker and a gush of foam comes rushing out are examples of an amassing chain reaction that takes on a life of its own.

During the initial creation of the atomic bomb, some of the scientists involved were concerned that if the atomic bomb was set off, it might begin a chain reaction due to igniting a fission explosion in the air, and would generate a globally wide conflagration of overpowering fire and brimstone.

According to historical reports, the famous physicist Edward Teller was chatting with other members of the Manhattan Project and asked them what might happen to the air during an atomic bomb explosion, and pointed out that via a nuclear reaction using deuterium there are two nitrogen nuclei that collide and turn into oxygen plus carbon, causing a burst of tremendous energy.

Would this essentially ignite our atmosphere, doing so again and again, causing a fiery incineration that would spread around the entire planet in record time?

Not good, and far beyond the scope of what they had earlier envisioned of what the atomic bomb might do.

Pretty much, the act of detonating even just one atomic bomb might destroy the air across the entire planet and end-up killing all inhabitants, including mankind, animals, insects (even those formidable cockroaches!), plants, and you name it.

Apparently, after studying the matter, most of the team declared that such a massive domino effect was either extremely unlikely or some argued that it was just plain impossible. Despite those mindful analyses, some still harbored their doubts as to what indeed would happen.

They decided to make a gentlemen's bet on whether the atomic inferno would really occur or not.

Lest you think this callous, apparently the basis for suggesting making a bet was to relieve the tension among the team, rather than being a genuine and serious wager.

As you know, the air didn't turn into a worldwide firestorm.

Thank goodness for small favors.

Any type of chain reaction that feeds upon itself can potentially have a good outcome or a bad outcome.

We might not know for sure, in advance, whether the outcome is going to be good or going to be bad.

We might have guesses, potentially educated guesses, yet it still doesn't mean that there is an ironclad guarantee of what's going to be unraveled.

There's another venue in which a chain reaction phenomenon is being bandied about by researchers and scientists.

It's in AI.

Intelligence Explosion As Chain Reaction

Before we get into the AI aspects, ponder for a moment the nature of human intelligence.

Some believe that intelligence begets intelligence.

In other words, the more intelligence that someone has, the more intelligent they can become, doing so by feeding off the intelligence that they already have.

Not everyone necessarily works this way.

There are people that seem to be intelligent and appear to have reached their peak, unable to reach any higher in their intelligence, thus, they don't exhibit this rule-of-thumb that intelligence begets more intelligence.

Another consideration is whether there is some minimum amount of intelligence needed to foster the intelligence that begets intelligence formulation.

It could be that if you have too little intelligence, it is like a vessel that is nearly empty, and there's not enough stuff in there to enable the chain reaction to get underway (akin to when pouring chemicals into a beaker to generate the chain reaction of foam, if you don't have sufficient amounts of the chemicals, the chain reaction won't catch hold).

Another twist is that maybe there are only certain kinds of intelligence that beget intelligence.

We are said to have a variety of different bits of intelligence, including the traditional mindpower kind, along with having a form of intelligence that allows you to do complicated arithmetic calculations in your head, or have a remarkable form of emotional intelligence allowing you to sense other people's emotions and respond to them.

Do all types of intelligence have an innate capability to feed off each other, or maybe only certain types can do this (we don't know)?

Using again the beaker example, you can't just mix together any chemicals, you need to have the right ones, in the right quantities and proportions, in order to get the chain reaction to materialize.

Let's consider how this all relates to AI.

Some vehemently assert that we are potentially going to have an AI "intelligence explosion" that will someday occur, and there are various bets that this might happen somewhere between the year 2050 and the year 2100.

To be clear, nobody knows.

Frankly, it might be hogwash and there will never be an AI intelligence explosion, never ever.

Or, there might be an AI intelligence explosion, and it will occur in the year 2500, far off in the future and none of us today will be around to see it happen (unless, I suppose, you quickly discover a miracle cure to stop aging, or put yourself into cold storage for later thawing out to be a witness to the AI wonderment of the intelligence explosion).

Maybe those prognosticators are right, and it will happen in the next thirty to eighty years.

Get yourself ready.

Backing up, consider what it means to suggest that there will be an AI intelligence explosion, and why we should care.

Here's the story.

Today's AI systems are decidedly not on par with human intelligence.

I realize some might be shocked by such a statement, but it is the case that AI isn't there as yet.

The computationally based AI of current times can do some rather tricky and impressive things, but it is at best "narrow AI" that can only work in limited scope or domains, and furthermore lacks any semblance of common-sense reasoning that we associate with human intelligence.

The true AI, something that can unreservedly pass the Turing Test (a popularized method for trying to figure out if something does exhibit intelligence, which is both famous and infamous, oftentimes is referred to as AGI (Artificial General Intelligence).

Thus, whenever you or others speak of AI, in the view of many, it is allowed to be narrow AI, and not be true AI, whilst those that are in-the-know would utter AGI to refer to what presumably will someday be true AI.

There isn't any AGI today.

Many attempts are underway to craft AGI.

Here's the rub.

Suppose we humans toil away at trying to create AGI, the true AI, and yet no matter how long we try, and no matter how hard we work at it, we ultimately don't achieve the vaunted AGI.

Sad face.

Or, smiley face if you are worried that true AI will decide to wipe us out or enslave us (for conspiracy theories about ways in which AI might end-up being our nemesis, or be our best buddy ever).

Okay, let's assume for the moment that humans don't have what it takes to invent true AI.

Does this mean that we'll forever not have true AI?

Time to invoke the chain reaction notion.

In theory, perhaps we can render a sufficiently "intelligent" AI system so that it then morphs into an intelligence explosion, the likes of which we've never seen, and voila, out pops the true AI.

Notice therefore that we didn't have to figure out what it takes to achieve AGI, and instead merely needed to put together the appropriate AI that would spark the chain reaction that would lead to true AI.

You could say that we might back into the advent of true AI.

Yes, potentially we could plan to have the chain reaction, in which case, kudos for being able to figure that out, while it could also be that we have no idea of how to reach the point of starting an intelligence chain reaction, and thus our AI efforts just suddenly and unexpectedly get into an intelligence firestorm by its own volition.

Design versus happenstance.

If that does come to pass, it could happen in a flash, an instant, so quickly that we didn't even realize it was happening, or, some believe it might be a more gradual emergence, one that could take its time, meanwhile we might be gaping in amazement as it unfolds.

How's That AI Intelligence Explosion Going Over There

Returning to the earlier discussion about human intelligence begetting human intelligence, we can ask the same types of questions about how the presumed AI intelligence explosion might work.

For example, once underway, how far along might the AI intelligence explosion go?

Some believe that it will stop at the point that it reaches the full equivalent of human intelligence.

Why so?

Because it is asserted that perhaps mankind exhibits the highest possible intelligence, and therefore there isn't anything beyond it (similar to believing that the speed of light is the fastest thing there is, with nothing faster beyond it, though of course not all agree and would say that the universe could very well be expanding faster than light).

Not many subscribe to the notion that humans harbor the highest caliber of intelligence.

Well, at least that we haven't activated our highest potential, perhaps hidden someone in our brains or someday to emerge from our brains.

So, another viewpoint is that the AI intelligence explosion is going to zoom past human intelligence and land somewhere around so-called super-intelligence, also referred to as ultra-intelligence.

How high is up?

Can't say.

Don't know.

One belief is that this super-intelligence will undoubtedly be beyond our level of intelligence, and yet it will itself also have a boundary or final edge to it. It won't be some amorphous intelligence that is all-consuming.

There are those though that suggest the AI intelligence explosion might be a never-ending chain reaction. AI intelligence might keep going and going, getting smarter and smarter, doing so for the rest of eternity.

This has the feel of the atomic chain reaction worries about a conflagration.

What would it mean for mankind if the AI intelligence explosion was something that once started was ever-expanding?

Again, this could be good, or it could be bad.

Maybe the AI intelligence that begets the AI super-intelligence that begets the AI super-duper intelligence that begets the AI supreme-super-duper intelligence, ad infinitum (or is that ad nauseam), will just keep getting better and better, and be beneficial in increasingly beneficial ways to mankind.

I'd like to hope for the glass-is-half-full outcome.

Those that argue in opposition to the AI super-intelligence emergence are apt to ask what is it that a super-intelligence can think or do or see or say that those of us with ordinary intelligence cannot think or do or see or say?

The usual answer is that a super-intelligence could presumably solve cancer, solve world hunger, explain how the universe began, and essentially answer all of the nagging open issues and questions that us humans, having only perfunctory intelligence, have yet to figure out.

Great!

A twist is that it could be that our ordinary intelligence is insufficient to even identify what a super-intelligence could think about, thus, we really don't have any clue about what a super-intelligence, let alone a super-duper intelligence, could conceive of.

It's too far beyond our paygrade.

As the old story goes, we might be ants in comparison, and the AI super-intelligence would either tolerate our existence, maybe aid our existence, perhaps attempt to push us up the intelligence ladder, might keep us as "pets" in an ant farm (possibly Earth, or maybe move us someplace else), teach us tricks, or decide we aren't worth the trouble and squash us.

Are we risking too much by daring to possibly attain an AI intelligence explosion?

There are two sides to any such coin.

The AI super-intelligence might wipe us out, a risk-adverse outcome (I'd claim), or maybe save us by showing us how to be peaceful and co-exist with each other and with AI.

Cornerstone Prediction

A cornerstone to the AI field on the topic of an AI intelligence explosion was first published in 1965 by John Good Irving in a paper entitled "Speculations Concerning The First Ultraintelligent Machine."

He states that in his opinion: "It is more probable than not that, within the twentieth century, an ultraintelligent machine will be built and that it will be the last invention that man need make, since it will lead to an "intelligence explosion." This will transform society in an unimaginable way."

Well, we're not there yet, though many are trying.

You might find of interest that some interpret those remarks in differing fashions.

For example, the aspect that the rise of an AI super-intelligence (ultra-intelligence in his parlance), would be the last invention that man need make is open to variations in meaning.

Such as:

- Is the statement indicating that the AI super-intelligence will henceforth make any and all new inventions, doing so without any aid or input by mankind?

- Or, does it mean that we won't need any other new inventions at all, since somehow having AI super-intelligence will meet all of our needs?

Another added twist is whether we might get intertwined with the AI intelligence explosion.

Here's the idea.

If the AI becomes super-intelligent, maybe this will rub-off on humans.

Consider how sometimes when with someone else that is really intelligent, it boosts your intelligence, and you glum off or absorb or somehow amplify your own intelligence due to the interaction with and exposure to the other person's intelligence.

Doesn't it seem reasonable to expect that if we did achieve AI super-intelligence, it would ergo inevitably lead to an increase in our own intelligence as a species?

Maybe, though if you believe that the brain has a certain limited capacity of intelligence, and if we are there already, the counter-argument is that the AI super-intelligence can't do much about our own physical limitations and thus we aren't going to become any further intelligent.

Darn!

Perhaps though the AI super-intelligence could make us some nifty thinking caps, which upon sitting on our head, augmented our otherwise puny and noggin brain-constrained intelligence.

See, there's always a way to solve any problem.

One additional quick point worthwhile to include here is the alleged coming of something referred to as the AI singularity.

The singularity is considered the time and point at which AI becomes sentient.

You might be thinking that certainly, the singularity must, therefore, be the point and time of the AI intelligence explosion, seemingly going hand-in-hand thereof.

Maybe, maybe not.

Suppose we don't have an AI intelligence explosion and otherwise reach singularity by our handcrafting of AI to that degree.

Another scenario is that we do reach the singularity, and at that juncture, the AI itself realizes that there's more to be done, and it somehow is able to spur or spark an intelligence explosion within itself to further its evolution (which it chooses to do, at its own discretion).

The gist is that the singularity and the AI intelligence explosion are not necessarily one and the same, and though they obviously have many potential in-common touchpoints, they aren't necessarily conjoined (though, despite this seeming apparent notion, some still argue they are most certainly coexistent and co-dependent).

AI Self-Driving Cars And An Intelligence Explosion

Let's add to this discussion the role of AI-based true self-driving cars.

True self-driving cars are ones that the AI drives the car entirely on its own and there isn't any human assistance during the driving task.

These driverless vehicles are considered a Level 4 and Level 5, while a car that requires a human driver to co-share the driving effort is usually considered at a Level 2 or Level 3. The cars that co-share the driving task are described as being semi-autonomous, and typically contain a variety of automated add-on's that are referred to as ADAS (Advanced Driver-Assistance Systems).

There is not yet a true self-driving car at Level 5, which we don't yet even know if this will be possible to achieve, and nor how long it will take to get there.

Meanwhile, the Level 4 efforts are gradually trying to get some traction by undergoing very narrow and selective public roadway trials, though there is controversy over whether this testing should be allowed per se (we are all life-or-death guinea pigs in an experiment taking place on our highways and byways, some point out).

For Level 4 and Level 5 true self-driving vehicles, there won't be a human driver involved in the driving task.

All occupants will be passengers.

The AI is doing the driving.

Let's consider three aspects of AI self-driving cars and the AI intelligence explosion:

(1) Could the rise of AI self-driving cars be the ingredients going into the beaker that's going to ferment and give forth the AI intelligence explosion?

(2) If AI self-driving cars aren't in the beaker per se, and if some other AI system beats them to the punch and becomes the AI intelligence explosion, would AI self-driving cars be carried along anyway, secondarily, into the AI intelligence explosion?

(3) Would AI self-driving cars as we have devised them be perhaps abandoned as archaic and ridiculous by an AI intelligence explosion that led to an AI super-intelligence, which might find something else or another means for transport that is so mightily superior that driverless cars seem like mere toys in comparison?

Hey, those are great questions.

Lots to discuss and debate.

One viewpoint is that it seems a bit unlikely that the AI self-driving cars that are being devised today are going to produce the AI intelligence explosion.

There's just not seemingly enough there for there to be a there.

Indeed, this brings up another whole debate about whether the effort to achieve true self-driving cars requires that we also discover and codify AGI or true AI.

CHAPTER 5

AI TRUTHTELLER AND
SELF-DRIVING CARS

Will AI lie to you?

Sure, why not.

Most people assume that AI is dispassionate, unbiased, objective rather than subjective, and indubitably a truth-teller.

Nope, it's a myth.

Often fostered by those sci-fi AI-based robots portrayed in movies, it seems that AI itself has managed to gain an assuredly unearned reputation, perhaps promulgated by a terrific Hollywood agent that keeps AI in generally good stead with the public-at-large (well, other than the cases where the AI decides to wipe out humanity and expunge us from the earth, a rather hurtful act, one would so suppose).

In the real world, there is no particular reason to believe that AI is going to be telling the truth.

Anyone that interacts with an AI system can get themselves into quite an untoward posture and suffer inadvertent adverse consequences by doting on every utterance of an AI system and blithely accepting such interaction as some form of ordained truth or gospel.

Let's start with the now known facet about AI potentially containing biases and make our way to the seemingly shocking aspect about AI lying through-its-teeth.

There is already a rising realization about the dreadful biases that an AI system can secretly harbor.

For example, an AI system that decides whether to grant a car loan could end-up doing so by using race as a key factor in the decision-making process, or perhaps an AI system that ascertains the approval of certain medical procedures for a healthcare insurer is using gender to provide a thumbs up or down on those requests.

All that you would know is that your effort to get a car loan was turned down, or that your urgently needed medical procedure got denied for coverage by your insurer. You would be unlikely to ever discover that it was due to an underlying AI-based system that made such a life-changing decision.

And nor know or be made aware that the choice was determined by your ethnicity or your gender.

Oftentimes referred to as Algorithmic Decision Making (ADM), our lives are gradually and inexorably becoming shaped and controlled by how these AI systems render their decisions.

The exquisiteness for any firm using those AI systems is that they can pretend to not know why the AI made its decision, and therefore attempt to deflect any angry response by those adversely impacted. It is easy for a company to simply shrug its shoulders and say the computer made them do it, and thus act as though they are the victim, even though they are the ones that put the AI into the middle of things, to begin with.

AI usage in this manner is undoubtedly a clever means to deflect blame, automate procedures, reduce manual effort, cut back on labor, and potentially get away scot-free when confronted with concerns about inappropriate biases infused into such matters.

How could an AI system get into the business of possessing and leveraging unsuitable biases?

Easy-peasy, one might say.

One of the most common means to have biases slip into the AI stream is via the use of Machine Learning (ML) and Deep Learning (DL), which have been so-far revered as magnificent ways to craft AI systems, though there is an ugly underbelly involved (that's kind of an insider secret, so don't tell anyone or you'll maybe have some clandestine AI looking over your shoulder).

ML/DL is a computational pattern matching approach and usually requires a trove of data for training purposes. Typically involving Artificial Neural Networks (ANNs), the AI attempts to find patterns in data, and then henceforth make use of those patterns to aid in making predictions or review newly provided data to indicate whether it comports to whatever patterns had already been detected.

Let's make clear that there is no "thinking" involved by this kind of AI.

Please do not fall into the common trap of ascribing sentience to such pattern matching techniques.

There isn't any there, there.

Some believe that all of this ML/DL might someday lead to the emergence of human-like intelligence, potentially appearing in a moment or flash that has been coined the singularity, but do not hold your breath for that day.

The use of ML/DL is handy as a somewhat sophisticated mathematical means to model data. A possible downside is that the underlying arithmetic is so arcane that there is no ready means to interpret how the AI ultimately has ascertained relationships among the data elements. Much of the ML/DL used today lacks any inherent explainability that can logically showcase how the AI is rendering its decisions, a sorely needed aspect that is known as XAI for explainable AI. In short, it means that the AI could have landed on race or gender as a factor within the data provided, and silently latched onto such a legally-troubling metric as a vital one for deciding whether to approve a car loan or accept a request for a medical procedure.

Even those that launched the ML/DL into existence might not be able to ferret out that race or gender had become the crucial factors embedded within the AI system.

Kind of an implicit case of plausible deniability built right into the nature of the effort itself.

We will need to wait and see if this is going to be allowed per se, since there are widening calls for regulation to catch such matters (see my assessment of such aspects, and the odds are too that civil lawsuits will be brought and won that then act to break firms from using inscrutable AI systems that encompass troublesome biases.

Shifting gears, consider how AI might similarly become a liar.

Maybe the best place to start involves the famous story of President George Washington and his reported remark that he could not tell a lie.

We have all grown up hearing the story, though only the outlined version.

The full version of the story about George Washington was originally brought to life by Mason Locke Weems, in the fifth edition of his book entitled "The Life and Memorable Actions of George Washington" which was published in 1806, several years after George Washington had already passed away in 1799.

As the story goes, George's father had said he would ride fifty miles to see his son, a long distance in those days, and that any such arduous trip was worth it since his little boy had a heart of honesty and lips that were pure, so much that all could depend on every word that the youth might say.

One day, the father came upon George and plainly could see that the boy had damaged a beloved cheery tree with a new hatchet that had been given to his son.

Reportedly, young George said: *"I can't tell a lie, Pa; you know I can't tell a lie. I did cut it with my hatchet."*

Did the father become enraged, or perhaps he might have instantly scolded his son for the sour deed?

No, supposedly instead the father while beaming with pride indicated: *"Glad am I, George, that you killed my tree; for you have paid me for it a thousand fold. Such an act of heroism in my son, is more worth than a thousand trees."*

Now that's the way a parent presumably ought to be, though if George proceeded to cut down all the other cherry trees on the property, one wonders how far this largesse would be extended.

Well, it is certainly a heartwarming tale, yet nobody knows for sure whether the story is true or not.

I'd like to think it is true and will continue to forever cling to such a belief.

In any case, an underlying theme too of the story is that George was raised in a manner that emphasized the importance of being truthful. Thus, it was not happenstance that he offered the truth, and instead of an upbringing that aided in his tending toward being truthful.

We can tie that same notion to AI.

Recall that we just discussed that the adverse biases of AI systems that incorporate ML/DL were essentially due to being trained in a means that led to such biases.

In the same manner, AI can be trained to lie.

If the data used to train an ML/DL AI system contains lies, the resulting AI is going to proceed to tell lies.

Before we get deeper into this surprising phenomenon, keep in mind that we are going to have AI systems immersed into our everyday lives in ways beyond deciding on loans or medical procedures, including life-or-death real-time circumstances such as self-driving cars.

Today's intriguing question then consists of this: *Will AI-based true self-driving cars potentially have AI that lies, and if so, what might that portend for our reliance upon and riding in self-driving cars?*

Let's unpack the matter and see.

Self-Driving Cars And Those Lies

For Level 4 and Level 5 true self-driving vehicles, there won't be a human driver involved in the driving task.

All occupants will be passengers.

The AI is doing the driving.

Rightfully, you might assume that the AI is going to drive you safely and with proper diligence, and otherwise the AI ought not to be driving a multi-ton vehicle that can readily kill the riders by crashing or kill others by hitting nearby cars or pedestrians.

Would you also expect that the AI is truthful?

This admittedly is not something on the radar of most automakers and self-driving tech developers, and nor on the minds of regulators that oversee driverless vehicles, and unlikely to be something asked by those currently going for a ride in a self-driving car.

Of course, one naturally assumes that the AI driving system unconditionally tells the truth and there would not seem to be any reason to doubt that it does.

How dare we suggest that the AI driving system might be a liar.

Those are fighting words, for sure.

But what does the act of lying consist of, one must first ask.

A common definition of lying is that it is the act of making a false statement with a deliberate intent to deceive.

There are two major elements involved in lying, firstly that a false statement or untruthful statement is being proffered, and secondly that the basis for doing so is a deliberate act intending to convey the lie.

The second part of that definition is somewhat problematic when it comes to being applied to AI.

Without taking us too far down a rabbit hole, there is a big loophole here about the meaning of intent.

Can you honestly say that AI can form intent?

Unless or until we reach sentience of AI, it is hard to ascribe intent to a form of automation. In other words, we usually consider the intention to be part-and-parcel of sentient beings. We would not regard a toaster as intending to burn the toast. It might indeed burn toast, but presumably not because it was "intending" to do so.

Today's AI would presumably be akin to the toaster, namely that AI cannot form intent, despite whatever elaborate ML/DL of a contemporary means we might wish to employ.

If you argue that a lie must have intent as a fundamental element, we cannot then explicitly characterize AI as a liar per se, since it has nothing as yet embodying human-like intent. One also wonders whether it is fair to say that AI is truthful since we might equally claim that truth involves intent as well, in which case, we are once again residing on the rather murky ground.

Of course, we already know that humans can sometimes intentionally tell a lie and in other cases unintentionally tell a lie.

A friend tells you that they saw a ghost, which they fervently believe to be true, and yet it later turns out that it was a trick played on them by some pranksters.

Was your friend lying to you?

Well, maybe yes, maybe no.

They were not intentionally lying, even though it turned out to be a lie.

There are also small lies and big lies, along with lies that are inconsequential and lies that can be overwhelmingly damaging.

Some lies are lies-by-omission, whereby the whole truth is not being told, while other lies are partial-truth and partial-lie, mixing the two together which can make the lying part seem more truthful by the afterglow of the adjacent truth-telling.

In short, lies come in all flavors and shapes and sizes, and we are bombarded by lies throughout our daily lives.

Consider a use case involving self-driving cars.

You get into a self-driving car and interact with the AI via its Natural Language Processing (NLP) interface, akin to an Alexa or Siri.

After telling the AI that you want to be driven to the local grocery store, you ask the AI how long will the trip take?

The AI responds that it will take 18 minutes to get there.

Upon getting underway, the journey ends up taking about 35 minutes, quite a relatively lengthier amount of time than the pledged 18 minutes (nearly double the estimated time given).

Did the AI lie to you?

You might instantly say that the AI did not lie, it merely estimated the driving time, and we all know that traffic conditions can mess-up any kind of such an estimate.

Suppose though that the AI had "known" that there was construction work going on that might impact the driving time, having access to online databases that log any roadway infrastructure projects. Upon obtaining such data, the AI had opted to not add any delaying time to the estimate, since the AI calculated that the time of day of the travel was unlikely to be impinged by the street repairs going on.

In short, the AI provided you with an estimate but hid facts about the estimate, such as the aspect that there was construction work ahead, and that the AI was not including the roadway efforts into assessing the journey time.

Is this a lie then by omission?

You could try to make the case that the AI provided an incomplete picture of the situation and was hiding material facts that led to the time estimation. If a human did the same, we would most likely call them a liar, or perhaps label them as being either untruthful or playing games with the truth.

Returning to the matter of intent, was the AI purposely trying to deceive you about the time involved in the trip?

As earlier pointed out, intent is a rather mushy topic when it comes to today's AI. As far as we can discern, the AI was not somehow choosing to lie, and it is presumably nonsensical to ascribe intent to the actions of the AI.

Imagine that the AI had been fed with data about the responses of human riders when being provided with time estimates for ride journeys. Perhaps an inward-facing camera captured the facial reaction when riders were told the estimated time for a trip. Via sentiment analysis, the facial expression was used to register either happiness or being upset and used as a predictor related to informing riders about the time estimates.

Using ML/DL, the AI system "learned" that people were happier when hearing shorter time estimates, and unhappier when hearing longer time estimates. Perhaps a stated goal for the AI driving system involves trying to have happy passengers, presumably, this would be good for the owner of the self-driving car since riders will then make use of their self-driving car ride-sharing service repeatedly.

In the case of providing the 18 minute ride time estimate, suppose the AI ascertained that the ride time could be up to 35 to 40 minutes in length, and "knew" that to be the case, though it also "knew" that indicating lengthy driving times led to unhappy passengers, and therefore the AI opted to "knowingly" offer the shorter time estimate, which it "knew" to be highly unlikely.

Is the AI telling a lie?

Conclusion

Utter balderdash, some of you might be thinking.

The AI developers that designed, coded and fielded the AI are the ones that are the "liars" in this example.

They devised automation that was primed to lie.

Don't look to the AI, look to the Wizard of Oz that sits behind the curtain.

Perhaps so, and we should certainly seek to hold those that craft and deploy AI systems to be accountable for what these AI-based decision-making systems do.

Some AI developers might argue that their AI creations go beyond what they were initially instructed to do, offering the advantage of "learning" on-the-fly, and as such, it is indeed the AI that is at fault for such considerations and not their maker.

CHAPTER 6

DRIVE-IN THEATRES
AND
SELF-DRIVING CARS

One of the post-pandemic "new normal" predictions is that we will no longer feel comfortable going to indoor movie theatres and will gravitate toward outdoor drive-ins instead.

That is a bountiful breath of fresh air for drive-ins and offers a chance to mount a comeback of seemingly insurmountable odds.

Go, drive-ins, go.

For those old enough to remember, the drive-in was once a dominant force in the movie-going foray and enjoyed tremendous success and growth.

According to industry stats, in the tail end of the 1950s there were an astounding 4,000 or so drive-in theatres across the United States (a peak year for the movie business), and gradually became less and less alluring over the years since.

Today, there are an estimated 300 drive-ins still remaining in the U.S., which actually is a surprisingly large number given that the interest in drive-in movie-going has waned so much.

Why are people going to avoid conventional movie theatres and suddenly shift toward drive-ins?

The answer seems rather straightforward.

From a virus spreading perspective, sitting in a seat at an enclosed movie theatre for several hours at a time seems like rolling the dice on getting infected with COVID-19.

It is hard to practice social distancing, even if somehow the theatre mandates that patrons sit a seat or two away from each other. There is also the difficulty of getting up to go get some more popcorn or soda, or perhaps make that mid-movie visit to the washroom, all of which means having to squeeze past the knees and elbows of others trying to enjoy the movie.

Wearing a facial covering or mask for several hours nonstop while trying to enjoy that action-filled or maybe rom-com cherished movie is going to be an arduous chore.

Plus, how can you comfortably munch on that candy bar or slurp your drink throughout the show while ensuring that the mask remains firmly secured to your face. Worse too, the act of merely moving aside your mask is one of increasing your exposures, and doing so will also likely have your hands end-up touching your face, which is another big no-no when trying to remain infection-free.

Okay, so going to a sit-down movie theatre is going inure some pretty rocky times, and yet meanwhile the public is raring to go out and see a movie.

Sure, the public has been watching an endless parade of movies while sheltering at home, but the so-called *island fever* of being cooped up at home is making people ache to go elsewhere to do their movie viewing. A change of venue can make the movie an entirely different and more enthralling experience.

Solution: *Go to a drive-in theatre.*

Doing so offers some quite sensible and compelling "new normal" benefits.

First and perhaps foremost, you are able to reside within your own self-contained environment while watching a movie at a drive-in.

Your car is your protective bubble.

Presumably, the interior of your car is already germ-free assuming you have kept it spotlessly clean, or worst-case, at least the germs are being confined within your own vehicle. And other moviegoers that might be nearby your car cannot readily spread their germs into your safety sphere.

In theory, friends or pals that are in the car with you are also presumably either infection-free or are loved ones or others that you are already cavorting with. In that sense, probably none of you are wearing masks during the movie-watching experience and have no need to do so per se (this is admittedly a debatable point).

You can, of course, eat to your heart's content.

You can watch a movie on a huge screen, a massive and awe-inspiring sized screen, rather than that puny one that you have at home.

You are outdoors, and mercifully outside of your claustrophobic domicile, including being able to cast your gaze upward to relish a few glances at the evening stars and the beauty of a nighttime sky.

I realize that those of you that used to go to drive-in movie theatres will instantly cringe at the idea of going to a drive-in because of the lousy sound systems and those ungainly metal-speakers that you had to hang onto the partially rolled-down window of the car.

If you might be willing to mentally shift in time, today's drive-ins are usually broadcasting the sound and it is easily picked-up via the sound system inside your vehicle. Generally, most modern-day cars have a snazzy speaker setup, meaning that you will get crisp sound, and hear all of the movie explosions and even the hushed whispers with amazingly clear-cut precision.

Another frequent complaint about drive-ins was that they tended to have older movies, ones that were already past their prime, and seemed to showcase one-off obscure movies, or focused on cheap scary films or those with decidedly low-production quality.

Again, you will need to change your mindset since today's drive-ins frequently offer newly released pictures and realize that they must do so to compete with the sit-down theatres.

I do not want to though leave you with the impression that drive-ins are a nirvana of movie-going.

Realistically, there are some serious downsides to be considered and dealt with.

For example, one of the greatest joys as a child when going to a drive-in was the opportunity to be let out of the car and go for a romp. You could walk past the parked cars and wave at people or carryon snippets of conversation.

Oftentimes, there was a playground at the base of the movie screen, allowing kids from all throughout the sea of parked cars to come together. You met other kids that you perhaps had never otherwise met before. The play area was in many ways more significant than the movie watching.

In a COVID-19 world, it seems doubtful that you would want your children to be rushing into a playground area that might be coated in germs and likewise be interacting openly with other children or nearby adults that might be infected.

Nix the playground aspects, for now.

Another concern would be the act of getting food.

Though you might bring your own home-cooked meals and snacks, there was something fresh and exciting about going over to the centrally located food huts in the drive-in lot and getting a fully embellished hot dog or a freshly made hot-buttered popcorn.

Doing so in today's era might be chancy in terms of not being able to maintain social distancing.

Fortunately, this is somewhat easy to solve, since there are drive-ins that provide delivery to your car, sometimes undertaken by a car-hop on roller skates.

Where there's a will, there's a way.

One other notable point is that going to use the bathroom at a drive-in is a tricky matter to resolve in the post-pandemic realm.

Besides the social distancing difficulties, the additional question is whether the drive-in will be able to keep the restrooms sufficiently clean and whether you or your accompanying loved ones will want to brave a visit to the lavatory. If not, those in your car are unlikely to want to ever again make a visit to a drive-in, assuming that they ended up having to hold-in their primal needs for the entire length of the movie and were forced to wait until getting home to undertake their rather pressing business.

Overall, as might be plainly evident, the drive-in theatre realm is not going to be entirely absent of any consequences in a "new normal" setting, and we will need to wait and see how things actually shake out.

Shifting gears, consider another kind of novel twist that is going to gradually arise.

The curious surprise is the advent of self-driving cars.

Here's then an intriguing question: *Will the emergence of AI-based true self-driving cars aid in drive-in theatre-going or will their adoption put a damper on the remerging outdoor movie watching experience?*

Let's unpack the matter and see.

Self-Driving Cars And Drive-In Movie Theatres

For Level 4 and Level 5 true self-driving vehicles, there won't be a human driver involved in the driving task.

All occupants will be passengers.

The AI is doing the driving.

Let's start with some of the positives or advantages of using true self-driving cars for the drive-in theatre movie-going experience.

Perhaps the biggest plus is that you won't need to drive the car.

Instead, you merely jump into the self-driving car, load it with your family or pals, and tell the car via its Natural Language Processing (NLP) to whisk you all to the nearest drive-in theatre.

Meanwhile, you are able to immediately start enjoying the excursion, doing so without having to worry about traffic or otherwise having to keep your eyes locked on the road ahead.

Party time!

Furthermore, while at the drive-in, whereas you or someone within your group had to remain sober to be the designated driver to get you all safely home, you can now drink (responsibly) and know that the AI is going to remain completely capable to drive when it comes time to leave the drive-in.

This act of the AI being able to drive the vehicle is a tremendous reduction in the friction of the drive-in theatre journey.

Another advantageous factor is the likely altered interior of cars that are self-driving vehicles.

For Level 4 and Level 5 self-driving cars, there is no longer a need to have the driving controls for human access, and thus the automakers can rip out the steering wheel and pedals, freeing up the interior space of the car.

The odds are that the seats inside a self-driving car will be of a swiveling nature, allowing the riders to rotate to-and-fro throughout a riding journey.

In addition, the seats are likely to be recliners, allowing you to fully recline and catch a nap while heading to work in the morning, or perhaps sleeping more fully while on a longer trip that is going to take you across a state and last for the better part of a day or so.

In short, this means that the interior of self-driving cars might be extraordinarily accommodating for the drive-in theatre experience. In today's cars, it can seem like you are a pretzel trying to find a means to conveniently watch the drive-in screen, while for the self-driving car passenger the odds are that the interior seating and reclining are ready-made for the drive-in trek.

What then is not to be liked about the use of self-driving cars for the drive-in going purpose?

One aspect that remains to be seen is whether true self-driving cars are going to be affordable for use in such a luxury-oriented use case of going to a drive-in movie theatre.

Allow me a moment to explain.

It is assumed that true self-driving cars will be somewhat pricey, which is partially due to the added cost of the suite of specialized sensory devices that aid in the self-driving effort. There is also the cost of the development that led to the crafting of self-driving cars. And, there will be some unknown and yet presumed significant ongoing cost to keep self-driving cars in pristine shape to keep safely working on our roadways.

In short, most pundits predict that self-driving cars will be operating nearly 24x7 on a nonstop basis, doing so on a ride-sharing basis to earn enough money to make them worthwhile or profitable as an undertaking.

The question then arises as to whether taking a self-driving car to a drive-in will make much sense.

The vehicle will sit doing nothing for several hours at a stretch.

Is that a cost-effective use of a self-driving car?

The quick answer would be that if there is a buying public that is willing to pay the per hour cost to simply be sitting inside the self-driving car, even while it is not in motion, the owners of such vehicles would be prudent to encourage such business.

On the other hand, one supposes there are pressures that would fight against it.

For example, suppose that an owner had a fleet of self-driving cars in a given geographical area, and the public became used to the self-driving cars being readily available for providing a lift. Meanwhile, on some evenings, a portion of those self-driving cars are "trapped" in a parking lot at a drive-in and not available as self-driving roamers that are ready to pick-up human passengers needing a ride.

Some foretell that we might see regulations that pop-up about the need for self-driving car owners to make sure their vehicles are performing rides, across the board, for everyone that needs a ride, and dutifully roaming around at all times to be readily available.

This is perhaps part of the mobility-for-all mantra.

Time will tell.

Overall, it could be that the cost involved and the other allied pressures are so sufficiently imposing that the use of a self-driving car for a drive-in going activity will be either implausible or might cause a backlash of sizable proportions.

As such, only conventional cars might be the drive-in theatre mode of transit.

But the number of conventional cars is anticipated to gradually dwindle, plus the remaining conventional cars are going to be seen as outcasts, by some, namely that it seems inappropriate to continue the use of human-driven cars if there are AI-driven cars to be had.

Why so?

One aspect is that the human-driven cars are reliant upon those unreliable human drivers that have all sorts of human faults and foibles. In the U.S. there are about 40,000 deaths each year due to car crashes, and perhaps 2.3 million injuries.

Assuming that AI-based true self-driving cars are proven to radically reduce that carnage, there is certainly going to be added pressure to get human-driven cars off the roads.

All told, it could mean that only those "malcontents" that are brushing back against society about giving up their conventional cars would be the only ones left to go to a drive-in theatre. In that case, it would seem unlikely that drive-ins would be able to make enough dough to remain open.

That would be the killjoy effect of the advent of self-driving cars.

Conclusion

Consider one other relatively obscure factor to also consider about self-driving cars and drive-in theatres.

You might recall that in the golden days of drive-ins that teenagers were often desirous of using their parent's car to go to the drive-in, which proffered a sense of independence and adulthood.

Plus, doing so could allow for the infamous "passion pit" aspects (well, we can think of it as an opportunity for teens to learn more about the birds and the bees, in real-life, while fumbling around as the movie played on the screen, rightfully or wrongly so).

You could make the case that the self-driving car would readily enable this kind of behavior.

The teens would not need to know how to drive. The car interior is ready for reclining and fertile for the undertaking of amorous activities.

Furthermore, some of the self-driving cars are predicted to have windows that can be made switchable to be opaque in appearance or be fully transparent, doing so at the push of a button. The basis for this feature would be that people might want privacy while inside their self-driving cars, such as taking that nap during the evening commute home, while at other times might wish to switch the windows into a transparent mode to blissfully observe the countryside as the AI does the driving for them.

The opaqueness is the kind of privacy that those frolicking teens might relish.

I suppose it would seem odd or ironic to go to a drive-in movie theatre and yet blackout the windows of the car, but I think it is obvious why that might be a popular capability for some moviegoers.

A parent's worst nightmare, perhaps, and emboldened due to the advent of true self-driving cars.

There is another side to that coin.

The odds are that self-driving cars will have inward-facing cameras, used to capture video of the internal activities and for ride-sharing purposes be able to detect and catch those that might opt to mark graffiti or tear-up the interior of the vehicle.

Presumably, a doting parent could forewarn the teenagers that the roving eye of the self-driving car will be watching them at all times.

Certainly, that would put a wet blanket on the shenanigans.

But, maybe not since those energetic and enterprising teens might be quite innovative and figure out a crafty way to circumvent the intrusive watcher.

Where there's a will, there's a way.

CHAPTER 7

AI MIND-COPYING

AND

SELF-DRIVING CARS

If you make a copy of something, is it the same as the original?

Suppose that you go to a local copier store and make a copy of your birth certificate, perhaps needing to have a handy copy available.

The copy might generally appear to be the same as the original, though by closer inspection perhaps the colors are slightly askew of the original and the lines are not as fully formed. In addition, there are numerous speckles or noise that managed to find their way onto the copy, perhaps due to the copier glass not being completely clean or due to the printing process overall.

So, the copy it turns out is actually somewhat inferior to the original and not truly a complete and purely exacting match.

On the other hand, it turns out that the birth certificate was quite faded and the newly made copy is much sharper in appearance. The clarity of the document has been greatly enhanced.

Thus, you could make the case that the copy is somewhat better than the original.

All in all, you did not end-up with exactly the same thing as the original, including some aspects that were not as desirable and other facets that were an added bonus.

Shift gears and let's discuss the human mind.

Can you make a copy of a human mind?

If so, would it be exactly the same as the original, or would it be better or worse?

That is an abundantly intriguing question and an aspect that continues to be a raging and indubitably controversial topic among philosophers, neuroscientists, cognitive specialists, and experts on Artificial Intelligence (AI), along with many other theorists and practitioners.

First, it is important to establish that there are no known means today to make a copy of a mind.

Presumably, doing so would require somehow gauging or collecting the byzantine biochemical and electrical states of the brain, miraculously recording or copying them, and then placing those states into another brain.

That is a tall order.

Today's methods such as MRI, CT Scan, and other experimental approaches are not up to the task.

Even if we could do such a feat, some question whether you would really be copying the totality of the mind of that original source.

In other words, perhaps there are other elements about the mind that do not arise via the mere mechanical-like aspects of the brain. This can range into the arena of whether we have a "soul" that is beyond the physically collective brain states and involves too some quizzical postulations about whether the mind is indivisibly intertwined with our bodies beyond just the brain elements alone.

If there is more to the mind than the brain states themselves, your copy is presumably going to be "inferior" to the original and not be a true copy. Of course, the counter-argument is that perhaps the copy would be superior, similar to the point made earlier about the copying of the birth certificate which led to some enhanced facets.

In short, we don't know if this mechanistic approach to physically copying a brain would result in an equal mind when ported into someone else's brain.

That brings up an allied point that makes for additional troubles.

Whose brain would receive the copy?

It would seem problematic to try and copy one complete brain-copy into another brain.

The structure of the target brain might not be the same as the source brain, likely containing a different number of neurons and their myriad of interconnections (plus a slew of other demonstrative differences). As such, it would not be readily feasible to simply map on a one-to-one basis from the source brain to the target brain.

Also, what happens to the contents that are already inside the target brain?

It could be that you would wipe out whatever was there or maybe cause an overlap. Perhaps it would be crucial to start with a blank slate, but this brings up the question of how a brain could be scratched such that there is no mind per se within the brain.

Dizzying.

And if it turns out that the mind is more than the collective set of states of the source brain, you might make the copy and have a resultant non-working mind in the target brain. The person receiving the mind-copy might be so mentally scrambled that they no longer can function.

A darned shame after going to all that trouble to make the brain-copy.

These are some of the issues confronting those that are trying to figure out how to make a Whole Brain Copy (WBC), also known as brain uploading, mind copying, mind transfer, and also at times referred to as Whole Brain Emulation (WBE).

WBE though is not quite the same as the other monikers since it tends to deal with emulating the brain, rather than focused solely on the notion of brain copying.

This though brings up a nifty transition to an affiliated topic, the role of AI in this matter.

AI And The Copycat

The overarching intent of AI is to achieve human intelligence or its equivalent, doing so into a machine.

Currently, AI researchers and AI developers are slaving away at trying to craft the equivalent of a human mind by using all sorts of computational approaches and algorithmic trickery.

Do not be misled by the popular press that suggests we are on the verge of cracking the code of the human mind and somehow readying to have AI that fully has achieved human intelligence.

Indeed, the discussions about arriving at sentience, considered the as-yet defined spark that makes humans into thinking humans, and the presumed moment known as the singularity when this switchover from an everyday computer into human-equivalent AI will occur, these such discussions and prognostications are indefatigably premature.

I am not saying that we shouldn't be discussing those momentous topics, we should be, but emphasizing that the realization of those lofty goals is still a faraway glimpse, at best.

Anyway, imagine how exciting it would be if we could potentially copy a human mind.

So far, the earlier points were about copying a human mind and placing that copy into another human.

Suppose that we could copy a human mind and place that copied mind into a computer.

On top of that supposition, suppose that the computer then was able to emulate a brain sufficiently that the now-copied mind would actually function properly.

One of the reasons that would be exciting is that it could mean that we do not need to construct a mind or AI from-scratch.

Right now, the laborious approach of deconstructing the mind is not necessarily going to proceed smoothly, and nor will the programming and coding necessarily produce the AI desired results of equating to human intelligence.

It might make sense that if you can't beat them, join them.

This is the copycat approach.

In other words, we should focus on creating an artificial brain that could house a human mind.

Don't worry about how to craft the human mind part of things. Instead, aim to craft a repository and then let the copied over mind do all the rest for us.

We change our attention to the matter of how to emulate a brain versus the other stickler of how to develop a mind or its equivalent.

Does this imply that we are currently going in the wrong direction and need to take a different fork in the road, aiming to build a shell for containing human minds rather than seeking to make a human mind from the ground up?

Well, it is a wild bet as to whichever direction you go.

Maybe the mind-from-nothing is the better approach, or maybe the brain computer-receptacle is the better approach or something that combines the two, or neither of them.

Nobody can say for sure.

Twists And Turns In The Human Mind Replicas Debate

I'll add some breathtaking twists to the topic.

Suppose we could copy a human mind into a computer-based brain shell and that this actually produced a computer-based mind, functioning fully and properly.

You could claim that AI was finally achieved.

Some would call it cheating.

It would presumably be cheating in that we might not necessarily know why the mind worked and only did a somewhat bland and wholescale copy of the mind from the source human brain. Purists believe that as part of the AI overarching goal, we ought to figure out how human intelligence comes to be. A bulk copying of a mind would seemingly not get us there.

Of course, you could easily argue that if we cracked how to do the copying, we might also ergo have cracked how the mind works, thus it could be a twofer.

Another twist involves the plentiful nature of copying.

When you make a copy of your birth certificate at the copier store, you can easily make as many copies as you want.

If we somehow could copy a human mind, let's assume we ask Joe or Jane to let us copy their mind, and we then upload that into our handy-dandy computer-based brain receptacle, we have then made one copy and apparently now have an equivalent of Joe or Jane (with respect to their mind).

Maybe it would be nifty to make more copies.

We could perhaps build a hundred of these brain receptacles and put the mind of Joe or Jane into each one of them.

Why would we do so?

Pretend that Einstein was alive today and we were able to copy his mind. If we made a hundred copies, some might argue that we would have a tremendous amount of brainpower to work with, perhaps leading to new theories about physics and the workings of the world, far beyond what a singular Einstein alone could ever have discovered.

That is the upside.

The downside would be making copies of a potentially devilish or evildoer mind, which keeps me up at night, nightmarishly envisioning a hundred copies of some dastardly mind that might be surge-powered to come up with ways to completely rule or ruin mankind.

Don't want that.

Coming back to the mind copying notion, perhaps we could craft an AI system that was the equivalent of human intelligence, an artificial mind as it were, and use that to be our source for copying.

Heavens, you say.

Yes, the implication is that we could do any of these:
- Copy a human mind to another human mind
- Copy a human mind into a computer-based brain receptacle and have the mind working there
- Copy an AI "mind" into a human mind
- Copy an AI "mind" into another AI "mind"

While you consider those possibilities, there is something else to be contemplated.

In theory, each human is unique with respect to their mind.

More so than even the uniqueness of your fingerprint, your mind is a constantly meshing conglomeration of all your experiences and thoughts. No other person on earth has had the exact same experiences and thoughts as you. Therefore, your mind is wholly unique, at any given in point of time, and entirely throughout your living existence.

Now, I'm not saying that this uniqueness necessarily makes a difference.

At the scale of looking at how a person behaves; we might say that two people are pretty much the same. Nonetheless, as far as we know, the detailed inner states of their brain and their mind are indeed different.

Okay, so we opt to copy the brain of Jane on Tuesday at precisely nine in the morning. A split second later, her mind is now different than it was at the moment of making the copy. And, for each second or minute or hour or day that passes, her mind continues to veer further and further away from the copy that was made.

As an aside, we are also assuming that the act of copying does not disturb or alter the original. In the analogous case of the birth certificate, presumably, the birth certificate is unchanged during the copying process. We do not know that the copying of a human mind could be said to be the same, and it might very well be that the copying action in some means mars or changes the mind, either for the good or for the bad.

Since we are already in fantastic theory-land, to begin with, assume for now that the mind copying is change-free.

When we put Jane's mind into another human, the instant we do so, presumably thereafter the mind is no longer the same as Jane's subsequently evolving mind, and the new Jane is going to essentially be a different mind.

The point here is that we do not know that having a working copy is going to produce necessarily the same results as would the original mind that is instantly veering off in other ways.

Those one hundred Einstein brains are each morphing and might or might not converge toward the Einstein original that is also morphing.

If we did do this kind of human cloning, doing so about minds and not about bodies (though, possibly that is also on the To-Do list), what rights would those minds have?

Would you say that those one hundred Einstein's should each be accorded human rights, and thus can do the things that any other human is considered rightfully able to do? As a simple example, could each one vote in an election?

I assume too that your answer might differ depending upon the target of the mind.

When the target is another human, it seems like you would be willing to agree that this human with the newly minted mind (though a copy), would retain their human rights. Meanwhile, if the human mind was placed into a brain computer-shell, the assertion of human rights might be more challenging.

The ethical implications are staggering, as are the legal ramifications.

There is no free lunch involved in mind copying.

AI Minds And Self-Driving Cars

We can use AI-based true self-driving cars as an exemplar for pondering these mindful matters.

True self-driving cars are ones that the AI drives the car entirely on its own and there isn't any human assistance during the driving task.

These driverless vehicles are considered a Level 4 and Level 5, while a car that requires a human driver to co-share the driving effort is usually considered at a Level 2 or Level 3. The cars that co-share the driving task are described as being semi-autonomous, and typically contain a variety of automated add-on's that are referred to as ADAS (Advanced Driver-Assistance Systems).

One question yet resolved is whether the AI that can drive a car is necessarily going to need the same capabilities as full human intelligence.

Some assert that there is no need to fully replicate human intelligence in the "narrow" act of being able to drive a car. In theory, the AI does not need to measure up to the AI aspirations, today referred to as Artificial General Intelligence (AGI), which is an alternative re-phrasing of the AI moniker that harks us back to the overarching goals of AI.

If we don't need the full ensemble of human intelligence to drive a car, it sure makes the task of developing an AI driving system easier, though realize that does not mean it is easy, and only suggests that it will require less of a reach than if we had to perform all facets of human intelligence.

Either way, it is appropriately labeled as a moonshot (see my discussion in the introduction).

Suppose after the many billions of dollars have been expended toward self-driving that we are not able to arrive at what would be considered suitably safe and proper driving by AI.

Then what?

Well, in theory, we could try the approach of making a computer-based brain receptacle and get a human mind that we would pour into that vessel.

Similar to how today there is a person that voiced the words you hear from an Alexa-like or Siri-like voice Natural Language Processing (NLP) system, imagine if we picked Joe or Jane as the person to be the key source for our AI self-driving car systems.

We grabbed up their mind, including all of their personality and idiosyncrasies, and download that into an AI driving system that would presumably now be able to drive a car.

It would seem prudent to make sure first that Joe or Jane did not have any outstanding warrants for illegal driving or had any traffic tickets outstanding. In fact, we might want to find a racecar driver as the human mind to be copied, though that could bite us too since the AI driving system might suddenly place the vehicle into high-gear and put the pedal to the metal (for my discussion about racecar performance for AI driving systems, see **the link here**).

Okay, this overall idea of mind copying for AI driving purposes is admittedly a bit of a stretch.

Let's aim a bit lower.

One practical consideration is that the AI driving systems that are being crafted today are generally oriented toward a particular make and model of a given brand of car.

This does bring up an interesting and useful question, namely how hard will it be to port the AI driving system (it is a "mind" in a pejorative sense) into other cars.

I hope you can see that this is the same kind of issue about copying, though a lot easier, by far, and we aren't talking about human minds in that case.

From the perspective of the automakers and self-driving tech developers, they will be happy, actually ecstatic, when being able to have an AI driving system that is safe and works appropriately, while the question about porting to other cars is something they would say is quite secondary and not worthy of undue attention right now.

Get the basics done, they contend and worry about the expansions later.

Conclusion

Throughout the existence of mankind, there have been dreams and even actual attempts at achieving immortality.

For those that have chosen to already freeze their bodies and go into a cryogenic state, some are hoping that when they are someday awakened, perhaps the illnesses racking their bodies will have new cures and they will once again have a healthy life. Or, perhaps an elixir will exist that provides them with long life and allows them in a reawakened state to live for hundreds of years.

Maybe we will someday have mind copying.

Would someone choose to be mind-copied into another human, or prefer instead to be placed into a computer-based brain receptacle (perhaps accompanied by a robotic body)?

But would this copying really be immortality, or merely a copy and not be offering the source mind to live forever per se.

You might say it is cheating and not the true version of immortality.

Guess we will deal with that vexing matter when the day arrives.

CHAPTER 8

MENTAL WAYFINDING

AND

SELF-DRIVING CARS

Do you know where you are right now

The odds are that you do.

I don't mean that you perhaps know that you are at a particular street address or sitting in your favorite chair at home, but instead, I am referring to the aspect that you spatially know where you are.

Via both your senses and your mind, you might realize that you are ten feet away from a nearby TV and that you are five feet away from the nearest window. As you sit inside a room, your mind has an abstract model that keeps track of where you are and where other nearby objects reside.

On top of that realization, your mind also knows that the room is within a building, the building is within a neighborhood of buildings, and the neighborhood is within a city, which is within a county, and within a state, and within a country, etc.

Imagine using something like a mental version of Google Earth and having your mind be able to zoom in and zoom outward, quickly imagining your position from a faraway location and at the same time being able to get close-in and know exactly where your feet are placed and your immediate and within reach surroundings.

This knack of cognition is typically referred to as mental wayfinding.

Humans seem to have a powerful capability of mental wayfinding.

To set the record straight, wayfinding is not solely a function found within humans and decidedly is an inherent facility of many living organisms.

We do though seem to take this wayfinding to a higher-level of thinking.

Here's what that means.

The notion of spatial orientation and spatial elements permeates a lot of what we do, far beyond the mere act of locomotion.

Sure, you use your mental wayfinding when trying to find the kitchen or while hiking in the woods and aiming to get back to your campground, but this is only a sliver of the wayfinding usage.

Wayfinding and spatial processing are subtly found in how we describe a lot of what we do.

You might describe a longtime friend as being a near-and-dear close friend and bring up to your distant aunt. Notice that the words "close" and "distant" are conventionally about spatial matters and would normally refer to physically being near to someone or something. In this alternative use, those words are more so about the relationships that you have with those people.

In short, we borrow lots of spatial meanings to be used in various other significant ways.

Why so?

One theory is that our minds are so immersed in spatial capabilities that it wants to try and use that built-in aptitude in as many ways as seems possible.

Presumably, we might as well leverage a handy feature that already is ingrained in our minds and use it to our Darwinian survival advantage. Spatial processing is akin to duct tape, namely, it has a lot of uses and we keep finding new ways to take advantage of it.

We can't help ourselves.

Let's then separate the use of spatial processing from that which aids our ordinary physical navigation and consider how spatial facets are used in more abstract and unheralded purposes.

As an aside, the traditional assumption is that spatial processing is intended principally for locomotion and movement within our physical world, a seemingly obvious point, though some try to argue that maybe spatial processes were intended really for our higher-level thinking and just so happened to get harangued into being used for bodily navigation. A fascinating proposition, though one that is hard to make as strong a case as being more likely the other way round.

Well, at least we do know that wayfinding is existent and quite exquisitely useful.

Consider your mind to be filled with knowledge and those gold nuggets are arranged somewhat like an everyday library or bookstore. When you go into a physical library or bookstore, you might know that the books on cooking are on aisle seventeen and that the books about car repair are stacked toward the back of the store.

Likewise, we often find ourselves trying to think about a subject or topic and roll our eyes, as though we are peering inward into our minds, seeking to find that location of an obscure fact about a great historical explorer or maybe trying to remember an algebraic equation we learned in grade school.

It seems as though we use wayfinding in how we store information within our minds.

The same spatial memory that remembers where you left your toothbrush is also able to remember the notable fact that Einstein developed the theory of relativity.

A toothbrush is a physical object in the real-world and has some position thereof, while the snippet of memory about Einstein is a piece of knowledge that conveniently is organized and stored inside your head, yet they both have in common the use of your cognitive spatial powers.

One can persuasively argue that mental wayfinding is a crucial cornerstone for humans being able to think.

Perhaps the aspect that we seem to be able to extend thinking far beyond that of other animals is that we have taken spatial processing to a heightened place. This does not suggest that wayfinding is the only basis for the incredible reaches of human thought, and merely emphasizes that it is seemingly a vital reason for the amazing aspect of human intelligence.

Why all the bother about this?

For those embarking upon crafting AI, the underlying vitalness of mental wayfinding needs to be given its due respect and attention.

One might say that wayfinding has earned such a right.

Not everyone necessarily sees things that way.

Time to back up and provide some context.

AI is intending to achieve artificial intelligence that presumably is the equivalent of human intelligence.

The vaunted quest involves grasping how human intelligence works, doing so to try and give us insights into what artificial intelligence is most likely to also need.

Some within AI are apt to argue that we do not necessarily need to deconstruct or reverse engineer human intelligence and instead can construct whatever we want, as long as outwardly it seems to showcase the same semblance of intelligent behavior.

That indeed is one means to approach the problem and lessens the difficulty of needing to crack open the inner secrets of how the human mind works. Don't worry about the human mind and just proceed ahead to make something that appears to have the same result.

Others believe that the treatment of the human mind as a kind of an impenetrable black box is a false path and ultimately doomed to failure. Rather than trying to devise the equivalent of a mind from the ground-up, the hope is that by figuring out the wonders of the brain we will be more likely to arrive at AI.

If you believe that the open-the-brain is the appropriate pathway to AI, we seem to already know that mental wayfinding is instrumental to human intelligence, and therefore logically we ought to be devising and implanting such wayfinding into AI systems.

For those on the other path, wayfinding offers some interesting considerations but does not loom as large as an essential component to be toyed with.

Some applications of AI readily make wayfinding a sensible and needed ingredient.

Consider this intriguing question: *Should AI-based true self-driving cars embody a type of mental wayfinding, not just for physical navigation, but also as a general knowledge-based model for operation and driving?*

Let's unpack the matter and see.

Self-Driving Cars And Mental Wayfinding

For Level 4 and Level 5 true self-driving vehicles, there won't be a human driver involved in the driving task.

All occupants will be passengers.

The AI is doing the driving.

First, let's cover the apparent aspects of physically-oriented navigational wayfinding.

Using GPS and other navigational aids, including the IMU (Inertial Measurement Unit), the AI driving system has to keep tabs on where the vehicle is and where it is going.

Also, similar to how robots navigate, the AI driving system makes use of SLAM (Simultaneous Localization and Mapping), a computational technique that enables the AI to do physical wayfinding.

Once AI self-driving cars become prevalent, humans will presumably no longer need to be especially concerned about wayfinding when traveling via an automobile since the AI will take care of that chore for them.

No more needing to consult a map before a journey or during your travels. Just sit back in the seat, maybe reclining as it is anticipated that self-driving cars will have seats that convert into beds, allowing for taking a nap during a lengthy ride, and enjoy the trip.

In the United States alone, we drive about 70 billion hours annually and need to keep our minds sharpened toward the driving task and the navigational considerations too. Of course, in modern times you can merely follow the GPS step-by-step instructions and not need to mentally have a larger image in your mind of where you are going, yet nonetheless, you are still exercising some amount of mental wayfinding.

Some worry that once we become reliant upon self-driving cars, our mental wayfinding related to navigation will wane.

It is potentially a skill that if not kept up-to-date will atrophy.

You might be thinking that it won't matter if we do weaken our physical wayfinding prowess since we will have those self-driving cars to do our bidding.

The rub consists of the potential leakage due to such a weakening.

One theory holds that if we begin to lose our physical wayfinding mentalism, we will see a similar degradation in the other realms of our mental wayfinding.

Trying to remember the name of that famous historical explorer or the fact about Einstein is going to become harder and harder for us humans to do. The belief is that the wayfinding as an overarching capability will diminish and therefore spill over into all other mental uses of wayfinding.

What do you think?

Will AI self-driving cars inadvertently lead to the human mind becoming less sharp and maybe we will become dumb and dumber?

It is a twofer, namely, we lose the ability to do wayfinding in the physical world, plus we undercut our mental prowess that relies upon wayfinding.

Here's a means to thicken the plot and make things even worse.

Some believe that we will opt to no longer walk as much, due to the advent of self-driving cars. Instead of walking down the block to visit a neighbor, we will hop into the handy-dandy self-driving car and have the AI drive us there.

If you go along with that theory, humans are possibly going to exercise less and potentially plump up.

The totality of this grand convergence results in humans becoming fattened and slovenly, along with losing their mental edge and becoming mental zombies, all as a result of the convenience and marvelous addition of self-driving cars into our world.

Wow, a lot of baggage seems to be piled on top of those self-driving cars.

Anyway, let's shift gears.

Can AI use mental wayfinding in ways other than purely for navigation?

Yes, absolutely.

One such approach involves the use of knowledge graphs, considered an AI-related technique that structures knowledge into a representation that might be construed as a tree that branches and stretches out in a multitude of directions.

Ponder how this might be used in an AI-based self-driving car. Suppose the AI is driving the self-driving car and getting near to railroad tracks.

You might not normally give much attention to railroad tracks while driving a car. The surprising aspect of railroad tracks is that nearly 500 deaths per year occur in the United States due to failing to safely cope with a railroad crossing. There are about 128,000 public railroad crossings and approximately 180,000 miles of railroad track in the U.S.

The AI could treat each railroad crossing as an individualistic and prior unseen type of driving circumstance. Or, the AI might have a treasure trove of aspects previously recorded when driving over railroad tracks, stored as part of its knowledge-base about driving.

Via the use of a mental wayfinding component in the AI, perhaps based on a knowledge-graph, access is made to those various techniques and possibly even prior experiences of having crossed railroad tracks. Those are then fused and utilized when approaching a railroad crossing that the AI has not previously encountered.

The AI-based mental wayfinding can be used in a wide variety of other contexts, including carrying on discussions with the passenger inside a self-driving car. Whereas today's self-driving cars have a quite limited Natural Language Processing (NLP) capacity, in the future it is anticipated that the NLP will be able to engage in rather wide-ranging dialogues with riders and possibly even offer a kind of therapeutic counselor as both your driver and emotional adviser.

CHAPTER 9

AUTOMATED MACHINE LEARNING

AND

SELF-DRIVING CARS

Suppose you could develop an AI application without having to lift a finger.

To some degree that is the goal of Automated Machine Learning, known as AutoML, which consists of an automated means to build on your behalf a Machine Learning application, requiring minimal by-hand effort on your part.

Just sit yourself down in front of a computer, make some selections on a few screens, and voila, out pops a Machine Learning app that does whatever it is you dreamed-up.

Well, that's the idea behind the AutoML movement, though please be aware that life is never that easy, thus do not set your expectations quite that high if embarking upon using the latest and greatest in Automated Machine Learning.

Nonetheless, AutoML can still provide a lot of heavy lifting for those crafting an AI application, and serve as a kind of over-the-shoulder buddy that can double-check your work.

Let's back up and consider what it takes to make use of Machine Learning tools, which are programs that essentially do pattern matching on data and you can then deploy those programs to do fieldwork as part of an overall AI system.

For those of you that have never tried to build an ML-based application, the closest that you might have come to do the same thing would involve having used a statistical package to do a statistical analysis.

Perhaps in school, you had to do a multiple regression statistical run on data about the relationship between the heights of basketball players and their weights. The effort probably was not especially enjoyable, and you might remember having to collect a bunch of data, get the data prepared for input, you had to run the statistics package, then interpret the results, and possibly do the whole thing over depending upon how the reports came out.

That is a pretty good overall perspective on the steps taken to craft a modern-day Machine Language application.

Indeed, anyone that has attempted to make use of today's Machine Learning building tools is familiar with the difficulties associated with making an AI application that relies upon Machine Learning as a core element.

There are a series of steps that you customarily need to undertake.

The typical set of steps includes:
- Identify the data that will be used for the ML training and testing
- Ascertain the feature engineering aspects such as feature selection and extraction
- Prepare the data so that it can be used by the ML tool
- Do preliminary analyses of the data and get it ready for the ML effort
- Choose an ML model that applies to the matter at hand
- Setup the hyperparameters with the ML model chosen
- Use the ML model for initial training and inspect the results
- Modify the hyperparameters as needed
- Potentially reexamine the data in light of the ML model results
- Rejigger the data and/or the ML model
- Loopback to re-selecting the ML model if so needed
- Undertake testing of the final ML model
- Ready the ML for use and deployment
- Over time make sure to monitor the ML and re-adjust

If you skip a step, the odds are that your budding AI application is going to be a mess.

If you badly perform a step, the chances are that your aspiring AI application is going to be faulty.

Even if you do a good job of undertaking the prerequisite steps, you could inadvertently make a goof, perhaps forgetting to do something or doing the wrong thing by accident, and yet would have an AI application that might falsely seem to be okay on the surface though it has some rotten apples in its core.

With the ongoing rush toward pushing AI applications out-the-door as quickly as possible and doing so with great fanfare, the "developers" doing this kind of Machine Learning work are no longer the prior insider core that it once was.

It used to be that you had to have a strong AI and computer programming related background to do Machine Learning. Also, you likely had a hefty dose of statistics under your belt, and you were in many ways a Data Scientist, which is the newer terminology used to refer to someone that has expertise in tinkering with data.

Nowadays, just about anyone can claim to be a Machine Learning guru.

As mentioned, in many respects the ML technologies are akin to a statistical package that does pattern matching. In that sense, you usually do not need to develop raw code in an obtuse programming language. The main task involves running a package and making sure that you do so with some (hopefully) appropriate aplomb.

With larger and larger masses of people opting to toy with ML, the dangerous aspect is that they are using a jackhammer but do not know the proper ways to do so.

Others around them might be clueless too that the person they have hired or sought to make the ML is also clueless.

This leads to the scary potential that the resulting ML application will not be in suitable shape for real-world use, though no one along this chain of "makers" realizes they are doing things wrongly.

What can happen?

An AI application based on a sour or poorly crafted ML core can contain inherent biases. Perhaps the AI app is intended to identify those that should be approved to get a car loan. It could be that the underlying ML pattern matching uses gender or race as a key factor in ascertaining whether the loan will be granted.

You might be thinking that wouldn't it be obvious that the AI app has such a foul underbelly?

The answer is no.

The biases might be deeply hidden within the guts of the ML portion.

It got in there because the "developer" of the ML app was not on the prowl to find such biases. It got in there too because the "developer" did not do sufficient testing. They did not do the needed data prescreening. They did not do the expected assessment of which ML techniques would be the best fit. and so on.

In short, for many of today's AI apps and the use of ML, it is the blind leading the blind.

Someone that does not properly know how to use ML is asked or paid to craft an ML-based application. Those making the request do not know how to judge that the ML is working prudently. In any case, deadlines must be met, and the AI app has to hit the ground quickly to keep up with the competition or to try and leapfrog those presumed lead-footed competitors not yet using AI.

In one sense, having an AutoML can provide handy-dandy guidance to those that are not especially versed in using ML. The AutoML does some crucial handholding and can offer keen advice about the data and the ML techniques being selected.

That's good.

The unfortunate side of that coin is that it can encourage even more neophytes to take a blind shot at doing ML and further widen an already opened can of worms.

That's bad.

Some argue that ML experts are essentially elite and that the use of AutoML will democratize the capability of leveraging Machine Learning. Rather than having ML capabilities only found within the hands of a few, the power of ML can be spread among experts and non-experts alike.

Historically, this same kind of debate has occurred in other facets of the computer field.

For example, writing code in conventional programming languages has always been subject to the same kind of expert versus non-expert criticisms. There have been numerous attempts at so-called fourth and fifth-generation programming languages, often indicated as 4GL and 5GL, trying to make programming easier for those that want to create applications.

Thus, this latest notion of putting something on top of Machine Learning tools to make things easier or more productive when using ML is not a wholly new idea or approach.

Those in the AI Ethics realm are worried that the ML add-ons that offer AutoML might undercut their call for being attentive to key principles underlying the stewardship of trustworthy AI.

The OECD has proffered these five foundational precepts as part of AI efforts (the OECD AI Ethics principles document):
1) AI should benefit people and the planet by driving inclusive growth, sustainable development and well-being.
2) AI systems should be designed in a way that respects the

rule of law, human rights, democratic values and diversity, and they should include appropriate safeguards – for example, enabling human intervention where necessary – to ensure a fair and just society.

3) There should be transparency and responsible disclosure around AI systems to ensure that people understand AI-based outcomes and can challenge them.

4) AI systems must function in a robust, secure and safe way throughout their life cycles and potential risks should be continually assessed and managed.

5) Organizations and individuals developing, deploying or operating AI systems should be held accountable for their proper functioning in line with the above principles.

Similarly, the Vatican has provided akin precepts and so has the U.S. DoD.

Will the use of AutoML spur attention to those precepts, allowing those that are making ML-based apps the needed time and capabilities to do so, or will the pell-mell ad hoc use of AutoML simply allow people to dodge or forgo those precepts?

Time will tell.

Some fervently clamor that any AutoML worth it's salt ought to be enforcing those kinds of AI Ethics precepts.

In other words, if the AutoML is "shallow" and just provides the surface-level accoutrements to make ML applications, it is likely more dangerous than it is good, while if the AutoML embraces fully and implements added capabilities to provide insight for the AI Ethics precepts it is hopefully going to do more good than harm.

How far the AutoML offerings will go in trying to imbue and showcase the AI Ethics guidelines and suggest or even "enforce" them upon the end-users of AutoML is yet to be seen.

In any case, the presence of AutoML is opening widely the possibilities of utilizing Machine Learning, doing so in nearly any domain, encompassing using AI/ML for medical uses, healthcare, financial, real estate, retail, agricultural, etc.

At this juncture, the AutoML is still in its infancy and some would say that the ML apps being crafted via AutoML are more so prototypes and pilot efforts, rather than full-fledged and robust ones (this is arguable, of course, and some AutoML tools providers would readily disagree with such an assessment).

What about in a domain that has already received intense focus on the use of Machine Learning?

For example, the emergence of today's state-of-the-art self-driving cars can be greatly attributed to advances already told in the crafting of AI and Machine Learning capabilities.

Here's how AI/ML comes to play in self-driving cars.

When a self-driving car is driving down a street, the sensors on-board the car are collecting vast amounts of data from the cameras, radar, LIDAR, ultrasonic, thermal imaging, and the rest, and then using Machine Learning apps that have been forged to analyze the data trove in real-time.

The AI driving the car then uses the ML-based interpretations to gauge what the street scene consists of.

This in turn enables the AI to make choices about whether to start to use the brakes or perhaps instead hit the gas and what direction to steer the vehicle.

Without the existent advances in ML, we would not nearly be as far along in the advent of self-driving cars as we are today.

Consider this intriguing question: *Will AI-based true self-driving cars be seeing much benefit from AutoML in the effort to craft AI/ML driving systems?*

Let's unpack the matter and see.

Self-Driving Cars And AutoML

For Level 4 and Level 5 true self-driving vehicles, there won't be a human driver involved in the driving task.

All occupants will be passengers.

The AI is doing the driving.

As earlier pointed out, the use of Machine Learning is a crucial element to the advent of self-driving cars.

Partially due to the maturity of using ML already, there is not yet much rapt attention going toward using AutoML for self-driving cars, at least not by those that have already made such advanced progress.

Why so?

The AutoML being provided today is usually suited more so for trying to explore a new domain that you've not previously tackled with ML.

This can be very handy since you can use the AutoML to quickly try out a multitude of different ML models and parameter settings.

For self-driving cars, much of that kind of work has already come and gone, and the crafting of ML has significantly evolved. At this juncture, the emphasis tends to be on pushing ML models to greater lengths.

Unless you are starting a self-driving car effort from scratch, the AutoML of today is not going to buy you much.

That being said, some enterprising experts are reshaping AutoML to provide specific functions for particular domains. If you want to make an ML for a medical domain, for example, the AutoML will have a prespecified approach already included for dealing with medical-related data and such.

Some are doing likewise by adding or detailing AutoML for self-driving car uses.

Whether this will be sought out by groups already well along with their self-driving car activity is still open to question.

It could be that the AutoML might be used for more ancillary aspects of self-driving cars.

The primary focus of AI/ML is naturally on the driving task, but there are lots of other ways that self-driving cars are likely to use AI.

One area that is still being figured out involves the interaction with riders or passengers that are inside a self-driving car.

Those with a much too narrow view are seemingly thinking that riders will merely state their desired destination and no other conversation with the in-car Natural Language Processing (NLP) will take place.

I have repeatedly exhorted that this is nonsense in that riders are going to want to converse robustly with the AI driving system. Imagine being inside a self-driving car and the likelihood that you want the AI to take a particular shortcut that you know or prefer, or you want to have the AI pick-up a friend that is a few blocks over, or you want to get a quick bite to eat by having the AI go to the drive-thru.

This is an aspect that can use AI/ML, and for which the AutoML might be of applicability.

Conclusion

Do you think that AutoML is going to be boon for making available Machine Learning apps on a wider basis and improve our lives accordingly?

Or, are you of the mind that AutoML is a Pandora's box that is going to allow every knucklehead to generate a Machine Learning app and swamp us with ill-advised ill-prepared AI apps that eat our lunch?

Those that are versed in ML are already eyeing AutoML with concerted qualms, worried that the potential dumbing down of ML is going to be an adverse slippery slope, meanwhile, they welcome well-crafted AutoML that can bolster professional work on Machine Learning.

In these days of being worried about AI putting people out of a job, you might be thinking that some of the AI/ML experts are perhaps furtively worried that AutoML is going to put them out of a job.

So far, that does not seem to be the case, and the worry generally is that those without the proper training and mindset are going to poison the societal elation for ML by churning out garbage ML with the ease of AutoML.

We could see the surge of excitement about ML suddenly shift into Machine Learning being the scourge of AI and needing to be banned.

That's decidedly not an outcome that it seems anyone wants, though if you conceive of AutoML as having Frankenstein-like potential, there is certainly a chance of wanton desolation and we should be keeping careful watch for any such onset.

CHAPTER 10
FAST AI ETHICS
AND
SELF-DRIVING CARS

There seems to be quite a rush to get AI systems out-the-door these days.

It is certainly understandable, partially attributed to the pandemic amidst the hope that using AI might aid in undercutting the COVID-19 scourge and potentially help spur the post-COVID reopening of the economy.

Unfortunately, there is a potential price to be paid for that rush to judgment and the associated flimsy assumption that the soonest AI is the best kind of AI.

For example, some have put together contact tracing apps that have AI capabilities to bolster the intended functionality of slowing or preventing the spread of the infectious virus, but insufferably those same apps oftentimes are dreadful privacy intrusion nightmares.

Had there been concentrated attention toward incorporating AI Ethics precepts, perhaps those scurrying to push out an AI beneficial application would have been more likely to consider the downsides of their creation too.

For clarification, AI Ethics is a set of ethics-oriented guidelines or principles that offer guidance when designing, building, testing, fielding, and maintaining an AI system. There is currently a multitude of such proposed AI Ethics indications and no single set has become the one-and-only globally accepted standard, though nonetheless they all pretty much adhere to a similar theme and core values.

In that sense, those that try to use as an excuse that there isn't an anointed all-hands standard are disingenuous at best, and by readily embracing nearly any of the bona fide ones they would be doing well and able to proceed unabated.

Okay, so let's hope that entities developing AI will see the light and opt to adopt a viable AI Ethics code set. Doing so is intended to make them aware of the qualms about AI such as the potential for privacy intrusions, the potential for inherent hidden biases in AI-based decision making, and so on.

One assumes that with that awareness will spark AI development efforts that foundationally detect those kinds of problematic and endangering issues, beforehand, rather than after shipping the AI into the hands of the public.

Letting the horse out of the barn prematurely is a bad idea and the goal ought to be making sure first and foremost that the horse is ready to be let loose.

But what happens to AI Ethics when it is crunch time and a kind of panic occurs to rollout AI?

While in the throes of a crisis, it can seem daunting to keep AI Ethics at the forefront, since the usual perception is that worrying about those AI Ethics codifications are bound to stymy the pace of development and undercut the urgent tempo to get AI into the hands of end-users.

That is a decidedly short-minded viewpoint and though it might seem like the value of being quick to market is a worthwhile tradeoff, the result can reverberate for a long time to come. The public will not especially remember that there was a presumed urgency and instead will only tend to know that the AI fostered into the world was insidious and ultimately nefarious.

If enough of those kinds of haphazard make-and-bake AI apps are tossed into the market, we will inevitably witness a colossal backlash that will make the so-far optional AI Ethics principles and guidelines into becoming mandatory and potentially overly onerous as a reaction to those that scrimped at the beginning.

Maybe AI will get banned entirely.

Somehow, there needs to be a balance found that can appropriately make use of the AI Ethics precepts and yet allow for flexibility when there is a real and fully tangible basis to partially cut corners, as it were.

Of course, some would likely abuse the possibility of a slimmer version and always go that route, regardless of any truly needed urgency of timing. Thus, there is a chance of opening a Pandora's box whereby a less-than fully AI Ethics protocol becomes the default norm, rather than serving as a break-glass exception when rarely so needed.

It can be hard to put the Genie back into the bottle.

In any case, there are already some attempts at trying to craft a fast-track variant of AI Ethics principles.

We can perhaps temper those that leverage the urgent version with both a stick and a carrot.

The carrot is obvious that they are seemingly able to get their AI completed sooner, while the stick is that they will be held wholly accountable for not having taken the full nine yards on the use of the AI Ethics. This is a crucial point that might be used against those taking such a route and be a means to extract penalties via a court of law, along with penalties in the court of public opinion.

Let's next take a look at a well-known set of AI Ethics, promulgated by the OECD, and see if we can shape those into offering a fast-track variant.

The OECD has proffered these five foundational precepts as part of undertaking AI:

6) AI should benefit people and the planet by driving inclusive growth, sustainable development, and well-being.
7) AI systems should be designed in a way that respects the rule of law, human rights, democratic values, and diversity, and they should include appropriate safeguards – for example, enabling human intervention where necessary – to ensure a fair and just society.
8) There should be transparency and responsible disclosure around AI systems to ensure that people understand AI-based outcomes and can challenge them.
9) AI systems must function in a robust, secure, and safe way throughout their life cycles and potential risks should be continually assessed and managed.
10) Organizations and individuals developing, deploying, or operating AI systems should be held accountable for their proper functioning in line with the above principles.

For ease of reference, this is the official shorthand list of the five AI Ethics principles:

1) Inclusive growth, sustainable development, and well-being
2) Human-centered values and fairness
3) Transparency and explainability
4) Robustness, security, and safety
5) Accountability

What can be done to fast-track this set of AI Ethics?

Some might leap to the easy way out by simply lopping one or more from the list.

In other words, just cut the stack down to four, or maybe three, or heaven forbid even just one or two of the precepts.

It isn't apparent as to which of the five would be "best" to ditch.

You could liken this to having to cut off a limb and be arguing about which appendage is the less vital one.

No, I don't think this will do.

Each of the five has a distinct purpose. None of the other five will make up for having omitted one of the other precepts. Knocking out any of them is akin to taking out the leg of a stool, wherein the stool no longer properly stands.

For those that have suggested to chop out one or more of the five, it seems to defy any reasonable logic and you are essentially arbitrarily willing to wholly weaken and undermine the concrete flooring upon which any AI has to be properly constructed.

Case rejected.

That might seem stubborn and unyielding, lest there are some other means to try and turn these precepts into a slimmer variant.

Consider these possibilities:

- **Prioritize the five and weight your effort accordingly** – they are all essential but you could argue that in a pinch they are not all equal, thus, for a given AI, assign weights to each of the five, and then structure your AI development effort according to those with the greater importance or weighting.

- **Take the shortened version of one or more of the precepts** – for each of the five there are lots of subordinated items to normally be considered, but for a bona fide crunch you could shorten some of those underlying elements and knowingly skip a few underlings, keep track as you do so and realize what you are missing accordingly.

- **Double-up on the precepts** – the principles do not need to necessarily be considered one-at-a-time, and there are synergies to be had by considering simultaneously more than one while undertaking your AI effort, thus a double-up is bound to reduce the time and effort, though be careful that it does not become a morass and a gigantic blur.

- **Borrow from a similar AI app** – many that are embarking upon developing AI are doing so for the first time and as such they have little or no prior base to build upon, yet for those that are actively in AI and have other AI systems under their belt they can readily reuse prior aspects that already passed the AI Ethics precepts (just be mindful and do not blindly and falsely borrow something unlike what you are doing now).

- **Parcel out wisely the precepts** – in some instances an AI effort places the rigors of the AI Ethics precepts onto the shoulder of one person that becomes the AI Ethics guru, this might be handy, unfortunately, this can also become a bottleneck and slows down the entire effort, reconsider if there is a single link in the chain and how to better parcel out the workload.

- **Cautiously crowdsource the precepts** – in an open-source manner some are doing AI that relishes using crowdsourcing to either perform the AI development or serve to scrutinize and test it, in which case you could have the AI Ethics become likewise crowdsourced, just as long as the crowd knows what it is doing and this is not an unbridled castoff that undermines the precepts.

- **Combine these fast-tracks** – the aforementioned fast-tracks can be combined in various sensible ways and produce even larger short-cuts accordingly, but do not cut to the bone and end-up losing the core by taking too many slimdowns at once.

As mentioned, you can use one or more of the fast-track facets at the same time.

How will you know that you have gone too far?

Here are the key supplementals for taking on a fast-track approach with the AI Ethics principles:

- **Establish internal checks-and-balances** – make sure to set up the responsibilities for the AI Ethics precepts and include numerous checks-and-balances for gauging how they are proceeding.

- **Potentially use an external third-party auditor** – in addition to internal checks-and-balances, it can be helpful to use an external auditor that does not presumably feel attached to what has been done and therefore will independently and forthrightly conduct their review.

- **Explicitly plan to include the AI Ethics considerations** – sometimes the AI Ethics considerations are belatedly shoved into an AI effort as though a second class citizen and not worthy of resources and nor priority, rate them instead as primary for all AI implementations and include them dutifully in all of your AI planning accordingly.

- **Boost the fail-safe catchall of the AI** – properly devised AI should already have fail-safe catchalls so that if it goes awry in the field the AI will presumably realize troubles are afoot and will do something prudent as a contingency, this is even more so a crucial component when taking the fast-track.

All told, I've provided a workable semblance of how to fast-track an AI effort as it pertains to using AI Ethics guidelines during the project.

Again, do not interpret this as a license to wildly proceed and merely try to skate through the AI Ethics precepts.

Your AI is going to be better if it undergoes a robust and complete AI Ethics effort, and likewise, those using your AI will benefit, and the totality of AI adoption will be kept enlivened.

Self-Driving Cars and AI Ethics Principles

You might be wondering how the AI Ethics principles come to play in real-world AI applications.

A handy exemplar would be the development of AI-based true self-driving cars.

For Level 4 and Level 5 true self-driving vehicles, there won't be a human driver involved in the driving task.

All occupants will be passengers.

The AI is doing the driving.

Many of the automakers and self-driving tech firms have been adopting the AI Ethics precepts (this varies from firm-to-firm).

One can argue that all of them ought to be doing so, which is worthwhile to mention herein as an impetus to get some of them off-the-dime and get in gear with including AI Ethics facets.

Please do so.

Let's next consider an example of how AI Ethics applies to self-driving cars.

Besides the bevy of sensors facing outward to detect the roadway, self-driving cars are likely to have a camera or two that are facing inward too.

Why so?

It is assumed that self-driving cars will be mainly used in fleets for purposes of ridesharing. The fleet owners will seemingly be large firms like automakers, car rental agencies, ridesharing firms, and the like (though, I am somewhat of a contrarian and argue that individuals will also own self-driving cars).

With those self-driving cars roaming around and taking on passengers, there is quite obviously the chance that a rowdy rider will decide to mark graffiti on the interior or maybe rip up the seats. By having a camera that points inward, the actions of those unruly people can be tracked. The AI might be trained to look for such behavior and immediately warn or scold the person, potentially stopping the miscreant from doing any further damage.

The inward-facing cameras are readily recording whatever happens inside the vehicle.

Seems innocent and sensible.

Consider another perspective.

Suppose you went to the bar after work and opted to take a self-driving car home, doing so rightfully rather than driving yourself in your conventional car while drunk. During the journey home, you blabber about your work, your personal life, and all sorts of confidential commentary that is spilling out of you while intoxicated.

It is all captured on video.

Who owns that video?

What will they do with it?

Currently, this is an open question and each self-driving car owner is presumably going to decide whatever they believe is appropriate to do about those videos.

Meanwhile, you personally have inadvertently created a personal privacy exposure for yourself and are potentially left in the lurch.

How does this relate to AI Ethics precepts?

Take a look again at the OECD five.

You might hopefully realize that at least one of the AI Ethics principles applies, and indeed it could readily be argued that all five apply to this scenario.

Some of the automakers and self-driving tech firms would

currently say that the inward-facing camera is merely a piece of technology and they would absolve themselves of any duty related to how it might be used.

Likewise, if they have an AI monitoring system that can examine the video in real-time or after-the-fact to catch those that are doing something untoward, the makers of that AI would almost surely claim that however it might be used is not their concern.

If those organizations were fully embracing the AI Ethics guidelines, they would instead be having serious and contemplative discussions about the societal implications of that feature. Also, they would aim to figure out how to best put the feature into use and including for those that buy their self-driving cars and opt to use them as ridesharing vehicles.

Without the nudge of the AI Ethics precepts, it can be quite easy to overlook important and societally impactful facets such as this and meanwhile naively profess a type of head-in-the-sand rationale for not dealing with thorny issues.

Conclusion

AI Ethics are only now becoming prominent and we will need to wait and see how those involved in making and fielding AI opt to adopt such guidelines.

The excuse that incorporating AI Ethics is too much effort or will needlessly delay getting AI onto the streets is false and frankly, hogwash.

You can potentially fast-track the AI Ethics facets when (and only when) there is an AI that might be instrumental for the benefit of humanity and for which the timing presupposes an urgency, but this is not the norm and those doing a wink-wink to undercut the AI Ethics elements are doing a disservice to themselves and the rest of us.

Maybe there ought to be an inward-facing camera watching those making AI and we could catch those kinds of scoundrels in the act.

CHAPTER 11

I THINK THEREFORE I AM

AND

SELF-DRIVING CARS

You have undoubtedly heard the famous phrase "I think, therefore I am."

Written oftentimes in its Latin form, the saying is known as *ergo cogito, ergo sum*.

If you want to be smarmy and outwit your friends, please be aware that Rene Descartes in 1637 had originally delineated the phrase in his French treatise *Discourse on the Method* and the words were shown as "Je pense, donc Je suis."

Make sure that when you opt to brandish this arcane fact over the snippety noses of your pals that you get the French pronunciation nailed down beforehand, otherwise your attempt to look extra smart will be undermined when they ding you for mispronouncing the French version.

There is an important added twist that you ought to also know.

The now-ubiquitous phrase leaves out an important part, without which the saying is not quite the same as what Descartes originally intended.

Turns out that a twitter-like reduction in the number of allowed characters has inadvertently caused his intended meaning to become shortchanged.

Here is the English translated passage that contains the famous embedded quote:

"I supposed that all the objects (presentations) that had ever entered into my mind when awake, had in them no more truth than the illusions of my dreams. But immediately upon this I observed that, whilst I thus wished to think that all was false, it was absolutely necessary that I, who thus thought, should be something; And as I observed that this truth, *I think, therefore I am*, was so certain and of such evidence that no ground of doubt, however extravagant, could be alleged by the Sceptics capable of shaking it, I concluded that I might, without scruple, accept it as the first principle of the philosophy of which I was in search."

Okay, so what does that exactly showcase?

It is interpreted by most scholars as an indication that Descartes was asserting that his real-world existence is affirmed as a consequence of being able to doubt that he did actually exist as a real-world entity.

Huh, you might say, somewhat puzzled by the seeming enigma.

The fact that he was able to doubt that he existed was sufficient proof that he does exist.

One might say that if he did not doubt that he existed, this would suggest that he might not exist and that in this non-existence there was no willingness and no attempt to question whether he exists or not. You see, failing to question your existence is tantamount to not seeking the truth of whether you exist, and as such, the way to establishing your existence is by challenging the veracity of the existence claim.

I realize that the passage is open to all kinds of other interpretations, but the infusion of this vaunted doubtfulness ingredient is generally considered essential by many that have closely studied his entire collection of work (not everyone agrees, thus, you'll need to make your private peace with the matter).

As a result of the viewpoint, that doubt was such a key factor, the fuller tweaked version of his intended saying is typically couched in Latin as *dubito, ergo cogito, ergo sum* and then indicated in English as this final revisionist proclamation:

- "I doubt, therefore I think, therefore I am."

Some recoil at this modified variant and believe that the beauty and poetry of his original words have been completely usurped and torn asunder. Meanwhile, others contend that the longer version is more fitting, and the shortened version is nothing less than an out-of-context sham.

Sorry about all this.

I hope that you are not shaken by the rancorous debate and discourse underlying something that you probably thought was a straightforward and settled matter.

Let's consider how the added element makes quite a difference.

The shorter version seems to suggest that by the mere act alone of thinking, one must therefore exist.

There is copious purity that "I think, therefore I am" is short and sweet, allowing any of us to contentedly utter the phrase with parsimonious satisfaction.

The longer version though is said to add a vital preamble, during which you must first express doubt, a kind of doubt that presumably underlies your existence, and once you've crossed that bridge, you can assert that this establishes that you can think, and finally you can proceed to put the proverbial icing on the cake by claiming that due to those propounding propositions you must indeed exist.

That's a lot of insidious if's and contortions, way beyond the realm of being easily wielded and readily flaunted in any everyday conversation over coffee or tea.

Charles Porterfield Krauth, a historically notable theologian, perhaps summed it up rather well in 1872 by wording the matter this way: "That cannot doubt which does not think, and that cannot think which does not exist. I doubt, I think, I exist."

Returning to the desire to be a know-it-all with your colleagues, the more advanced and rather torturous approach to impress your friends would be to first ask them if they have any doubts about their existence.

Assuming that they say yes, you can share with them that as a result of their willfully admitting such doubt, it proves that they can think.

And, since they have now proven that they can think, they are in fact in existence, and by these brazen rules are undeniably a certified card-carrying "am" (based irreducibly on "I doubt, therefore I think, therefore I am").

This brings up a popular joke that generates much glee and uncontrollable laughter among impassioned philosophers.

Are you ready?

Rene Descartes walks into a bar. The bartender asks Descartes if he would like his normal drink. In response, Descartes says "I think not."

Instantaneously, Descartes disappears.

Ha!

Get it, he admitted straight out that he does not think (well, sort of), and thusly if he does not think, he must not exist, and by not existing he wouldn't be in the bar, and as a result miraculously disappears.

Whoa, you exclaim, doesn't the joke omit the point about having doubt.

Yes, your eagle eye caught that missing facet in that this particular piece of humor was shaped around the shortened version of the infamous saying.

Good catch.

There are lots of ingenious and at times devilish ways to play around with this lofty topic.

Some try to contend that by simply stopping their mind from thinking, they will cease to exist, similar to the joke about Descartes.

A small problem with that theory is that your mind is always thinking, as far as we know, including when you are sleeping and even when you go into a mind-numbing state of meditation and believe that you have emptied all your thoughts.

Your mind is the engine that will not stop.

Of course, upon death, your mind does come to a stop, which by the way there is a great deal of interesting research on how long the brain sometimes keeps going even though the rest of your body might be considered legally dead. You might be queasy on this line of research and consider the question to be rather gruesome, but it does have fascinating implications and stokes our innate curiosity about how the brain works.

With your mind always thinking, do not confuse that with the notion of thinking clearly. Your mind might be racing along, but the thoughts could be a scrambled mess and not especially intelligible. I dare say most of us know someone that has an active mind, yet very little of value to report (I'll say this, among my colleagues, they know exactly who I mean).

Overall, you might conclude that if you don't think, you don't exist, assuming that the meaning of existence is to be essentially sentient.

That added tidbit about sentience is a crucial clarification since a deceased human that does not think is obviously still here and for all intended purposes does exist as a thing, which you can see and touch, but the point is that the human no longer exists as a fellow active human that can interact with the rest of us living souls.

You cannot be an "am" unless you are alive, most would proclaim.

Well, that proclamation might be shortsighted, and perhaps there are other dimensions of existence that we have yet to tap into and as such we do not know what those are and nor quite how to span over into them.

What about someone caught in a deep coma?

The usual argument is that despite the coma, their brain is still functioning, at least to the degree that it is aiding in maintaining the various autonomic bodily activities.

Plus there is a chance that the brain is maybe dreaming of beautiful sunsets and wide balmy beaches, yet we have no means to peer into the person's mind to see this, and nor is the person able to use their sensory apparatus such as their voice or hand motions to convey this thinking action to us.

In that case, the person is still an "am" though they are not able to particularly interact with us.

This brings up another potential can of worms.

Your beloved dog can speak (we'll count barking), it can shake your hand, it rolls over, it comes when you call (depending upon the mood of the moment, it seems), and by all appearances is a living creature that we can interact with readily.

Does that cherished dog fit into the "am" category?

Some would immediately exhort that a dog cannot think.

Really?

How exactly does it fetch the morning newspaper, or know that when you come in the door after a hard day's work that it quickly moves to comfort you and tries unabashedly to brighten your day?

Here's where some party-poopers might turn the Descartes elongated version against you as a type of lunging conceptual foil.

The dog cannot think because it cannot doubt.

In other words, since a dog presumably does not doubt its existence, it cannot, therefore, be said to think, and in that meaning, it is decidedly not an "am" per se.

The dog is likely to be in existence, even the most argumentative type of philosopher would hopefully acknowledge, but the pooch does not get into the exclusive "am" club because it is not of the same kind of thinking that we humans employ, which requires the seemingly requisite iridescent doubt.

Thus, there are lots of things in existence, all around us, but just as a rock or a car are irrefutably in existence it does not mean they are an "am" (as an aside, perhaps only you exist and all those other things are a figment of your imagination, which if so, I appreciate that you are imagining these words and envisaging that I have written them, thanks much for doing so).

You might be outrageously steamed that your dog is not being counted as an "am" and I certainly can understand your angst.

Please do not tell your dog about this downright exasperating point since it might upset the poor canine and cause them to doubt their own existence.

Hey, wait a minute, that solves the dilemma.

Switching gears, I just mentioned that neither a rock and nor your car qualifies as an "am."

Most of us would tend to agree with that line of reasoning, though some believe that all things have a soul and in that case, the rock and car might well be an "am."

Put aside the soul related considerations for the moment.

Having done so, consider that perhaps we still might be shortsighted in declaring that a car cannot be an "am."

Why so?

There is a multi-billion dollar-sized worldwide effort underway to craft AI-based true self-driving cars.

Here is an intriguing question: *Will AI-based true self-driving cars be able to think and if so then are they in existence in the same "am" manner as us, everyday humans?*

Let's unpack the matter and see.

Self-Driving Cars And Whether AI Is Am

For Level 4 and Level 5 true self-driving vehicles, there won't be a human driver involved in the driving task.

All occupants will be passengers.

The AI is doing the driving.

Let's first focus on the AI side of things, notwithstanding the car aspects, which we'll loop back into.

Despite the fake news about AI, which I continue to fight with my heart and soul, there isn't any AI yet that is sentient.

We are not even in the ballpark of sentience.

Some firmly believe that there will be a moment of singularity that suddenly and perhaps unexpectedly causes AI to spring forth vigorously by begetting intelligence with more intelligence, ultimately arising into becoming sentient.

Do not hold your breath for that to happen.

Okay, if you accept that premise, it means that if we are going to discuss and debate the topic of "I think, therefore I am" in the context of AI then we will, for now, need to do so without looming sentience peeking around the corner (it might someday appear, long from now).

This also brings up an underlying conundrum, namely, does the act of thinking require sentience?

If thinking does not require sentience, you might be on the somewhat less shaky ground to assert that AI, as we can conceive of it, might achieve thinking, in some closer time frame, perhaps via the route of crafting massively scaled Artificial Neural Networks (ANN) making use of Machine Learning (ML) and Deep Learning (DL) techniques and technologies.

Optimists might argue that upon such a machine being able to essentially simulate a human brain, sentience will naturally arise, doing so without necessarily a mankind created capability and more so as a synergistic effect that we did not directly divine.

In any case, suppose that we did get this thinking style AI to pass a Turing Test, a type of testing process named by its author the famous mathematician Alan Turing, which consists of pitting the AI against a human in a series of intellectual challenges, and the result was that we could not discern any difference between the two. The AI would then be considered the equivalent of exhibiting human intelligence, in whatever way we managed to achieve it, whether by clever computational means or by lots of toy Lego's and a bunch of duct tape.

Okay, now sit down, and get ready for the plot twist.

Would that AI, the stuff that has passed the Turing Test, qualify to become known as an "am" in the semblance of the venerated "I think, therefore I am" context?

Well, of course, it must, since we have agreed that the AI can think, and by the act of thinking it exists in the meaning of "am" that the Descartes rule seems to imply.

While you ponder that mind-bender, perhaps we ought to resurrect the question of doubt. Recall, the presumed full Descartes rule is "I doubt, therefore I think, therefore I am."

Maybe we found a loophole about the AI being an "am" since it might be that it doesn't express any doubts about its existence, and therefore it cannot be said to be thinking, and though it might exist as a thing, we can toss it into the classification of those entities that are not an "am" such as your treasured pet dog. The AI is pretty much saying this: "I do not doubt, therefore I do not think, and I, therefore, am not an am." Somehow, that logic seems doubtful, if you know what I mean.

Conclusion

An AI-based true self-driving car comes down your street.

Is that car realistically "thinking" or is it just some very tricked-out computer programming?

Some believe that we will not achieve Level 5 self-driving cars unless we can make AI that truly thinks. Others contend that requiring the act of thinking is an extraordinarily high bar, higher than required for the act of driving. We don't have any Level 5 as yet, and though some argue that the Level 4's being tried out will gradually and inexorably be transformed into Level 5, there is no means to proffer inarguable proof of that supposition.

Maybe we will end-up with AI that is characterized this way: "I think, therefore I am not." Or, for clarity: "I think, but not the way you do, apparently, so I guess that I am a not." One thing that we might have learned from Descartes is that if the AI begins to doubt its existence, we ought to realize the gig is up, and either run for the hills or extend a hand in friendship to our newest member of the "am" exclusive club.

CHAPTER 12
AI POLITENESS
AND
SELF-DRIVING CARS

Does it seem to you that civility and politeness are on the wane?

Many would surely agree that politeness appears to have been placed on the back-burner, or perhaps dropped altogether from our lexicon.

No one can put their finger on the precise reason for this increasingly slippery slope of tossing politeness to the winds.

Some point to the advent of social media and exhort that because people can bark out whatever they want to say, doing so from the other side of a computer display screen, oftentimes anonymously, this relatively recent capability and phenomena has led to the near demise of being polite.

Yet another social media-related connection could be that we are finding ourselves communicating in shorter and shorter bursts of words, amid too the use of clever emoticons and acronyms. We do so while texting to each other (usually a self-imposed limit), trying to be as succinct as possible, and we find ourselves facing character length limits when using feeds such as Twitter (typically a system-imposed limit).

Perhaps there is just not any room left to be polite.

Indeed, some have generally disfavored politeness as being added fluff and have always been eager to cast aside the extra baggage of polite discourse.

For colleagues that you might know, they perhaps over time have seemingly dropped from their vocabulary the use of the word "please" and the phrase "thank you," vehemently arguing that it takes too much verbal effort, uses up cherished breath, and fails to contribute any substantive meaning to what they have otherwise uttered.

This brings up the now-classic debate about content.

Allow me a moment to explain, thanks.

Suppose I was to say to you: "Let's stay in touch."

You presumably get the gist that I am asking you to consider remaining in touch, likely periodically and not necessarily regularly so. It is not a demand per se, and instead couched as a type of request, which offers a virtual handshake toward you in hopes that you might take it up and affirm that mutual interest exists.

I'll rephrase the line to this: "Please, let's stay in touch."

Does the inclusion of the word "please" add value?

Well, perhaps, since the original line could be construed as an order or edict, meaning that I was commanding you to stay in touch. Meanwhile, the added word "please" softens the utterance, and showcases that I am presumably beseeching you to stay in touch, imploring it rather than insisting on it.

Those that believe fervently in the economy of their words would likely decry the added use of the word "please" in this and most instances and argue that it is not needed and merely bloats the matter. Just get to the meat, they would contend, and skip those fluffy sugar coatings.

Returning to my earlier mention of the debate about content, here's where that comes to play.

Does the added word of "please" belong in the rubric of considered as content of the message, or would you say that the please is outside of the content?

In other words, those that espouse the politeness-as-fluff viewpoint would undoubtedly insist that the word "please" in this instance is not content and nothing more than an add-on, thus, you can delete it without any loss of content and nor any loss of meaning to the sentence.

A counterargument is that the word "please" is demonstrative and changes the nature and character of the message. The "please" is not simply a vacuous word that exists exclusively as filler in this context, and instead, it dramatically and notably alters the semblance of the entire line.

I suppose we might be beating a dead horse, as it were, and trying to wring a bit much out of the example, though it does help highlight some interesting and telltale facets about politeness.

Let's establish that there are three ways for an utterance to go:
a) Polite
b) Non-Polite (neutral)
c) Impolite

Let's explore those three mannerisms.

When somebody writes or speaks, they are bound to express things that are at times perceived as being polite, which is a culturally dependent matter and varies from place to place and likewise varies over time (what was polite some fifty years ago might no longer be considered as such, and vice versa).

If someone states something that does not appear to have the cultural dressings of politeness, the utterance could be classified as being neutral. A neutral utterance is labeled as being non-polite. Unfortunately, using the moniker of "non-polite" kind of sounds like a bad thing, but we should not leap to that conclusion and there's a third classification to handle the devilish versions of utterances.

That third category is known as being impolite. We will reserve the "impolite" naming to refer to circumstances whereby the message is worded to seemingly be lacking in politeness and it goes an extra step by thumbing its nose at being polite, causing the meaning to lurch into outright impoliteness.

Of course, all of this is squishy due to cultural and societal norms and the context makes a whopper of a difference.

In any case, consider these three variants of the exemplar sentence:

- Polite: "Please, let's stay in touch."
- Non-Polite (neutral): "Let's stay in touch."
- Impolite: "Let's stay in touch, you dolt."

You can argue readily about whether those three examples neatly fit within those classifications.

Perhaps the third instance, calling someone a dolt, might be an endearing remark and meant positively, so it deserves to be reclassified in that case into the politeness category.

Or, the sentence might be stated in a jokingly manner, whereby the "you dolt" is done with laughter and intended to lighten up the request, thus maybe the line belongs in the non-polite grouping.

Words alone on a page are not sufficient to always know what the context of an utterance signifies.

Similarly, if you heard an audio clip of someone stating any of those three lines, it might be difficult to discern the full meaning without hearing what came before and after the utterances, along with the tone and measured inflection.

What makes matters further confounding involves the potential meaningfulness gap between what the speaker intended versus what the receiver interpreted the intent to be.

You might have added the word "please" and done so out of the goodness of your heart. You genuinely are trying to be polite and were raised to include the word please whenever possible. It is your sense of good manners and a desire to always be courteous.

The other person that you are saying "please" to might not know any of that background.

As such, when you use the word "please" it might be taken as an insult, appearing as though you are trying to stuck-up, or standoffish, or putting on airs.

Imagine your shock that the other person reacts negatively, given that you were sure that by the use of "please" that the other person would understand your belief in respect toward others. Oddly, to you, the effort to be polite has veered not simply into the non-polite grouping, it has fallen all the way down into the sullied category of being impolite.

What a mess!

The person intending to be polite has offended by doing so, and the attempt has backfired.

Round and round, these kinds of situations can spiral out-of-control.

The person attempting to be polite might ratchet even higher their politeness quotient, thinking that perhaps their politeness is just not being fully appreciated, and meanwhile, the other person takes the politeness on steroids to be stoking the fires of excruciatingly being impolite.

Sometimes, the politeness portions or attempts can completely overshadow the "content" and all of the attention shifts toward the politeness bits and pieces, skirting or neglecting whatever else the messaging was about.

If you said "Please, let's keep in touch" and the use of the word "please" becomes the entire focus, it is easy to imagine that the part about keeping in touch gets lost among the angst and concerns over the politeness infusion.

Being polite can inadvertent obscure content, it can confound the content, it can burden the content, and have lots of similar undercutting properties.

In that case, some give up trying to be polite and decide they will try to be neutral (the non-polite).

Sorry, that will not get you out of the conundrum.

The other person might be anticipating that you were going to be polite and notice that you instead went the neutral route, and then become disturbed that you were not "polite" per se.

Darned if you, darned if you don't.

All these twists and turns are pretty hard for humans to deal with.

And, not just for humans, but for AI too.

There is a veritable tsunami of AI systems being developed and fielded, many of which make use of Natural Language Processing (NLP). You are likely familiar with Alexa and Siri, which are prime examples of today's capabilities at NLP and how such state-of-the-art AI systems interact with humans.

At first, the use of AI NLP was undertaken in a somewhat neutral or non-polite mode.

The thought by AI developers was that the messages emitted by the AI should be direct and to the point, thus, no need to add those (assumed) superfluous aspects to make the wording perceived as being polite.

Gradually, it was realized that the starkness of the wording was a giveaway that the AI was a machine and not a human. As such, many NLP systems not only added the politeness trimmings, they went further and have added pauses as though the AI is "thinking" and included filler sounds that a human might proffer such as "uh-huh" and other common human-like expressions.

On the surface, this effort to make AI seem more conversational appears to make a lot of sense.

People will be put at ease and feel more comfortable chatting with AI. The interaction would be less clumsily disjointed.

Others worry, rightfully so, that people will get a false or misleading impression of what the AI can do.

By adding the bells and whistles of human-to-human interaction into AI-to-human interaction, there is a real danger of leading people down a primrose path. You might inadvertently assume that the AI has a fully conversant and sentient capacity, along with believing that the AI has common-sense reasoning (all of these are human qualities that AI has yet to fully achieve).

Typically, when AI acts in this way, humans will anthropomorphize the system and fall into the mental trap that the AI is truly equal to human intelligence.

Politeness is a dual-edged sword that provides an added indicator potentially of human qualities and thus could be considered part of the anthropomorphizing tendency sway.

Using politeness in AI is darned if you do, darned if you don't, kind of challenge.

When you are polite, it oftentimes is done as part of social interaction dynamics and can encompass power differentials. Being impolite to someone can be an obvious way to showcase one person's greater social status over another.

Too, being polite can have a similar effect.

Consider these three somewhat vexing questions:
- Should AI be polite?
- Should AI be neutral (non-polite)?
- Should AI be impolite?

You might be tempted to say that the AI can be any of those three, at any time, in any mixture, as dependent upon the context and the culture so involved.

That's quite a mouthful and trying to discern the right level of politeness for the right moment and to the person(s) involved can be trickily problematic.

There are various AI research efforts trying to figure out these aspects, including taking non-polite human utterances and doing an automated translation into polite versions, using Machine Learning and Deep Learning, for which this is a lot harder than you might think (for an interesting research paper by researchers at Carnegie Mellon University on politeness transfer).

Shifting gears, consider the various situations that we will inevitably be interacting with an AI NLP.

One such instance consists of the advent of AI-based true self-driving cars and the need for people to interact with the AI driving system.

Here's an intriguing question: *Does AI politeness bode for positive or negative aspects when humans are passengers in AI-based true self-driving cars?*

Let's unpack the matter and see.

Self-Driving Cars And Politeness

For Level 4 and Level 5 true self-driving vehicles, there won't be a human driver involved in the driving task.

All occupants will be passengers.

The AI is doing the driving. When you are a passenger in a human-driven car, the driver might be polite, they might be non-polite, and of course, they at times might be impolite.

What should the AI driving system be like?

Imagine that you are heading to work and using a self-driving car.

The AI explores behind-the-scenes your usual morning rides via data stored in the cloud by the automakers and self-driving car tech firms and detects a pattern that you usually opt to have the AI swing through a Starbucks to get your favored latte, helping to awaken you for the day's work efforts ahead.

Rather than waiting for you to suggest the driving diversion, the AI instead talks to you via the AI NLP capability and actively prompts you about it.

Here's what the AI might say (three variants):
- Polite: "If it pleases you, I can visit the Starbucks drive-through so you can get your morning latte."
- Non-Polite (neutral): "Should I visit the Starbucks drive-through so you can get your morning latte?"
- Impolite: "Hey, baggy-eyed, do you want me to visit the Starbucks drive-through so you can get your morning latte?"

The polite version includes an elongated instance of the "please" aspects, which the non-polite excludes, and meanwhile the impolite throws a barb at you about being baggy-eyed (perhaps the inward-facing camera analyzed your face using facial recognition and determined that your eyes are baggy, though even if so, it seems impolite to especially make note of that morning time facial feature).

Some people might be creeped out that the AI "knew" about their morning routine of getting a latte, and I just note that this is part of the upcoming privacy intrusion issues that will rear its ugly head as true self-driving cars become prevalent.

Anyway, some people meanwhile will relish having a "chauffeur" type of personalized driver.

Back to the politeness topic, you might be upset and disgusted at being called baggy-eyed. It could ruin your day and cause you to render a complaint with the owner of the self-driving car.

Or, one supposes, you might be tickled by the remark, taking it as a wake-up call, as it were, and nod your head approvingly that you did stay out last night until the late hours and today seem to be paying the price.

You could even argue that the polite version has gone too far, mentioning "if it pleases you" and this might upset a rider. What pleases me is for you to shut-up, the passenger might retort.

Okay, so it is not blatantly obvious which of the utterances is best, and the AI ought to be considering contextual parameters to ascertain the politeness level and encumbrances to be used (not easy for the AI, and not easy for humans to do either).

Conclusion

There is an added twist to self-driving cars politeness as a use case. Keep in mind that the AI is undertaking life-or-death driving actions when serving as the driving system for the self-driving car.

Suppose the AI has detected an upcoming dangerous roadway condition and wants to interact with the passenger about options available for dealing with the pending matter. Ultimately, the AI is going to decide what to do but wants any input or preferences from the passenger.

This might involve urgently asking questions of the rider, any wording of which might be easily misunderstood or misinterpreted by the passenger, and thus the human in this AI-to-human interaction might provide an answer that is askew of what otherwise would have been intended.

Or, the AI might be seeking to forewarn the passenger, such as the AI is alerting the passenger to get ready for a rapid and jarring stop because a pedestrian has unexpectedly jaywalked in front of the in-motion self-driving car. Some wonder whether politeness might get in the way of those crucial interactions.

CHAPTER 13

INCOME SHARING

AND

SELF-DRIVING CARS

There is a trend called "Pod Up" that is taking place these days as a result of the COVID-19 pandemic.

At first, the pod-up phenomena had to do with trying to identify local friends or family that you could potentially team-up with to seek some semblance of familial interaction and friendly socialization during this scourge of a pandemic.

All of those in a designated inner circle or pod would pledge to try and refrain from getting the COVID virus and thus avoid infecting others in their chosen collective. The idea was to seek a viable means of remaining sane and interactive with fellow humans, despite being charged to maintain social distancing and avoid contact with those beyond your immediate household.

You might for example agree with parents down the street that has children the same age as your kids to form a "pod" and allow everyone to physically get together accordingly. You take your kids over to their house, and they likewise feel comfortable bringing their kids over to your house. The respective parents can directly meet and converse, perhaps undertaking a barbeque, and meanwhile, the youngsters relish the company of each other.

Assuming that none of you have coronavirus and that you all steadfastly observe social distancing and mask-wearing wherever else you go and upon interacting with anyone outside of the pod, the hope is that you have established a cloistered enclave that is free of the virus, allowing open and everyday interaction without distancing and masks.

Essentially, the notion is to bring back in a truncated way what just six months ago we would have all considered a normal form of living. It is a festering nostalgia for a lifestyle that seems ancient though was commonplace earlier this very same year.

Medical and healthcare experts tend to denounce these pods.

This sour outlook aligns with their view that the direct interaction that you have when unmasked and without social distancing should be the minimalist variant that you can create. In other words, if your existing family consists of you and your loved one as parents, along with say two children, you ought to only be a pod of four people and no more. This keeps the chances of contracting and spreading the virus to just a set of four people.

Meanwhile, forming a pod with a family down the street that has one child and two parents, plus maybe another neighbor that has one parent and three children, now amounts to a pod of eleven people.

It is presumably a no-brainer that trying to keep COVID at bay for four people is going to be more readily handled than with eleven.

All it takes is for one of the members of the pod to get the virus, perhaps unknowingly and by some seemingly innocent act, and that infected member will surely spread it to all other members of the pod.

And this could happen without anyone in the pod realizing that the dispersal is taking place, possibly because the spreader is not showcasing any symptoms and the others in the pod are too early in the infectious cycle to display the infection.

In brief, mathematically, the smallest set of those that stick together without undertaking proper precautions is crucial since it means that the odds of getting the infection and having it propagate is lessened, and the number of people that will possibly get infected is lower than it would in a larger collective.

Some localities are taking a somewhat considered extreme stance and indicating that those within a household of say four people should always be social distancing and wearing masks, even when solely remaining within the confines of the home itself. This kind of requirement is a bit much for most people to the stomach and can be exceedingly arduous to maintain for any length of time.

In any case, the pod-up movement is surely a sign that people crave being with other people, and we are at our instinctive core ardent social creatures.

The magnetic allure of being with others comes at a cost. Those that are doing these pod-up efforts are lamentably increasing their individual risks by sharing the overall risks across the collective and taking dicey chances that someone will otherwise get the virus and then pump it unfettered through all the unprotected and unsuspecting members.

There is a new pivot taking place in the pod-up realm.

It has to do with schooling.

Once the summer months conclude, there is a huge question about whether physically going back to school is a good idea or a bad idea. Some assert that the virus risks are still too high and thus all schooling should be done via remote instruction, while others contend that schooling undertaken in cautious ways is feasible and also necessary for a variety of social, economic, and livelihood reasons.

Here's how the pod-up comes to play.

There are parents eyeing homeschooling like never before, contemplating trying to home school their children and therefore explicitly decide to not have them attend public and nor private school per se. This though is harder than it might seem at first glance since the parents might not have the time to do the homeschooling or might feel unqualified in doing so, etc.

Voila, the idea of doing a pod returns to the forefront.

In the prior example of eleven people formed into a pod, they might decide that henceforth they will conduct their home-schooling in a pod-up setup, consisting of all eleven participating. The parents might tradeoff doing the instruction, dependent upon availability, work schedules, and areas of expertise.

Those that are planning on this approach would likely assert that this pod formation would be safer than the kids going to a physical school whereby there are zillions of potential virus-infecting opportunities.

In that way of thinking, they might acknowledge that the pod does have its risks, but those risks are now presumably less so than the risks of attending regular school in-person.

There are variants on this pod-up homeschooling notion.

For example, rather than performing homeschooling as led and instructed by the parents, some pods are intending to leverage the remote schooling options and have their children learn in a somewhat "customary" remote schooling fashion by using the online learning facets via their local school.

What makes this a variation of the pod is that those parents might decide to bring together their children for the remote schooling sessions.

Perhaps on Monday's, all the kids of the pod are dropped off at one of the homes, and they all play and interact in-person, minus masks and social distancing, and meanwhile attend their classes remotely. One viewpoint is that this keeps the kids amid interaction with their fellow youngsters and simultaneously gets them the educational aspects needed too.

As you might imagine, this is once again generally considered a bad idea as it can spread the virus to those in the pod, though one can be sympathetic that there is a desire to have the children interact more so than simply via online screens.

Shift gears for a moment.

What else are pods and this pod-up trend possibly good for?

Here's an interesting twist: *Might the use of a pod-up approach be utilized during the advent of AI-based true self-driving cars as a means to enable the masses to own, earn income, and have available the touted mobility-for-all that is supposed to emerge?*

Let's unpack the matter and see.

Self-Driving Cars And Pod Up

For Level 4 and Level 5 true self-driving vehicles, there won't be a human driver involved in the driving task.

All occupants will be passengers.

The AI is doing the driving.

What in the world does a pod-up phenomenon have to do with AI-based true self-driving cars?

Ditch the pandemic aspects underlying the existing pod-up trend and focus instead on the concept of small collectives that band together for beneficial purposes as a grouping.

Here's how that comes to matter in the case of self-driving cars.

First, some believe that the price tag for a self-driving car is going to be quite high, much higher than the purchase price for today's conventional cars. This might be as a result of the added cost of the various hardware and electronics needed for a self-driving car, plus the costs for the self-driving software.

Some are worried that self-driving cars might only be available to the rich and famous due to stratospheric pricing.

It has meanwhile been hoped by most pundits that self-driving cars are going to become a mobility-for-all option, enabling everyone to finally have ready access to car transport. Those today that are mobility disadvantaged will presumably have access to car travel and be able to experience a mobile inspired lifestyle accordingly.

Can the mobility-for-all be achieved if the cost of self-driving cars is through the roof?

Well, the argument goes that self-driving cars will only be owned by large companies. Those entities will have the big bucks needed to buy self-driving cars and they will turnaround and have those expensive assets become money-making ride-sharing vehicles (so-called robo-taxis). In short, self-driving cars will only be owned in fleets.

This would seem like a quite logical proposition.

We do not yet know whether the owners of these fleets would be someone like an Uber or Lyft, or might be the automakers, or could be rental car firms, or perhaps just about any large corporation that thinks the deployment of self-driving cars will bring them a dandy profit.

Under this way of thinking, there will no longer be individually owned cars, at least not self-driving cars, though as mentioned earlier perhaps outsized wealthy people might opt to get them for their use and amusement.

I am known as a contrarian on this topic and fervently believe that we will still likely have individual car ownership, even for self-driving cars.

My logic is that if there is a buck to be made off of a self-driving car, entrepreneurs and even everyday consumers are going to be tempted to make that buck too.

Today's conventional cars are difficult to rent out as an individual owner because you need to provide a human driver. In the future, if you own a self-driving car, you can have it take you to work, and during the workday it could be out doing ride-sharing, earning you a supplemental income. The same could happen at nighttime after you get home, and perhaps the self-driving car is providing rides while you are nestled in your bed and sleeping throughout the night.

Today's cars are a wasted asset that sits idle about 95% of the time. Also, they require the added cost of a human driver.

With self-driving cars, they can be put into use nearly 24/7. And, importantly, no human driver is needed.

There is a bit of a rub though.

Besides the purchase price, there is the matter of maintaining the car and making sure it keeps in top form. The sensitive electronics and systems are not necessarily going to be as readily able to withstand the rigors of day-to-day wear-and-tear.

A fleet owner of self-driving cars is likely to set up special maintenance bays or equivalent centers whereby the vehicles come to get their needed ongoing fixes and repairs. This adds cost and makes owning self-driving cars more complex than it might otherwise seem at first glance.

If an individual owns a self-driving car, how are they going to make sure that this maintenance gets done?

Also, the individual owner is at risk that their self-driving car might or might not be sought as a self-driving ride-sharing option and thus end-up forking over a lot of dough for an asset that might not offer the expected monetary returns.

Into this conundrum enters the Pod Up movement.

Rather than buying a self-driving car on your own, you might instead enter into a pod of others that collectively have agreed to share the ownership and responsibility for a self-driving car.

Let's use the earlier example of the pod that had eleven people in it, consisting of three distinct families.

They decide to pool their monies and buy a self-driving car. Also, they determine where and how maintenance will be performed. These details are important and would need to be worked out, though eventually there is likely to be a contractual template readily available for those wishing to collectively own and operate self-driving cars.

During parts of the day, the members of this pod might have agreed to use the self-driving car for the sole purposes of the pod.

They might individually ride in the self-driving car, or with their family, or with other members of the pod. At some points during the day, they might have agreed that the self-driving car is listed on a ride-sharing online network and shown as being available to provide rides.

Overall, some of the time, the self-driving car will be making money by doing ride-sharing, and at other times will not be earning money per se and instead simply be providing rides for those members of the pod. There will be a trade-off involved as to how much money the pod wants to make versus the convenience of having their shared self-driving car for traveling purposes.

In one sense, you could liken this sharing arrangement to timeshares, though of course conventional timeshares have gotten a bit of a bad reputation and there are undeniably lessons to be learned from those kinds of ventures.

Hopefully, the shared self-driving cars arena will avoid the pitfalls of other such agreements.

Conclusion

The possibility of pods for self-driving car ownership has the potential for reducing the wasted time of meandering and somewhat aimless self-driving cars. Those within a pod would presumably seek to utilize the self-driving in optimal ways, including for their personal use and for when it is made available for ride-sharing activities.

CHAPTER 14

MAN ON HOOD

AND

SELF-DRIVING CARS

Multiple videos captured an unlikely scene on a Saturday when a semi-truck was spotted barreling along a Florida highway with a man clinging wildly to the hood, bashing the windshield with his head and fists. The oddity of the situation seemed to defy comprehension and was evocative of something that a Hollywood studio might stage for a film production.

This was no stunt.

According to news reports, the semi-truck had earlier been flagged down by the man while on foot along the turnpike, and once the trucker came to halt the man then shockingly leaped onto the hood, opting to inexplicably start smashing away. The truck driver then instinctively drove forward amid the belief that the man would opt to get off the truck, but instead, the determined intruder continued to stay affixed, and so the truck driver continued apace on the highway, driving jerkily from side-to-side and alternating braking and accelerating, seeking to dislodge the alleged marauder.

Cars driving near to the semi-truck were awestruck by the incident and of course pointed their smartphone cameras toward the spectacle, seeking to video a moment-in-time that might not ever arise in a lifetime, akin to catching a bird's eye glimpse of Haley's comet.

For about nine miles the semi-truck proceeded as though it was like a bucking bull trying to dismount an unwanted castigator. The news indicated that the police ultimately showed up, the truck came to a halt, the clinging man was disengaged from the hood, questioned, and summarily taken into custody. So far, no apparent motive or rationale for the activity has been clearly identified.

It would be easy to write-off or dismiss the matter as an offhanded curiosity, but perhaps there is more to this than otherwise meets the eye.

Consider this intriguing question: *In an era of AI-based true self-driving cars, what would happen if someone opted to unexpectedly cling to the hood of an AI-driven vehicle?*

We already know what a human driver might do, such as potentially driving ahead in a manner to shake-off the clinging person (rightfully or wrongly), so it seems worthwhile to ponder what an AI driving system might do in a similar circumstance.

Let's unpack the matter and see.

Self-Driving Cars And Unwelcomed Hood Riders

For Level 4 and Level 5 true self-driving vehicles, there won't be a human driver involved in the driving task.

All occupants will be passengers.

The AI is doing the driving.

Suppose that a person climbed onto the hood of an AI-based true self-driving car.

Before we consider what the AI might do, if you are wondering why anyone would opt to get onto the hood of a car, especially a self-driving car, there are presumably lots of reasonable explanations and equally abundant nonsensical reasons.

On the reasonableness side of things, maybe someone is unable to get inside the car and is anxiously trying to get away from a foul situation, such as being confronted by an evildoer aiming to harm them, so the frightened person leaps onto the hood in hopes of being spirited away from their existing endangerment. The risky ploy could backfire in that the AI might suddenly halt the self-driving car, leaving the person a sitting duck, as it were, but it is also conceivable that the

AI would proceed and potentially enable the escape of the terrified person.

Another possibility, marginally in the reasonableness camp, consists of someone seeking to go for a joyride. A person might consider it funny or exhilarating to hitch a ride on a self-driving car, either doing so as a prank or maybe on a dare, all of which is certainly dangerous and undesirable. You might remember the spate two years of people jumping out of a moving car as part of the Drake song *In My Feelings* viral challenge that momentarily became a popular but foolish trend (for my coverage at the time regarding the phenomenon as it related to self-driving cars).

Let's hope that people do not come up with similar foolhardy stunts involving self-driving cars.

Yet another angle might be someone wanting to stop a self-driving car and believing that by jumping on the hood it will cause the AI to halt the vehicle. This might be done by a protestor that is seeking to hinder traffic. More ominously, there are concerns that if the AI driving systems are too easily fooled, it could foster acts of robo-jacking, which is similar to carjacking but has to do with tricking the AI into allowing a wrongdoer to possibly commandeer a vehicle and its riders.

Shifting gears, an example of a nonsensical reason might consist of someone that is not right in their mind and gets onto the hood due to hallucinations or other irrational thoughts. We might not ever know what possessed someone to take the action and only know that they chose of their own volition to do so.

Okay, so it is entirely within the realm of possibility that a person might end-up getting onto the hood of an AI self-driving car. I think we can all agree that this is not a farfetched notion.

You might be wondering, well, why hasn't it already been occurring?

It hasn't particularly happened due to the paucity of self-driving cars on the roadways, plus there is usually a human back-up driver inside the self-driving car, thus it would seem unlikely that we would be encountering many hood-riding incidents to-date.

Once self-driving cars become widespread, you ought to assume and naturally expect that all kinds of oddball activities will come out of the woodwork. There are already reported instances of people trying to trick the AI driving systems, such as jaywalkers that "know" they can illegally cross the street and the AI driving system will not challenge them, which a human driver would likely do (this is a high-risk gambit, by the way, since the AI is not infallible and those human interlopers are imprudent to bet their lives on such matters).

All in all, as strange as it might seem to be discussing the act of getting onto the hood of a car, this is a bona fide topic and one that AI developers fielding self-driving cars need to give proper consideration.

One of the first reactions by some AI developers is that the chances of someone getting onto the hood for any reason whatsoever are so infinitesimal and unlikely that it is not worth any semblance of contemplation. Those with this rather dogmatic viewpoint would pointedly ask how many times such an act occurs with today's human-driven cars, for which there aren't any available statistics to showcase that it happens with any modicum of frequency.

Of course, this might be like trying to compare apples and oranges, in the sense that what happens today with human-driven cars might end-up being a lot different in an era of AI-driven cars. Acts that people will not do due to a human driver at the wheel are likely to arise once there is no longer in fact a human at the wheel.

We do not yet know how people are going to react to a world of plentiful self-driving cars and thus can convincingly argue that all bets are off as to what people perchance do today, and instead, we need to think ahead about what people will do in the future and especially how they will react to an abundance of self-driving cars around them.

I mention this quandary because there are some automakers and self-driving car tech firms that would dismiss out-of-hand facets such as people leaping onto the hood of a self-driving car. Besides the belief that it is an unlikely scenario, they admittedly already have their hands full trying to simply make self-driving cars that can safely drive from point A to point B, getting from a house to the grocery store, doing so without getting into a car accident or otherwise having troubles.

In that viewpoint, the hood clinging use case is admittedly an edge or corner-case, meaning that it is something placed way down on the priority list of things deserving attention. AI developers for self-driving cars already have a lot on their plate and trying to chew too many things at once can end-up diluting their efforts, leading to delays in getting the core stuff done.

Let's then go ahead and concur that the hood clinger is a rarity and an edge problem. Once so stipulated, we can nonetheless still give it some focus and explore what the AI might or might not do in such a seemingly bizarre or improbable occurrence (though, as I say, this might be regrettably end-up being more common than we expect).

What The AI Might Do Or Not Do

We can begin this assessment by first establishing that the hood clinging act might occur when the self-driving car is motionless, or it might occur once the self-driving is already in motion.

If a self-driving car is not in motion, and yet someone opts to get onto the hood, the question arises as to whether the AI will be able to detect that a person has gotten onto the hood of the vehicle. Furthermore, once making that determination, if feasible to do so, the AI would need to ascertain whether to proceed with having the car go into motion or whether to remain motionless.

Put aside, for now, the use case of a parked self-driving car. Though someone could certainly crawl onto the hood of a parked self-driving car, let's not worry about this per se, and instead focus on the more somber circumstance of a self-driving car that is temporarily stopped such as at a red light or a stop sign. To clarify, I am not suggesting that having someone on top of a parked self-driving car is somehow okay, and also to be clear cut, the AI would need to deal with this situation at the time of the self-driving car seeking to get underway, so those all need to ultimately be factored into these mechanizations.

The other major and crucial use case is when the self-driving car is already in motion and someone chooses to get onto the hood. For those that think it nearly impossible to somehow navigate your way onto the hood of a moving car, keep in mind that if the self-driving car is say going down an alleyway at a speed of 3 miles per hour, it would be relatively easy to have someone run alongside or otherwise jump onto the hood.

Thus, the in-motion variant is clearly a real-world possibility and cannot be patently dismissed.

We are now at the prized moment of asking a seemingly straightforward question, namely whether the AI could detect that someone is on the hood of the self-driving car.

An initial reaction by many would be that this has to be detectable and that it would seem impossible or outlandish to think that the AI could not figure out that a person has landed onto the hood of the vehicle.

Do not be so quick with your assumptions.

Depending upon where the sensors are arrayed on the self-driving car, there could very well be a kind of blind spot in terms of someone clinging to the hood. The cameras are usually aimed at the street ahead, thus, someone standing directly in front of the car is likely to be detected, but a person laying down on the hood is not so readily seen. The same could be said of the radar and LIDAR, suggesting that they too might not detect a person that is straddled on the hood of the vehicle.

One key would be how the person got onto the hood.

There is a solid chance that the sensors would have detected the person as they approached the vehicle, thus, the AI would be able to ascertain that a person was near to the car. If the person suddenly disappears, so to speak, and no longer is at the sides or front of the car, the AI as normally being crafted today would not somehow be curious about where the person went. As long as the person is no longer an impediment to proceeding, that's all the AI would generally be programmed to consider.

Keep in mind that AI is not sentient as yet, and we are a long way away from getting there. Further, realize too that AI does not have any kind of common-sense reasoning, at least not that which humans have today, and so the AI doesn't "reason" that if a person was nearby and now is "gone" that they must be on the hood of the vehicle.

A human driver sitting at the steering wheel would obviously see a person on the hood and react in some fashion. The cameras of the self-driving car do not necessarily watch the roadway from the same perspective of a human driver. Oftentimes, the cameras are placed at the very front of the vehicle, therefore beyond the scope of seeing the hood. There might be cameras atop the roof of the car, in which case there is then a heightened chance of detecting the person.

This discussion about detection is crucial since the AI needs to discover that a person exists on the hood to do something about the situation.

But even if the detection occurs, since the AI has no common-sense as yet and is not sentient, it is unlikely that the AI is otherwise programmed today to consider what to do about a person being on the hood. In other words, even if detection occurs, the AI might have no provision of what to do. This is because the edge case is considered so rare that there is nothing as yet programmed into the AI to cope with the matter.

As such, the AI could presumably proceed to drive the car as though there wasn't someone clinging to the hood. This would certainly seem undesirable and be quite dangerous.

If there were passengers inside the self-driving car, they might yell to the AI's Natural Language Processing (NLP) system, which is normally focused on gleaning driving preferences from riders, such as where to go, and those riders might insist that the AI stop the car to allow the hood clinger to get off.

This brings up an allied and mind-bending topic, venturing into the arena of AI Ethics, as to whether those riders are in some sense obligated to warn the AI about such a predicament.

You might assume that base humanity would be to of course alert the AI, though suppose that there is a solo rider in the vehicle, perhaps they know the person that's on the hood, and they wish ill will toward that person. In that case, the rider might remain silent and wait and see what happens. Or, suppose the person on the hood is trying to get to the rider, aiming to harm the rider, and therefore the rider is hoping that the AI will continue driving the car and the hood clinging adversary will fall off the car.

Those are factors worth contemplating.

What else might happen?

There is a chance that a person on the hood might end-up obscuring some of the sensors, blocking the sensors from being used, or possibly damage sensors in the act of flailing around on the hood. In that case, the AI is usually already prepared to try and cope with sensor malfunctions or sensors that have gotten blocked by say mud or debris. The AI will not necessarily come to a halt if it can proceed reasonably safely, though by-and-large any substantive detriment to the detection will usually be a signal to the AI that the self-driving car should be brought to a safe halt.

Conclusion

One overarching point is that unlike a human driver, AI driving systems are not yet especially versed in dealing with the admittedly one-off act of a hood-clinging trespasser. Welcome to the world of AI Ethics, which is going to increasingly become a salient and vital ingredient in the existing pell-mell adoption of AI.

CHAPTER 15

PUDDLES

AND

SELF-DRIVING CARS

Have you ever encountered roadway puddles that turned out to be worse than you thought?

It is easy to misjudge a puddle and assume that there is no need for concern.

One time, I took a puddle at full speed on a major street and discovered to my jarring dismay that there was a sizable pothole hidden by the grimy layer of water. Besides shaking up the car and giving me a bit of a scare, turns out one of the front tires took the brunt of the matter and quickly went flat soon after hitting the camouflaged roadway pit.

A puddle of water can oftentimes be a cloak that hides roadway dangers. How deep is the water? Is the road surface intact underneath the layer of water? Might there be debris submerged in the puddle and potentially going to become a hazard to driving?

Another factor involves the potential for hydroplaning.

If the puddle is large enough, being wide and sufficiently deep, there is a chance that the tires might lose contact with the roadway and a precarious moment of surfing on top of the water can arise. Trying to control a car that is hydroplaning is notoriously tricky, and though there are advisable driving techniques that can be attempted, many drivers go into a semi-panic and are unable to apply rational thought to cope with the surprising predicament.

Some drivers opt to steer around a puddle, but they might do so without forewarning other nearby cars. All of a sudden, a driver opts to veer into another lane, causing all nearby cars to go into a cascading set of maneuvers to try and avoid banging into each other. Whether it was worth the risk to all the other cars, simply for the one driver to avoid a puddle, remains an open question, though much of the time those last-minute acts are likely to cause more harm to everyone and a questionable move by the one skittish driver.

What happens with one puddle can be magnified when there are numerous such puddles all in the same vicinity.

A slew of puddles can be like an obstacle course that needs to be threaded. A car ahead of you edges into the next lane, seeking to avoid a puddle, and meanwhile, a car to your right seeks to get into your lane, trying to avoid a separate puddle. Drivers are veering right and left, playing a game of dodgeball, and in their desire to avoid puddles are endangering each other as ramming machines.

For those situations involving rainstorms that have flooded the roadways, some puddles drain right away and other puddles sit around for much too long. Depending upon the depth of the water that remains, there is a chance of hydro-locking your car. This involves the water getting into the engine compartment or otherwise messing with the operation of the vehicle, including perhaps disturbing the brakes or other key components.

There is also the splashing effect of driving through a puddle.

A sizable puddle at a corner where pedestrians are crossing can become a splashy affair in terms of cars causing a large swoosh of sooty water to fly toward those innocents that are waiting to cross the street. This might seem funny, almost like a cartoon, but anyone that has gotten blotted with filthy street water is likely to tell you that it was not an enjoyable experience.

All in all, there is more to puddles than perhaps at first meets the eye.

Novice drivers are often clueless about puddles and take no action whatsoever. A doting parent that is sitting in the car when their young adult is learning to drive might find themselves urging their beloved offspring to slow down and take it easy when a puddle is encountered. The parent might be looking around the car to see if the other lanes are clear for the newbie driver to switch away from running through a suspicious looking puddle.

Of course, some drivers relish the excitement and unknown lurking dangers of puddles. These maniac drivers love to speed through puddles. The bigger the splash, the better. If they can get the water to obscure the windshield of a nearby car, it is decidedly worth bonus points. Getting the puddle to act like a tsunami and soak pedestrians is the ultimate pinnacle of puddle running for these driving demons.

The point overall is that puddles are worthy of consideration while driving a car. Most people learn via the seat-of-their-pants how to cope with puddles, discovering over time the variety of puddles and how to try and gauge the ominous ones from the more mundane ones. As they say about a box of chocolates, you never know what really is in a puddle, and so it is prudent to be wary and alert.

This brings us to today's intriguing question: *How will AI-based true self-driving cars fare in coping with puddles on the public roadways?*

Let's unpack the matter and see.

Self-Driving Cars And Puddles

For Level 4 and Level 5 true self-driving vehicles, there won't be a human driver involved in the driving task.

All occupants will be passengers.

The AI is doing the driving.

You might naturally assume that the AI driving system would be an expert at handling puddles.

Not necessarily.

For many of the automakers and self-driving tech firms, crafting the AI components for dealing with puddles is typically low on the list of priorities. Considered an edge or corner case problem, the belief is that puddles can be treated as though they essentially do not exist, and merely classified as a wet roadway. Someday, once the core of driving is established sufficiently, the AI can be enhanced to cope with puddle-specific facets.

This might be a shortsighted perspective.

Whether the street or highway has a dash of water or is coated with water, the AI is usually written to categorize the road as simply wet, thus not especially concerned about the depth of the water per se, and nor what might be underneath the water. This somewhat makes sense in that you would ordinarily assume that an asphalt road is tidy and well kept, which is a sharp contrast to a puddle that might be found on a rutty dirt road or while going off-roading.

Speaking of off-road driving, the military is closely exploring the detection of puddles for Autonomous Vehicles (AV) such as cars and trucks that they use while going across unpaved terrain. Dealing with puddles in the wild, as it were, versus on the everyday roadways is indeed a serious concern and one getting devoted attention.

Nonetheless, as earlier assessed, just because a puddle happens to be on a highway or be on your neighborhood street does not mean that it can be simply ignored or treated with disdain. Does putting a puddle into the same overall category of a wet street really make sense? It provides some hint of a warning but tends to ignore the multitude of bad effects that can arise due to driving through a puddle.

Since we can expect that both human-driven cars and self-driving cars are going to intermix on our roadways, an AI driving system that does not realize that human drivers might perform extreme driving actions when confronting a puddle means that the AI can get caught unawares. Anyone or anything driving a car should be considering not only the conditions of the roads, they also need to consider the actions and reactions by other drivers on the roadways too.

You might be tempted to argue that any crazed driving by human drivers is the fault of those humans, and therefore the AI should not need to be burdened with worrying about human drivers. Unfortunately, that head-in-the-sand attitude doesn't particularly helpful in terms of the AI possibly getting into a car wreck via the unanticipated antics of a human driver that could have possibly been predicted.

We ought to reasonably expect that the AI will be able to anticipate how humans drive, else the AI perhaps should not be driving on the public roadways.

If a contemporary self-driving car is unlikely to be particularly prepared to cope with puddles, it means too that the AI is probably not trying to calculate whether to avoid a puddle, nor whether to possibly slow down upon encountering a puddle. Similar to my own experience of getting caught off-guard by a pothole hidden inside a puddle, today's AI driving systems could end up in the same boat.

Part of the issue involves the sensors used by the self-driving car to detect the roadway conditions. Cameras and video streaming are the predominant mode of sensory detection and ferreting out the magnitude and dangers of a puddle by visual processing alone can be problematic. Humans do the same, of course, and look at a puddle to try and guess at the nature of it, which can be tricky to size up.

One common ploy involves watching other drivers as they go into the puddle. If you perchance have any cars ahead of you, once they strike the puddle, you tend to quickly know what the puddle seems to contain or be hiding. While there might be a sizable splash of water from the puddle, you can usually discern whether the car itself was jolted, giving you a visual clue that there might be something worse about the puddle than can be seen with the naked eye.

AI that is advanced sufficiently can do the same kind of detection. Rather than having to necessarily peer through the puddle, which few sensors can readily do (though, you might find of interest the potential advent of Ground Penetrating Radar or GPR), the AI can observe the reactions of other cars. Based on what happens to those other cars, the AI can try to deduce what the condition of the puddle might be.

Furthermore, it is expected that V2V (vehicle-to-vehicle) electronic communications will be a key aspect of self-driving cars. By sending electronic messages from self-driving cars to self-driving cars, the AI driving systems can warn each other about the traffic and roadway status. In the use case of puddles, it would presumably be feasible to have a self-driving car that first figured out that a puddle is dangerous to then alert any other upcoming self-driving cars, so they are prepared accordingly.

Also planned for the future is V2I (vehicle-to-infrastructure) electronic communications, allowing the roadway infrastructure to send out messages to self-driving cars. Traffic signals can beam messages that indicate the timing of the red and green lights, along with bridges being able to send signals when a bridge is unpassable. In theory, when puddles are bad enough on a stretch of road, perhaps there will be computer-based edge devices set up along the road that will transmit the dangers via V2I to any self-driving cars coming along that stretch.

Conclusion

For the moment, expect that a self-driving car is bound to cause a splash of water from a puddle at a corner, doing so not because it intentionally wants to soak the nearby pedestrians, but merely due to not being programmed to consider what will happen when plowing through a puddle. This naïve innocence might be of little solace to the pedestrians, and they can certainly curse those AI developers that hadn't yet established the AI to cope with puddles.

At some point, it is likely that the AI driving systems will be rather adept at puddles.

CHAPTER 16

UNHINGED

AND

SELF-DRIVING CARS

This past weekend the highly anticipated movie "Unhinged" starring actor extraordinaire Russell Crowe opened in U.S. movie theatres. Given the extraordinary circumstances facing the movie industry, the film did surprisingly well at the box office.

If you don't know anything about the movie, you might want to close your eyes for a moment and then skip quickly to the next paragraph. That being said, via the movie trailers and the overall buzz about the movie, it has already been widely publicized that a key hook to the storyline involves a spate of road rage. In fact, over the last several months, Crowe did several mock Public Service Announcements that elucidated the dangers of road rage and simultaneously helped promote his new film.

I sincerely hope that you've never experienced road rage, though it seems that anyone driving on the highways and byways for any length of time is bound to inevitably come upon a road rage incident. You might witness two cars wildly chasing after each other or perhaps have a driver that abruptly cuts you off in traffic because they believe you have somehow transgressed their driving activities. Seems like road rage can happen at any time of the day, in any locale, and for whatever type of reason, including no bona fide reason at all (to be clear, even if there is a reason, this still does not justify and nor warrant carrying out a road rage act).

We certainly expect that human drivers are apt to occasionally go wacky and flareup into a road rage fit. To try and avoid this outcome, cautious drivers are especially civil to other drivers amid an outside hope that doing so will keep those on-edge drivers from suddenly boiling over. Meanwhile, there are those hardened drivers that do not seem to care whether their behavior produces a feverish combustion of road rage. One supposes that the potential spark for a road rage confrontation is as varied as people are, thus, perhaps there is no ready way to predict what will ignite a road rage (though, discourteous driving would seem a high potential toward triggering it).

If human drivers are prone at times to slide into a road rage cataclysm, there seem to be one means to incontrovertibly avert those shady moments, namely by replacing human drivers with AI driving systems. Some pundits look with great anticipation to the day that human drivers are no longer sitting at the wheel anymore. In short, if those darned humans cannot take the heat, get them out of the kitchen entirely. The mantra becomes: AI driving systems to the rescue.

But is it really the case that AI-based true self-driving cars will obviate the road rage phenomena?

Let's unpack the matter and see.

Self-Driving Cars And Road Rage

For Level 4 and Level 5 true self-driving vehicles, there won't be a human driver involved in the driving task.

All occupants will be passengers.

The AI is doing the driving.

Great, you might assume, since we would not expect AI to launch into a road rage driving fit.

Well, yes, this sentiment is generally true, though keep in mind that the AI driving system can be whatever the developers want it to be. In other words, presumably no automaker or self-driving tech firm in its right mind is crafting AI that will drive in a manic manner. One would surely hope that being a crazed or even systemic "unhinged driver" is not on the list of AI-based self-driving car desired requirements. That seems to be rather axiomatic.

Nonetheless, it would be foolish to assume that any AI system is always going to be strictly proper as though there is some natural law that governs the AI's behavior. Like any kind of automation, there is still a chance that the AI could go astray, for which the developers have hopefully done their best to try and detect and prevent from occurring.

Some seem to ascribe a semblance of perfection to AI. Whether this is due to how science fiction stories have sometimes portrayed AI, or maybe because we do not think of AI as having emotions, the overall point is that the AI being devised for self-driving cars is decidedly not perfect and you ought not to fall into the mental trap that it is going to be.

Realizing that there is an oddball chance of AI going rogue, let's put that to the side and consider it a rather unlikely possibility.

Does this then resolve the road rage phenomena and we can summarily put it aside too?

I'm afraid not.

Here's the rub.

For quite a while, many years, likely many decades, we are going to have human-driven cars that are intermixing on our streets with AI-driven cars.

That's a fact.

Those that believe in a Utopian world of entirely and exclusively self-driving cars are dreamers. You can readily bet your bottom dollar that there are going to be humans that will insist on being able to drive a car, vowing that you will only be able to take away the steering wheel by prying it from dead cold hands. People are quite enamored of the "right" to drive (well, it is considered a privilege, at least on public roadways), and attempts to somehow prevent humans from driving a car are going to be met with a protest storm of unimaginable proportions.

Some that wish to do away with the act of human driving are quick to point to the number of car-related fatalities that are incurred each year, which is around 40,000 deaths per year in the United States alone, and emphasize that if self-driving cars can substantively reduce that number, we should all voluntarily give up our driver's licenses. For any leftover resisters, perhaps new laws would be established that outlaw driving a car on public roads. Inevitably, all new cars might be made without any driving controls for human access, thus, presumably making it nearly impossible for those scalawag humans to drive a car.

This whole matter is going to take a long time to figure out and meanwhile, the vastness and fierceness of resistance to giving up driving are going to be steep. An alternative would be to have streets and highways that are designated for human drivers versus self-driving cars, whether for the entire set of roads or possibly by splitting lanes for each type of driver. Do not fall into the falsehood that this is going to be easy. Sure, painting new lines on the roads are simple, but deciding where human drivers can go and where they cannot go, this once again is brewing for a huge battle.

Suppose self-driving cars are allotted special lanes and can get from point A to point B in say 30 minutes, while the lanes for human-driven cars are boxed-in and end-up causing the drivers to experience a 60-minute drive. If you are in favor of self-driving cars, you would assume that this difference would inspire the human drivers to forego doing the driving and switch over to using self-driving cars. Maybe, but it could also be that the human drivers become upset that they got the short end of the stick and the lanes they have are not as good, or that if they could also drive in the self-driving car lanes then the time for their trips would be shortened accordingly.

This is a merry-go-round that is going to keep on spinning for a protracted time.

Essentially, in any practical sense of the adoption of self-driving cars, there is going to be a mixing of human-driven cars and self-driving cars.

And that's how road rage is going to continue.

A human-driven car is coming up to a stop sign. The driver is in a rush, perhaps late to an important meeting, or wanting to get home to watch a notable baseball game that is just getting started. Ahead of the human driver is a self-driving car. The self-driving car comes to the stop sign and obediently comes to a stop. Not a rolling stop, but a full honest-to-goodness complete stop.

The human driver that is waiting behind the self-driving car is going bananas. There's no reason for the self-driving car to come to a complete stop since there isn't any other traffic nearby. Just run the darned stop sign or at least roll through it. The human driver is getting exasperated. It was a tough day at work and this idiotic AI driving system is the fuse on the powder keg of this human driver.

Finally, the self-driving car proceeds. The human driver zips past the stop sign, comes up to the self-driving car, and makes a rude gesture at the self-driving car.

Your first thought might be that it makes little sense to vent anger towards the AI. It won't care. It likely won't even notice.

Perhaps true, but this is not what is going through the mind of the road rage driver. Toss rational thought out the window, as it were.

Okay, so the human driver is irked and makes a futile gesture at the AI. Case closed.

Maybe not.

Suppose there is a human passenger inside the self-driving car. Perhaps the passenger, upon seeing the rude gesture, decides to do likewise in return and includes a showy and smirking smile as though suggesting that the human driver is stupid to be rebuffing an AI driving system. The human driver is now utterly steamed.

The human driver decides to cut off the self-driving car, getting the AI to swerve to avoid hitting the human-driven car. Next, the human driver gets directly in front of the self-driving car and comes to a halt. This causes the AI driving system to bring the self-driving car to a halt too.

So far, the AI has done what we might expect it to do, including avoiding a car crash and also coming to a halt when being blocked by a car ahead of it. The thing is, what about the passenger inside the self-driving car. You might suggest that the passenger is now a sitting duck.

If the self-driving car was being driven by a human rather than an AI system, let's imagine this is an Uber or Lyft, the human driver would presumably attempt to go around the road rage driver and the now halted car. The passenger could be imploring the ride-sharing driver to quickly get away from the nutty driver that has blocked their path forward.

What will the AI do?

Likely, not much. The odds are that the AI is not going to become "convinced" that you need to have the self-driving car skyrocket around the halted car. This is not programmed into the AI and nor a scenario that most of the self-driving car developers are considering right now (it would be rated as an edge or corner case, something of low priority and maybe gotten to once the everyday driving capabilities are fully developed).

The odds are that the self-driving car will have some form of OnStar-like capability, allowing the passenger to make a call to an agent to indicate that assistance is needed. The remote agent might or might not have an ability to activate the car and take over the driving (likely not, for now). The agent might be able to communicate electronically to the AI and command the AI to get underway, but this is also a tough situation to rectify because the AI might not have a provision for dealing with a predicament of being blocked by another car.

The agent might call 911, meanwhile, the human road rage nut is already outside the self-driving car and banging on the windows of the vehicle.

All told, the point being that as long as there are human drivers, there remains the opportunity for road rage to be enacted. And, per the earlier assertion that human drivers will be around for quite a while, this means that road rage is not going away simply due to the adoption of self-driving cars.

Conclusion

There are more mind-busting facets to consider.

In the example, the human driver started the road rage. The scenario could readily be turned around, somewhat, by having a passenger inside a self-driving car that purposely attempts to goad a human driver in a nearby vehicle. The passenger might make a rude gesture or stick their head out the window of the self-driving car and berate the human driver in the other car.

At that juncture, the human driver reacts by undertaking a road rage driving action.

To make things really topsy-turvy, consider that people riding in self-driving cars might begin to realize the "sitting duck" nature of doing so, and thus decide that they would rather be driving a car than riding as a passenger in a self-driving car. I know that this logic seems somewhat backward since the culprit to go after are the human drivers that are acting out, but if that is not easily done, the concern for being at the mercy of a road rage driver might be a stimulus to get riders back into driving a car versus being a rider in a self-driving car.

This is of course sad and beguiling.

If there is any kind of silver lining or path out of this conundrum, one is that the self-driving car is apt to be chockful of sensors such as cameras, radar, LIDAR, and the like. This is handy in that it can be used for the AI to drive the car, plus it also can record whatever happens outside of the self-driving car. In that manner, the road rage undertaken is going to get recorded.

The downside is that it is not clear that just because the road rage is going to be recorded that it will necessarily dissuade the road rage drivers. We earlier conceded that they are bound to lose their rational thinking and thus the facet that they are being recorded might not cause them to alter their violence precipitated efforts.

Another helpful element consists of the V2V (vehicle-to-vehicle) electronic communications and V2I (vehicle-to-infrastructure) messaging that self-driving cars are likely to have. In theory, if the AI suspects that a road rage is taking place, it might convey as such via V2V to other nearby cars, seeking help, or alert the police or other authorities via the V2I. This might bring help quickly and aid in preventing the road rage instigator from fully carrying out their actions.

Gloomily, none of that can especially stop a road rage crazed radical from ramming into the self-driving car. Some keep saying that self-driving cars will never get into car crashes, but this is nonsensical since a determined human driver can readily smash into a self-driving car. The AI cannot overcome the law of physics, such that even if the AI tries to maneuver out of the way, a human driver seeking to do evil can still manage to smack into a self-driving car.

Maybe the "good news" is that there would not be any road rage induced car chases involving a self-driving car per se. A human driver might opt to follow a self-driving car, but it is unlikely that the AI is programmed to try and run away and become part of a determined car chase. Instead, the AI will tend to obey the rules of the road and make it's way along, at safe speeds in a legally driven manner, for which this is not much of a car chase since the AI isn't trying to escape.

Shifting gears, a concluding thought for now. Once we have some prevalence of self-driving cars, the movies showing car chases will begin to look outdated, perhaps nostalgic. Wishfully, it would be nice if the movies could no longer showcase road rage, due to the aspect that self-driving cars will have made road rage a distant memory, but it seems that actors and actresses will still be able to get roles as the incensed and unhinged driver, despite the wonderment of AI-based true self-driving cars being on our roadways.

CHAPTER 17

REVERSIBILITY

AND

SELF-DRIVING CARS

The new sci-fi thriller *Tenet* has brought palindromes to the forefront of our minds, along with jolting us all to think outside of the box about time.

You'll see in a moment how palindromes and time appear to tie together, ingeniously so.

Writer and director extraordinaire Christopher Nolan have once again decided to get us all to think carefully about time, doing so in his latest provocative blockbuster-to-be film and further extends his legacy of toying with time in his prior films including having cleverly done so in *Inception, Interstellar, Dunkirk, Memento,* and so on. To avoid spoiling his latest movie, let's avert discussing any of the details about how time is utilized in *Tenet,* though we can certainly discuss the name of the film, which serves as an immediate and telltale clue.

In case you didn't already know, the word "TENET" is an especially famous example of a palindrome. A palindrome is a word, name, phrase, sentence, verse, or essentially any general sequence that can be read the same when doing so both forwards and backward. For example, the word "level" is read the same in either direction, reading either from left to right (forwards), or reading from right to left (backward or perhaps more aptly, in reverse). Likewise, the word "kayak" and the word "racecar" are examples of palindromes too, as are the names "Bob" and "Anna."

The instances of palindromes consisting of phrases or sentences can get a bit more complicated. Sometimes the reading process is straightforward in either direction, such as "step on no pets" is the same whether reading forwards or in reverse. Meanwhile, a trickier palindrome is "was it a car or a cat I saw" and for which you need to mindfully break up the letters into correspondingly aligned words when reading the phrase in reverse. Numbers can be labeled as palindromic and mathematicians seem to delight in finding interesting examples, such as the prime numbers of 101 and 353.

What makes TENET especially notable is its inclusion in the famous Sator Square. Historically, the Sator Square is a well-known exemplar of a palindrome and has stoked intense mystery and overall intrigue. There are five words in the Sator Square, each in Latin, and collected together to create a 5-by-5 square, consisting of the words SATOR, AREPO, TENET, OPERA, and ROTAS. No one is exactly sure what the message is supposed to mean, though many believe it is a story about a farmer named Arepo. Depending upon how you decide to translate the Latin words, perhaps there is a sentence composed of the five words that roughly indicates that the farmer Arepo works to rotate wheels (such as a plow), or maybe the farmer Arepo holds the wheels with difficulty, or effort.

Instances of the Sator Square have been discovered in many places and presumably must be of some significance, which has also led to a wide range and at times wild speculation about the alleged powers or magic that are imbued within this collection of five palindromes.

The palindrome TENET is a word that generally is indicative of the notion to hold or keep or comprehend something. You might suggest that this is somewhat similar to the everyday word "tenet" which generally means to hold a belief or principle to be considered true.

Okay, so we have the palindrome TENET that can be read forwards and backward (in reverse), along with a meaning associated with holding or comprehending something, plus it is famously used in the Sator Square, which might or might not be somehow magical, and there is a new movie made by a director seemingly obsessed with time that has opted to name the film as *Tenet*.

What do you get?

Well, focus on the idea of being able to read a word or sentence both forwards and in reverse. Suppose that we could do the same thing with time. Right now, we assume that time can only flow in one direction, namely forward. Mankind has seemingly dreamt forever that it would be nifty if time could be reversed. There are gobs and gobs of science fiction stories, movies, TV shows, poetry and you name it that have sought to explore what could happen and what might be done if time could flow in reverse.

Time reversibility is undoubtedly a fascinating topic.

Shifting gears, you might be surprised to know that time reversibility has been given some strident attention in the realm of computers and computing machines, doing so in a field of study known as reversible computing. Most people have never heard of such a thing. Indeed, even those within the computer field are often taken aback to discover that research and attention are being put toward reversible computing.

The usual reaction is in three stages. First, amazement that such a field of study exists. Second, a doubtfulness that it makes any sense to study the notion and that it might very well be an utter waste of time (a bit of a pun there). Third, curiosity about what exactly reversible computing is, and how it might be of use.

Generally, there are two major ways to categorize reversible computing facets. One is a means of performing a physical reversibility of computational activities, while the other has to do with undertaking a logical semblance of computational reversibility. These two categories tend to work hand-in-hand.

A simple example might suffice to get you started on the topic of reversible computing.

It seems that everyone nowadays knows that there are usually computer bits consisting of the binary values of 1 and 0. We could construct an electronic chip that would take as input a bit, either in the state of 1 or the state of 0 and produce as output the so-called opposite or inversion of the bit (i.e., if the input is a 1 then output a 0, while if the input is a 0 then output a 1). Those of you familiar with such matters would recognize this as the NOT operation (confusing perhaps that this is known as NOT, which might seem like not doing something, when in fact it will produce the outputs as mentioned herein). More commonly, this is referred to as an inverter.

Could you receive the output of a NOT operation and make things go in reverse, returning back to whatever you started with?

Yes, it would certainly seem straightforward to do so. If the output was a 0, you know that the input must have been a 1, while if the output is 1 then you know that the input must have been a 0 (assuming of course that the operation worked flawlessly). Now, keep in mind that most electronic chips are not made to work in reverse. We have logically identified how to go in reverse, but the electronics might not be set up to allow a reverse physical operation to occur. As such, if we wanted this to happen in a real-world sense, we might need to adapt the electronics accordingly.

A reversible electronic circuit then is a circuit that allows for bits to flow in either direction, forward or in reverse, through the circuitry. There is no longer a fixed indication of what is an input and what is output since either side of the circuitry could be considered available for input and equally available for output.

Where this can be usefully employed involves a somewhat complex understanding of entropy in computing and computers. Generally, it is posited that a reversible computing or computer system could potentially consume much less energy than a conventional forwards-only computer. There would in theory be less heat dissipated for a reversible computing system. That's important because computers are getting smaller and smaller, and limitations are being approached involving what to do about the heat production, for which the give-off of energy can adversely affect the electronics and otherwise undermine attempts to reduce the size of chips. It is hoped that the per Joule of energy that you can squeeze out of the computer hardware would be significantly enhanced via adopting reversible computing approaches.

For those of you more interested in software than hardware, you might enjoy knowing that there is reversible computing with respect to aspects of software too. For example, most software engineers value the notion of being able to stepwise execute their computer programs when doing debugging. This is usually done in a forward motion, proceeding with each line of code to the next in sequence or the intended next line to be performed, moving from the start to the finish. Some debugging tools will allow you to also work in reverse, such that you can essentially go back to a prior line of code, retracting what has just happened, and thus invoke your code to effectively perform in a reverse direction (this is not as easy a thing to do as it might seem on the surface).

If you stop to think about it, we are seemingly conditioned to always be thinking about going forward, and less so about going in reverse. We think of computers for example as going in a forward motion, performing a series of steps in a progression from start to finish. Rarely do you think about going from the end to the start.

There's another place that we tend to be primarily focused on going forward, entailing the driving of a car.

It is a pretty good bet that you spend most of your time driving in a forward direction. Sure, you do use the reverse capability of the car, such as when backing out of a parking spot or trying to back down your driveway. The preponderance of your time though at the wheel is likely going forward and only a tiny fraction of the time involved in reverse driving.

Some people are quite rusty at driving in reverse. You see them moving an inch at a time when backing up. They aren't sure whether to look over their shoulder or whether to look in the rearview mirror. Their heads twist back and forth, trying to figure out what is behind them. Luckily, technology has progressed that many cars now have a back-up camera built-in, aiding the reverse driving chore. Besides the camera, there are at times sensors that scan the area behind the car as you are driving in reverse, attempting to alert you if there are any objects detected. Nonetheless, a lot of older cars still exist on our roadways and they generally lack the back-up camera and allied technologies.

Since we are discussing the notion of thinking outside the box and coupled with mulling over palindromes and going in reverse, here's an additional twist for your day: *Will AI-based self-driving cars reconsider the act of driving in reverse, or will the task of reverse driving remain as it is today?*

Let's unpack the matter and see.

Self-Driving Cars And Going In Reverse

For Level 4 and Level 5 true self-driving vehicles, there won't be a human driver involved in the driving task.

All occupants will be passengers.

The AI is doing the driving.

Will the AI be able to drive the self-driving car in reverse?

Yes, if the AI has been set up to do so, and for which you can reasonably expect that nearly all automakers and self-driving tech firms are putting such capabilities into place.

There are some important caveats to keep in mind.

First, by-and-large, the mainstay of the sensors on a self-driving car are oriented towards going forwards, not going in reverse. There is usually not as much sensory capability installed at going in reverse as there is in going forwards, which somewhat makes sense since presumably, a self-driving car is predominantly to be used going forwards versus going backward.

Second, this means that even if the AI has been programmed or otherwise established to drive in reverse, it is doing so in a less than optimal way than it can drive going forwards. Presumably, the slow speeds usually involved in driving in reverse are sufficiently low enough that the amount of sensory gear will be good enough for reverse oriented driving.

But, this is potentially a legal liability issue that might ultimately rear its ugly head, as it were. If a self-driving car, while going in reverse, runs into say a child or harms or kills someone, you can be sure that lawyers are going to be asking pointed questions about how the reverse driving capabilities were designed and implemented. A case could be made that any shortchanges on how the reverse driving was devised are tantamount to insufficiencies that contributed to whatever regrettable incident might have occurred.

You might be tempted to assert that human drivers are relatively poor at driving in reverse, therefore if the AI is similarly insufficient at driving in reverse than we are no worse off than with human drivers. I doubt that logic will prevail. The public is likely to have higher expectations about the AI driving system, and especially so when going in reverse. In fact, people oftentimes assume that the AI to-date is safer at driving in reverse than humans are, which, debatably might be the case in comparison to rather newbies at driving, but not necessarily better than say human drivers that have honed their reverse driving skills.

Another consideration to contemplate about cars is that the design and construction of most conventional cars are entirely oriented toward forward driving. You cannot drive in reverse in any prolonged manner and nor at the same heightened speeds and fluidity as you can when driving forwards (in most cars). This is not simply due to the human driver, but also due to how the reverse driving mechanisms are devised.

Of course, it seems entirely sensible that the car is structured for forward driving, including that there are a front windshield and nothing comparable on the back (the back window is not usually the same as a windshield). Our seats for drivers are oriented toward the front of the car, and the driving controls are intended to be used while facing forward.

Here's a mind-bender for you.

For true self-driving cars, the driving controls do not need to be available in the car per se, since the AI is doing the driving. Furthermore, the seats inside a self-driving car do not need to be facing in a fixed manner forward. The typical interior design for a self-driving car consists of seats that swivel, allowing the passengers to face in any desired direction. Plus, the seats are oftentimes designed to recline, allowing you to catch a snooze while the AI is doing the driving.

The AI doesn't especially care that there is a so-called forward and a so-called backward (going in reverse). It can be crafted to drive in either direction.

As such, some question why we would use a conventional car design for the use in creating self-driving cars. Sure, it is easier to do things that way, since those car designs already exist. But, perhaps we ought to be reconsidering that a conventional car is oriented towards a forward driving role, and instead allow for an equal capability of self-driving cars to go in reverse as it does when proceeding forwards.

Akin to the earlier point about electronic chips that might allow for reversibility, recall that there isn't any designated side that has exclusively the inputs or exclusively the outputs, thus, perhaps our self-driving cars should be made to go in either direction too, doing so to an equal capacity.

Some pointedly ask, why should we continue to limit self-driving cars to driving in the ways that have been structured to accommodate human drivers?

Some readers might realize that I've discussed this topic in prior articles, including pointing out that Zoox has had a core goal of attaining self-driving cars that can equally proceed forward and "in reverse."

Conclusion

There is more to the debate about self-driving cars going forwards versus going in reverse, but this hopefully opens your eyes to the reversibility topic.

CHAPTER 18

DRIVING NUDE

AND

SELF-DRIVING CARS

Time to share some lighthearted news, though with surprisingly useful insights included.

A recent news item that received some rather startling reactions involved an Oklahoman that decided to get some fast food by using a drive-thru at a Taco Bell, which might not seem especially newsworthy except for the fact that the man was driving his car while completely unclothed. Yes, he was driving around in the raw, as it were, and the police upon responding to a call from the fast-food chain's staff were able to catch-up with the driver, stop him, and then detain him for his societal transgression.

According to the police, the man was mystified at being stopped and said that his clothes were being washed, thus the sans clothing journey to get a quick bite to eat, and that he had not realized that driving in that stark manner might be an illegal act.

This seemingly quirky story sparked some to question whether it indeed is somehow illegal to drive without a stitch on you and summarily rejected the notion that he should have been detained by the police. Bitter remarks showcased that are those in society that believe driving around in such a manner is perfectly fine (perhaps they also frequent clothing-optional beaches). Interestingly, a British newspaper earlier this year claimed that perhaps a million Britons have admitted to driving in their most natural condition, though the reporting needs to be taken with a grain of salt since it was based on a small poll and the results potentially can be questioned. In any case, if those stats are to be believed, perhaps those across the pond are more amenable to the unusual driving approach.

Meanwhile, it seems a relatively safe bet that most of the public here would probably never even give the absence-of-clothes driving method a moment's thought or consideration.

When analyzed as a lawful versus lawless act, the overall gist appears to be that driving in the nude is not necessarily a crime unto itself, by-and-large across the states throughout the United States, but that if someone is seen in that condition they are then susceptible to being ascribed with lewdness or indecent exposure. In the case of the drive-thru, the man was reportedly completely in view by the window workers of the fast-food eatery. One can imagine that other instances might naturally and inevitably arise, such as a local transit bus that perhaps travels alongside such a car driver, and then those seated within the bus get an unwanted and unfettered glimpse.

An intriguing offshoot of the overall scenario is the assumption by many drivers that shoes are a requirement when driving a car. As such, someone that is entirely without any clothing, presumably meaning that there are not wearing shoes either, those shoeless drivers would presumably be subject to getting pinched by the police, while the tangential aspect that they have nothing else on would be logically superfluous. On this point, it seems that the requirement to wear shoes while driving is predominantly a myth since catalogs of state-by-state driving laws suggest that there is rarely such a law. That being said, authorities generally and strongly recommend that shoes always be worn while driving, considered a much safer way to drive in contrast to doing so barefoot.

All of this brings up a captivating question about the future: *Once there are AI-based true self-driving cars avidly on our public roadways, will the clothing question be put to bed or will it continue to be a potential open issue?*

Let's unpack the matter and see.

Self-Driving Cars And Going In Reverse

For Level 4 and Level 5 true self-driving vehicles, there won't be a human driver involved in the driving task.

All occupants will be passengers.

The AI is doing the driving.

Okay, that seems to settle the matter about whether a human driver needs to be clothed or not, since for AI-based true self-driving cars there isn't any human driver involved. No human driver means there is no need to contemplate whether they should be with or without clothes and nor whether they need shoes. If you are wondering whether the AI needs to be wearing clothing, it's a smarmy thought and silly due to the aspect that the AI driving system is not a humanoid robot (and, even if it were, would we really be debating the clothes issue about the robot?).

Realize that likely for decades there will be an intermixing of both self-driving cars and conventional cars on our streets and byways, thus, those conventional cars will still have human drivers and the clothing matter for them will still be existent for quite some time ahead.

It would seem that self-driving cars are then off the hook on this topic.

Not so fast.

Suppose the passengers inside a self-driving car opt to go without clothing. There aren't any regulations yet about whether you can be completely unclothed while inside a self-driving car. With so few self-driving cars currently being tried out, this is not a topic that has yet come to noticeable attention. Perhaps, once self-driving cars are abundant, the matter will surface and become one of those hand-wringing considerations about rights and freedoms.

Returning to the earlier point that the act of being without clothing while inside a car is not unto itself the problem per se, and instead, it is the chance of being seen by someone outside the vehicle, this does indeed pose a concern for self-driving cars. A local transit bus that arrives at a red light at the same time as a self-driving car might allow for the bus riders to see more than they bargained for when having paid their bus token.

Yes, self-driving cars are squarely in the same stew.

The twist of course is whether self-driving cars are going to have windows, and also if they do have windows whether those windows need to be visibly transparent.

Some self-driving cars are being devised to have no windows at all.

The concept is that you will be riding inside a shell. For those that cannot tolerate an absence of windows, the interior walls of the self-driving car will have LED display screens and the cameras of the self-driving car will be able to showcase the outdoors for you. When you look "out the window" this will instead be you looking at a screen which is showing the video from a camera on the exterior of the self-driving car.

The beauty of the *no windows* approach is that you can have utter privacy while inside the self-driving car. Besides privacy, since the walls are lined with electronic LED screens, you can carry on Zoom or Skype kinds of interactive dialogues with others that are remote from your vehicle. You can take a class or simply watch a movie or relish your favorite cat videos. And so on.

In theory, you could presumably be fully bereft of clothing while inside such a self-driving car. But, we also don't yet know what the owners of self-driving cars are going to require. For example, suppose a large company decides to buy thousands of self-driving cars and deploy them in a ride-sharing fleet. The fleet owner might declare that anyone riding in their self-driving cars must be clothed. If you do not like such a rule, they would seemingly instruct you to use someone else's self-driving cars.

This brings up the notion of self-driving cars that are oriented towards particular interests. There might be some fleet owners that decide they want to court certain kinds of riders. Just imagine a fleet that is purposely aimed at those that prefer to ride around without wearing any clothing. Makes the mind boggle. And yet, where there is a buck to be made, service will be provided, it seems.

The scofflaws amongst you might be tempted to think that you will ride without clothing inside a self-driving car despite any fleet owner that might have declared it is against the rules to do so. Your first thought is that they will never know that you flaunted the rules. You've outfoxed them.

Maybe you can do so, though you might readily get caught.

Here's how.

Self-driving cars are likely to have cameras pointing inward, doing so to allow the fleet owners to detect whether riders are spray painting graffiti or ripping to shreds the seats. Those same cameras are also used to enable you to undertake those Zoom and Skype sessions. In any case, there are other potential uses of the cameras, including catching rule-breakers. The video streaming from inside the self-driving car might be monitored by remote agents, hired by the fleet owner to watch over their vehicles.

Likely, the labor-intensive act of monitoring will gradually be replaced by the AI doing the same thing. The AI will be watching you, during your driving journey, and can detect various conditions. This is something we might welcome. For example, suppose a sole rider suddenly has a heart attack. The AI might detect this occurrence and immediately contact 911, plus the AI could reroute the self-driving car to the nearest hospital.

The downside to these inward-facing cameras will be the privacy of those riding in self-driving cars. Undoubtedly, not everyone is going to be elated to have their every move captured on video while riding in a self-driving car. Imagine that you went out to the bars after work, and took a self-driving car home, doing so while drunk as a skunk inside the self-driving car. Where will that video go? Who owns the video? These are questions yet to be resolved.

Going back to the notion of windowless self-driving cars, not everyone believes that the absence of windows is the way to go. Most of the automakers and self-driving tech firms are assuming that riders will likely want to have windows. The question then becomes what the nature of the windows will be.

One clever approach consists of a special kind of glass that can be electronically switched from being transparent to being opaque. This would allow you to make the windows clear when you want to joyfully observe the roadway and revel in the scenery. Then, at the mere push of a button, the windows would become dense and potentially impenetrable. The nice thing about switching to the opaque condition is that you might be heading to work and want to catch a nap, thus, you can blot out the light from outside of the car and get a snooze. Or, you might want the privacy to do the sans clothing, one supposes.

Conclusion

Consider these emerging questions:

- Should passengers inside self-driving cars be allowed to have privacy regarding <u>not</u> being seen by outsiders?

- Is there a societal basis for requiring that the inside of self-driving cars must be viewable by those outside the vehicle, such as police or other authorities?

- Should videos of riders that were inside a self-driving car be owned and utilized by the fleet or by the rider or by whom?

- Will the ability to switch from transparency to opaqueness be in the hands of the riders, or by the fleet, or possibly by authorities?

- Does it make sense to have cars, self-driving cars, which have no windows whatsoever, or does an enclosed shell have downsides such as not being able to readily escape during a crash, thus otherwise negating the utility of a shell structure?

- And so on.

CHAPTER 19

TOWING OF

SELF-DRIVING CARS

One of the worst feelings when walking out to your parked car entails seeing a slip of paper and an ominous envelope sitting on the windshield and tucked under the wiper blade. You know in your heart of hearts that it must be a parking ticket.

If you aren't sure why you are the bearer of a parking ticket, you might look around frantically, trying to figure out whether you have parked in a no-parking zone, or perhaps parked longer than allowed or parked your car askew, and so on. On the other hand, if you knew beforehand that you had parked illegally and were taking a chance, lo and behold the hands of fate decided it was your time to come up on the foul side of the odds and get a parking citation. Probably best to not try next buying a lottery ticket given that instance of bad luck.

You might be wondering, what could be worse than seeing that gosh-darned parking ticket flapping around on your car windshield?

Well, suppose you came out to your parked car and it wasn't there anymore.

Gone. History. No longer where you parked it.

That will get you into a panic, for sure.

It could be that your car was stolen. That usually is the first thought that might pop into your head, though if you are unsure of where you had parked, to begin with, then you might be having anxious thoughts about where in fact you actually parked your car.

Assuming that you truly know that you parked where you parked and that your car is no longer present, and if you didn't overtly park in a spot that you knew was illegal to park in, it seems like a reasonable assumption that your car was purloined by some dastardly thieves. Meanwhile, if you were playing fancy and loose, opting to park in a dicey spot, realizing now that your car was gone would be that same feeling as your poker chips being all in at a poker game and getting beat by a surprise royal flush. Yes, you knew that the cards could turn out that way, and likewise, you knew there was a chance your car might get towed, but, hey, those just seemed at the time like wayward likelihoods.

According to various analyses of cars that got towed by the authorities, the most common top reasons for getting such an unrequested or involuntary tow are:

- Unpaid parking tickets
- Expired car registration
- Illegally parked

Notice that I mentioned that these are instances of involuntary tow. Besides getting towed without your explicit request, there are plenty of times that people purposely seek to have their cars towed. Perhaps your car breaks down on the highway and it cannot be driven due to a severe mechanical problem. In that case, you might call a towing service to come and get your vehicle. This might be described as a voluntary tow, which is somewhat an irritating way to depict the situation since you weren't especially hopeful of having your car breakdown and then getting it towed.

The towing industry in the United States is relatively sizable, amounting to about $7 billion or more in revenue each year. This includes towing for passenger cars and all other types of vehicles, both light ones, and heavy ones. In addition to towing, those revenues encompass facets such as bringing petrol to your car, doing a battery charge-up on the scene, and other roadway services.

For the towing that involves nabbing cars that are considered lawbreaking, such as when illegally parked or when the owner is rated as a scofflaw by having too many outstanding tickets, those tows are relatively significant moneymakers for local governments. To clarify, it is not necessarily the case that the authorities are prompting to generate the income, and instead, they are merely attempting to ensure that the laws are being properly obeyed. You might complain about your car getting involuntarily towed, but presumably, there is some legal basis for the act (and if not, this can be fought in court, albeit not something any of us relishes having to try and battle).

In any case, over the years, many local governments have become accustomed to a predictable amount of revenue based on the involuntary towing of cars. The anticipated funds are cooked into the budget of the local government and are allocated to a variety of governmental services. In brief, if there is a shortfall in the towing related revenues, this can lead to cuts in other government services that otherwise have nothing whatsoever to do with people's cars.

Of course, critics wonder whether local governments might become overzealous in pursuing those involuntary tows. The logic seems straightforward. If the local government has become dependent upon that line of revenue, it seems they are incentivized to pursue and expand the possibilities of deriving that income. Some assert that a vicious cycle arises of the local government ratcheting up the range and extent of reasons to tow, not for safety purposes but instead for the singular goal of raising monies to support government programs.

There is another angle of attack about involuntary towing. Some express concern for "poverty tows" that entail towing of cars that ultimately are denying the car owner access to their car, which can lead to loss of access to a job, or reduces access to education, shelter, medical care, etc. Thus, there are pressures applied to local governments to be more mindful about doing tows and consider the full semblance of ramifications.

Shifting gears, ponder what the future might consist of.

Here's an intriguing question: *Will the advent of AI-based true self-driving cars obviate the need for car towing and thus there will no longer be any towing activities?*

Self-Driving Cars And Going In Reverse

For Level 4 and Level 5 true self-driving vehicles, there won't be a human driver involved in the driving task.

175

All occupants will be passengers.

The AI is doing the driving.

Some pundits have predicted that there will never be a need to tow a self-driving car.

Sorry, but that's a fantasy land mirage.

The most frequent basis for claiming that self-driving cars won't ever be towed is that they will presumably never park illegally. The AI will be programmed to always park legally. Thus, in theory, there will never be any justification to tow a self-driving car.

First, we can immediately shoot down such a viewpoint by pointing out that there is the involuntary tow versus the voluntary tow. Both of those conditions need to be taken into account. We can start with the voluntary tow since it is the easiest to quickly illustrate.

A self-driving car is driving on a highway. All of a sudden, a mechanical problem occurs inside the car, perhaps in the engine or maybe in the transmission of the vehicle (or, whatever). The AI is supposed to be programmed to cope with such situations and will attempt to pull the car over to a safe spot, if possible. In the parlance of the self-driving car realm, this is considered an act involving the Dynamic Driving Task (DDT) for which after an occurrence of performance-relevant system failure, such as a catastrophic mechanical failure, there is a need to have the car repositioned into a minimal risk condition, perhaps pulling over to the side of the road or taking the next available exit from the highway and then coming to a halt.

Suppose the AI chooses to park on the side of the highway since the self-driving car is in dire straits and cannot otherwise continue on a driving journey. There is now a dead car, as it were, sitting on the edge of the highway. One way or another, the odds are that it will end up being towed.

In theory, the AI will have the capability of contacting the owner to indicate that the car is in an emergency state and has been pulled over. In addition to informing the owner, the AI is likely to have a communications capability to contact an emergency road service, whether one contracted by the owner of the self-driving car or perhaps something more on-the-fly.

Okay, so that's how a voluntary tow will happen to a self-driving car.

Those that reject this possibility are apt to suggest that self-driving cars will never breakdown. This is pure nonsense and they need to get themselves out of that Utopian world they are dreaming of. There is absolutely going to be self-driving cars that have mechanical problems and breakdown. A car is still a car, including self-driving cars.

The usual retort is that if that's the case, why don't we see self-driving cars parked on the side of roads today. This is easily answered. Today's self-driving cars are pampered beyond belief, perhaps more so than race cars. For the self-driving cars being tried out on the public roadways, they are nightly taken to a special depot whereby they are tuned-up and ready for the next day of trial runs. Furthermore, these are mainly new cars, ones with very few miles and thus less prone to having mechanical failures.

Upon the widespread advent of self-driving cars, it is unfathomable to expect that those self-driving cars are going to get that same white-glove treatment. This is just overly expensive and unlikely to take place. Also, over time, the self-driving cars will be racking up miles, lots of miles, since the owners will want to earn every dollar possible, and the only way to do so will be to keep those self-driving cars moving and serving primarily as ride-sharing vehicles.

I have predicted that the self-driving car repairs marketplace will be booming, though keep in mind that will occur many years from now and you would be especially gutsy to already begin gearing up for that faraway future. Nonetheless, assuming that self-driving cars become as popular as hotcakes, there will be zillions of them, and zillions of hours of repairs and maintenance will be required.

The overarching point is that self-driving cars will most certainly be towed, at least concerning the voluntary towing acts.

Does this imply that self-driving cars will avert any involuntary towing?

Nope.

Return to the scenario about the self-driving car that has gone to a halt on the side of the highway. If the AI is unable to make contact with the owner or some pre-determined towing service, an authority that comes upon the stalled vehicle will potentially take action if they see the self-driving car sitting there, endangering traffic.

Sure, the authority might try to contact the owner, but that might not work, or if the owner seems hesitant about taking rapid action, the authority might decide it is safest to have the self-driving car towed right away. Best to get the self-driving car off the highway and eliminate any chances of other cars somehow getting entangled with the self-driving car.

Voila, the involuntary tow.

The usual retort to this point is that if all other cars on the highway are self-driving cars, then the one that is sitting and stalled at the side of the highway will merely use V2V (vehicle-to-vehicle) electronic communications to forewarn all of the upcoming self-driving cars. The traffic will electronically be clued that there is a stalled vehicle and therefore move over or otherwise avoid hitting the motionless self-driving car. In that sense, there is no need to carry out an involuntary tow and the self-driving car can sit there until the cows come home, if necessary.

Well, that introduces several problems that need to be pointed out. One is that the highways and roads are <u>not</u> going to be exclusively used by self-driving cars, at least not for any foreseeable near-term future. We are likely to have self-driving cars and human-driven cars mixing together on our roadways for many years, likely many decades. There are about 250 million conventional cars today on the roads and they are not going to magically disappear or be replaced overnight. Furthermore, some drivers insist you will take away their driving privileges by prying their dead cold hands from their steering wheel.

Another problem with the assertion that the self-driving car can just sit there is that you are assuming the V2V is viable and still working. It could be that the mechanical issues of the self-driving car have somehow corrupted the V2V capability, in which case the self-driving car is not able to forewarn other vehicles.

And so on.

All told, self-driving cars are going to be towed, either by voluntary means or by involuntary means.

The Involuntary Towing Of Self-Driving Cars

The most obvious example and least argumentative about involuntary towing of self-driving cars is the breakdown use case (though some do argue it, so I clearly said *least argumentative* and did not claim it was *unargumentative*).

Recall that earlier that I had cited three primary ways that an involuntary tow of a car seems to most frequently be inspired, namely due to outstanding parking tickets, or expired car registration, or illegal parking (and, potentially any combination thereof).

You might believe that a self-respecting self-driving car would never fall into any of those three categories, but you would be wrong.

Let's tackle the expired car registration.

If the method of car registration is similar to how it is done today, there is no ironclad guarantee that a self-driving car will never have an expired tag. This matter of the tag is up to the self-driving car owner. In theory, a self-driving car owner ought to make sure that the self-driving car has a valid tag, but there is nothing axiomatic about this. Whether a fleet owner or an individual owner, they could goof and fail to renew the tag, or possibly renew it and drop the ball by failing to put the tag on the vehicle.

The only seemingly way to ensure that the tag issue never arises would be to put in place widespread electronic car registration. Presumably, the AI of the self-driving car would be programmed to check and make sure it has a valid tag. Also, rather than the tag being a sticker, it might be displayed electronically or communicated electronically, thus any authority desiring the status of the tag can just do an electronic check. All of this is possible, but one wonders if or when this will happen, and if so, will it occur before self-driving cars start to become widespread. As long as the tag aspects are essentially manually based, there is a chance that the self-driving car will end-up with expired tags and possibly get towed.

The outstanding parking tickets involves the same kind of logic as I've expressed about the tags, though this takes us to the other claim by some pundits that a self-driving car will never get a parking ticket. Thus, in that viewpoint, there is zero chance of outstanding parking tickets.

Will a self-driving car never get a parking ticket?

The use of the word "never" is pretty awe-inspiring and sets a rather high bar or hurdle. As I have expressed in several of my other articles, self-driving cars are going to end-up driving "illegally" at times, and included in that category is the act of being illegally parked. Those that think the AI will flawlessly ensure that a self-driving car is never parked illegally are envisioning a world of lollipops and candies.

In the real world, there is a substantive chance of self-driving cars getting caught illegally parked, and you can bet that it will happen.

Conclusion

Overall, the amount of involuntary towing of self-driving cars will likely be a lot less than the involuntary towing of conventional human-driven cars. In that case, it means that the revenue dollars for local governments as funded by involuntary tows will drop, potentially precipitously so.

CHAPTER 20

CONSUMER REPORTS

AND

FULL SELF-DRIVING

The well-known and highly recognized evaluator of consumer products, *Consumer Reports (CR)*, released an eagerly awaited review of Tesla's Full Self-Driving (FSD) feature set, and the evocative title of the CR posted piece makes abundantly clear the results of the overarching assessment: "Tesla's 'Full-Self-Driving Capability' Falls Short of Its Name" (the online posting also includes a quick-paced seven and a half minute video depicting the evaluation conducted).

For those that are already versed in self-driving tech, the assessment by CR is a welcome voice that adds more weight to the ongoing qualm by most such experts concerning Tesla and Elon Musk overpromising on what their so-called Full Self-Driving can currently do.

It is one thing to overpromise in general, and it is something else altogether to overpromise when dealing with the somber life-and-death matters involved in driving cars. If a vendor overpromised about say their laundry detergent, those that relied upon that vow would not likely suffer much harm by misjudging the use when washing their clothes. Making misjudgments when at the wheel of a car, a vehicle on our public roadways, one that weighs multi-tons and can readily crash into or kill someone, portends rather serious and disconcerting outcomes.

Let's start by considering the naming of the feature set, and then proceed into the details of what the features do and most importantly, what they do not yet do.

Those that favor the Full Self-Driving moniker are apt to quickly point out that it is merely an aspirational naming. Thus, they would likely concede that of course, the Tesla FSD does not yet operate on a fully autonomous basis, as though this is an obvious fact, and they would then exhort that the goal will be to someday achieve that kind of autonomy. In that sense, they would argue that it is reasonable to call the product what it is destined to become since otherwise you would need to rename the product at a future date and that would be costly and exhibit a lack of prophetic vision when getting ready for the future.

Well, a German court doesn't quite see things this same way, having in July rendered a court ruling that the Tesla brand name of Autopilot was falsely misleading, proffering exaggerated promises, and emphasized that as a driver-assistance capability the reuse of the everyday word "autopilot" implied a fully autonomous system rather than one that requires by-hand control. For those that felt the Autopilot naming allowed some leeway in the interpretation of autonomous or not (and therefore had angst over the German court ruling), certainly, the naming of "Full Self-Driving" seems to completely eviscerate that alleged loophole in semantics.

A frequently cited concern about Tesla drivers is that via the use of the existing "Full Self-Driving" capability is that they will become lax at driving and be lulled into relying upon driving automation that is decidedly not fully autonomous. Besides the name of the product giving them that illusion, the features themselves can be deceptively alluring and lead someone down the ill-advised path of letting the car drive when the human driver is supposed to be doing so.

A common retort by Tesla owners is that any driver of a Tesla that is either fooled by the FSD name or that becomes complacent when driving is essentially exceedingly dense and does not represent the preponderance of Tesla drivers. Even if that is true, what percentage of Tesla drivers are we as a society willing to accede is okay to have that semblance of falseness while at the wheel and potentially end-up in a car crash? At nearly any percentage you might pick, whether less than 1% or perhaps 10% or higher, that amounts to a lot of drivers with the potential for veering off the ranch, at it were, and presumably would not be so captivated if the FSD naming was less enchantingly oracular.

An additional debating point involves the notion that Tesla owners are paying extra for FSD, and yet they are not getting full self-driving per se, at least not now (instead, they are getting the less-than feature set that exists currently). It is promised that someday the entire incarnation of FSD can be downloaded into their vehicles via the use of OTA (Over-The-Air) electronic updates to the car, once so readied.

For those that try to include this latter issue in the debate about the FSD naming, it is somewhat of a distractor and not especially at the core of notable life-or-death concerns per se.

Here's why.

The Tesla buyers can readily assert that they have voluntarily chosen to put out the extra dough for the FSD and that therefore it isn't anyone else's business to judge them. If they want to spend their money in that manner, it is up to them. Furthermore, they would contend that since they can leverage the existing FSD feature set, it is not as though they are purchasing vaporware, though if they wanted to do so (i.e. buy a non-existent product), it still would be entirely on their own shoulders. Essentially, the tone typically is to butt out of how they want to spend their hard-earned bucks.

The counterargument made is that these people are being scammed into buying something that doesn't yet exist and for which it is unknown if it will ever exist. Of course, such a counterargument is somewhat weakened by the facet that there is something they are getting, namely the existing less-than FSD features, plus we do not yet know conclusively know that the FSD will never be achieved.

In short, this whole topic about the money is likely to ultimately makes its way through the courts, presumably via lawsuits by Tesla owners that would seek restitution if the FSD is never provided, or by legal authorities that might believe the public was wronged by pledges that were not ever honored.

Overall, the debate over the added cost of the FSD is a bit of a tangent and does not immediately and directly relate to the on-the-road dangers associated with this overall theme.

As a brief sidebar, just for completeness, anyone that tries to argue that FSD is indeed fully autonomous driving right now is really outside the realm of rational discussion. They are either completely unaware of what the Tesla FSD feature set is, or they utterly miscomprehend what it means when referring to a fully autonomous self-driving car.

To set the record straight, let's take a moment to clarify what self-driving truly means.

Features and Issues of Today's Tesla FSD Capabilities

For Level 4 and Level 5 true self-driving vehicles, there won't be a human driver involved in the driving task. All occupants will be passengers. The AI is doing the driving.

Tesla's today that employ the FSD are considered at a Level 2, and not as yet at a Level 3, and most certainly not anywhere akin to a Level 4 or Level 5.

The point is that the "Full Self-Driving" naming is irrefutably not what the feature set can do today. This is really inarguable and as mentioned earlier, anyone trying to assert that FSD is currently full self-driving is not willing to carry on the discourse rationally or sensibly.

As per the CR posting: "Though it has made significant strides in automated driving, owners should not rely on Tesla's driver assistance features to necessarily add safety or to make driving easier, based on Consumer Reports' extensive testing and experience."

Returning to the title of the Consumer Reports piece, they were perhaps generous when stating that the FSD falls short of its name, a generosity based on a twofold logic.

First, in a sense, everyone that knows about self-driving cars already knew that FSD of today is not true full self-driving. Nonetheless, it is seemingly helpful to have CR officially say it, and thus aid in promulgating this extremely crucial sentiment, perhaps too helping to put a dent in the ongoing public frontage of the "Full Self-Driving" moniker that appears in ads and for which many embellished media postings seem to contribute to its overinflated meaning.

Second, some would vehemently insist that the title should have been "FSD falls way short" or "FSD misses by a country mile" in the sense that today's FSD is so extensively far afield of what a true self-driving car would be.

This lack of emphasis in the title of the piece about how much a shortfall there is would potentially allow some to shrug off the review. The shrugging would presumably be that sure, there is always some tiny thing that might not be perfect, but that's to be expected in any product.

In a manner of speaking, this casual reference to a shortfall might be likened to an alleged super-cleaning laundry detergent that was characterized as falling short, when the detergent was undeniably unable to super-clean, and unable to clean nearly at all, plus potentially had the adverse potential of making your clothes dirtier too (all of this being an imperfect analogous situation without any life-threatening possibilities, which a car axiomatically has).

Now that we've covered the basics on this matter, next let's forge into the FSD details and the CR review thereof.

For those of you not especially familiar with Tesla's and the Autopilot versus the FSD, here's how CR succinctly stated it: "Tesla's active driving assistance systems are split into two parts: The first, Autopilot—which includes adaptive cruise control (Tesla refers to this as Traffic-Aware Cruise Control) and lane-keeping assistance capabilities (Autosteer in Tesla terminology)—is now standard on every new Tesla. For this evaluation, we focused on the optional Full Self-Driving Capability suite of driving assistance systems: Autopark, Auto Lane Change, Summon, Smart Summon, Navigate on Autopilot, and Traffic Light and Stop Sign Control."

As an exemplar herein, let's examine the Smart Summon feature.

The notion underlying Smart Summon is that you can use a Tesla provided smartphone app and request the Tesla car to come to you or go to a destination that you specify on the smartphone map. This would undoubtedly be handy when trying to park your car in a busy mall parking lot, allowing you to get out of your Tesla at the entrance of the mall stores, and then have the Tesla proceed to park itself. Likewise, you might have come out of an office building and it might be raining out, thus, you could use the Smart Summon to have the Tesla drive itself from the parking lot to the front of the office building where you are waiting.

Here's what CR said about the Smart Summon: "We tried out Smart Summon in a number of scenarios, including the parking lot at CR headquarters in Yonkers, N.Y. Overall, the system proved to be unreliable."

You might be wondering what kinds of reliability issues arose.

Noted problems included:
- Tesla vehicle at times did not stop or even pause at posted Stop signs
- Tesla vehicle at times went into the opposing lane (wrong lane) of traffic
- Tesla vehicle at times took wide turns, heading toward other parked cars
- Tesla vehicle at times sought to back-up due to nearing other parked cars
- Etc.

If you think those are nitpicky points, keep in mind that this is a multi-ton car, operating essentially on its own, in a potentially populated parking lot or other areas, being amongst other cars in motion, amid pedestrians that are walking along, and so on. As indicated by CR: "These are all situations that could cause confusion to other drivers, as well as be a potential hazard for any pedestrians in the car's path."

Fortuitously, the vehicle is usually going at slow speeds during the

Smart Summon, providing some margin of reaction time for those that perchance see and react to its poor driving.

Should we though be putting the onus onto other drivers to give clearance to a somewhat wayward driver, as it were, versus holding that driver's feet (the automation) to the fire as to driving properly and safely?

The same can be said about pedestrians.

Should pedestrians have to be on their special guard for a wayward (automation) driver?

You might try to argue that pedestrians need to also be wary of human-driven vehicles. Yes, that is indeed the case, but are we willing to have a "self-driving" vehicle that is driving in a manner of wayward human drivers? It certainly seems that we would expect a fully autonomous driving system to do a much better job than a distracted human driver or otherwise wayward human driver.

The shortfalls of the Smart Summon are somewhat whisked away by the Tesla posted indication that the person holding the smartphone that has invoked the Tesla app is the responsible party: "You are still responsible for your car and must monitor it and its surroundings at all times and be within your line of sight because it may not detect all obstacles."

This provides little solace to other drivers and those pedestrians that come upon a Smart Summon in-motion Tesla. Consider these pointed questions:

- Is the person that is activating the Smart Summon close enough to see what is happening?
- Will they react appropriately and in time?
- Are they continuously paying attention while the Smart Summon is underway?
- Suppose the person is talking with someone else and only partially paying attention?
- If the person has used the Smart Summon previously, might they be lulled into not paying attention this time?

- Can someone not in the driver's seat be trusted to be as mindful about a roaming car when they are standing at a distance from the vehicle?
- And so on.

Here's what self-driving car gurus also worry about.

CR reported that at times, during the Smart Summon, the Tesla would proceed ahead at a T-shaped intersection that required a left or right turn, nearing other parked cars at the edge of the T-shape. Upon getting close to those parked cars, the Tesla then stopped, went into reverse, backed up since it was now overly close to those parked cars and could not readily make a left or right turn, straightened out while in an active lane of traffic, and then was able to make the needed turn.

What's up with that?

Imagine a human driver doing the same kind of action. Perhaps think of a student learning to drive. They came up to the T-shaped interaction, drove straight ahead, and finally realized they need to make a turn. But they had failed to start the turn early enough, and now, in the middle of the movement, bring the car to a halt, back-up while in an active lane of traffic, and then ultimately crank the wheel and make the turn.

I'd bet that most of us have seen that kind of newbie driving behavior. If you are a parent sitting in the passenger's seat, it usually takes your breath away, and you pray that the car doesn't hit any of the parked cars and that no other in-motion cars nearby ram into your car while making the awkward turn. And, that any pedestrians nearby are willing to keep away or walk around the whole morass.

It's a mess.

One likely assumption is that the Tesla FSD capability is doing an insufficient job at the driving planning stage of the driving task. Upon reaching the T-shaped location, or even before getting there, the system ought to be anticipating that a turn will be required. The turn should not wait until already upon the other parked cars at the edge of the T-shaped locale. Instead, as the Tesla comes to the T-shaped emergence, the car should begin to make the turn or be prepared to do so, assuming too that it first has tried to detect if there are any other cars coming or pedestrians.

This inadequate operation at the T-shaped scenario could also be an indication of limitations in the sensor suite and detection capabilities of the FSD.

Perhaps the sensors were unable to detect that there were parked cars on the other side of the T-shaped locale, or was unable to figure out where drivable road existed (a key aspect of a driving system is the detection of the roadway and where driving is allowed).

Given that Tesla and Elon Musk have vociferously eschewed the use of LIDAR, indeed known famously within the self-driving car industry for their anti-LIDAR stance, it is conceivable that the use of their cameras and radar are presently unable to properly surveil the scene.

If so, this is perhaps another mark against the anti-LIDAR insistence and could be used against Tesla for potential court cases involving Tesla car crashes.

Yet another possibility is that the on-board hardware is not fast enough to process what is going on during the T-shaped turn. Suppose the driving system enters into the active lane, moving ahead without hesitation, and then the computational aspects catch-up and alert the rest of the driving system that parked cars are sitting there, blocking the way forward.

There are numerous ways in which these driving behaviors can be explained, though since the Tesla driving system is proprietary and unpublished, there are no direct means for outsiders to inspect the code and identify why the driving actions are inadequate.

Conclusion

In the CR posting, a quote by Kelly Funkhouser, head of connected and automated vehicle testing at CR, seems quite telling about the results of their assessment: "It seems like Tesla is focused on being the automaker with the most features rather than ensuring that the features work well."

CHAPTER 21

TIRE BLOWOUTS

AND

SELF-DRIVING CARS

Have you ever had a tire go bad on you?

Sometimes, a tire can seemingly obliterate and become a tangled mess of rubber and threads.

If this happens, a driver is likely to be taken by utter surprise, oftentimes reacting instinctively by doing the wrong things. For example, jamming on the brakes is not necessarily the wisest course of action in such a situation. Usually, taking firm control of the car and gradually bringing the vehicle to a stop is the more prudent approach. There is also the question of directional movement, such that you normally would remain in a straight-ahead driving motion overall, and slowly angle over to get out of the way of other cars. Sudden moves such as a radical turn are not apt to provide the desired results.

With today's tires, fortunately, there is a lessened chance of those wild blowouts than used to be relatively commonplace. The types of materials that tires are made of and how they are constructed has advanced dramatically over the years. Specialized tires that are built to remain self-supporting when there is a tire issue have also become more widely available.

You might be tempted to think that run-flat tires (RFT's) are prevalent these days and somehow found on all cars, but industry figures show that just 14% of new cars are outfitted with RFT's. The preponderance of cars on the roadways do not yet have run-flats on them.

Speaking of run-flat tires, there are several myths worth exploring.

First, it is possible to have a blowout of an RFT, though it would be unusual and tend to occur due to a driver that was exceedingly foolhardy. Here's how that can happen. The driver realizes they have a flat, but figure that since they have run-flat tires it is no big deal. For RFT's, the typical recommendation is to drive at reduced speeds once a flat occurs and aim to put on no more than a few dozen miles while it is punctured, limiting to less than a hundred miles all told. Despite these recommendations, an aggressive driver that decides to drive all out and disregard the tire malady can end-up pummeling the run-flat into mulch.

Another frequent assumption is that everyone wants run-flat tires more so than conventional tires. Turns out that some people prefer a conventional tire, though not necessarily for the reason that you might expect. One of the primary reasons given is to then have a spare tire available. In short, with conventional tires, usually, there is a spare tire provided in the trunk or somewhere attached to the vehicle, while with run-flat tires there is rarely a spare provided. Some people seem to like the idea of having a spare as a handy precaution, rather than betting on using the run-flat and getting to someplace where the tire can be either repaired or replaced.

Of course, we also know that sometimes people do not keep their spare in good shape. As such, when they find themselves in a bind and need to use the spare, it is not ready for primetime. There is also the concern that when people do have a spare, they might be tempted to change their tires amid a busy highway or byway. With the run-flat tires, you aren't likely to be changing one on your own and thus no temptation to pull to the side of the road to do so.

The other twist is that your car might have conventional tires and yet lack a spare tire altogether. Assuming that the spare wasn't somehow lost or stolen, it turns out that some cars these days are provided with a tire repair or inflator kit, in lieu of an actual spare tire. Some drivers are shocked to realize they did not have a spare and just assumed there must be one that is hidden inside the trunk of the vehicle. There seems no worse a feeling than going to get your spare out of the trunk, and then realizing that you are supposed to contend with a repair kit and an inflator. The AAA has pointed out that this is a double-whammy for car drivers in that they are apt to find it harder to use those kits than changing a tire (which already was hard enough) and might find themselves taking longer to cope with a kit and possibly being more endangered if doing so on the edge of a roadway (they suggest you call for service instead).

Well, life certainly has its tradeoffs, including when it comes to tires.

According to one set of statistics, nearly one-quarter of all roadside emergencies are due to a tire issue. It is further claimed that about 220 million flat tires are occurring each year in the United States alone, though the numbers on this facet are not entirely accurate and should be considered an approximation. There is also the astounding assertion that the average U.S. driver will experience about five flat tires throughout their driving lifetime.

How many flat tires have you had?

Presumably, if less than five such occurrences to-date, better prepare yourself for the chances of ultimately arriving at five or more, unless you decide to stop driving cars.

Whoa, that brings up a related point.

Once there are true self-driving cars, will there be any tire blowouts or flat tires?

Some that believe in magic are apt to say that the incredible nature of true self-driving cars will mean that they will never experience a flat tire. To make abundantly clear, that's pure nonsense. A tire is a tire, regardless of one on a conventional human-driven car or one that is mounted on a true self-driving car.

Flat tires will occur with true self-driving cars. That's a fact.

Here's the more interesting and open-ended question to consider: *Will the AI-based driving systems of true self-driving cars be able to cope with situations involving flat tires and tire blowouts?*

Let's unpack the matter and see.

Flat Tires and Tire Blowouts With Self-Driving Cars

For Level 4 and Level 5 true self-driving vehicles, there won't be a human driver involved in the driving task.

All occupants will be passengers.

The AI is doing the driving.

Will the AI know how to handle a flat tire or a tire blowout?

Maybe, maybe not.

It all depends on what the automaker and the self-driving tech firm have done to ready the AI for such a situation. Some developers are so busy with the fundamental aspects of getting the AI to drive a car that they have put the chore of handling a tire issue as a secondary matter. Such secondary conditions or issues are usually referred to as edge or corner cases, relegated to a lower priority, and will be dealt with at some later time. This means that there isn't any special provision in the AI to deal with a tire predicament in those self-driving cars. At a later date, when the developers can get around to it, they will craft such a provision and then proceed to do an update or upgrade of the AI accordingly (via the OTA or Over-The-Air electronic connection, if feasible).

This might seem rather shocking that the top priority of an AI driving system does not encompass what to do about a blown tire. The assumption generally by the developers is that if the AI "realizes" that something about the car is amiss, it has been programmed to try and safely bring the car to a halt. As such, whether the matter is a fouled tire or any myriad of mechanical problems, those are all lumped together into a contingency component of the AI that attempts to get the vehicle out of traffic and into a safe posture. The hope is that this catchall can sufficiently deal with a wide variety of untoward conditions, serving as a backstop before advancing the AI programming for specific handling of particular situations.

Some believe that this overarching mitigation is not adequate and that the allowance for how to deal with a tire issue ought to be higher on the priority list.

In any case, let's consider what has to happen for the AI to undertake a flat tire scenario.

First, the AI has to become aware that a flat tire or its equivalent has taken place.

This is not as easy as it might seem.

A human driver would likely feel the car becoming unstable and potentially hear the dreaded thudding of the tire. The vehicle would tend to pull in the direction of the marred tire. Attempts to steer the car would possibly become more forced and less seamless. Noises coming from the tire as it flops along on the roadway would become apparent and the roughness of the ride would be felt as rattling in your bones.

The AI is not a human and not even a robot driver. As such, there is no immediate way for the AI to experience the same ramifications or sensations that a human driver would feel. That being said, the AI would potentially detect that the steering is not being as responsive as it had been. When the AI sends commands to the steering mechanism and it is not producing the expected result, the AI would be able to detect that something is amiss.

Unless the self-driving car is equipped with special listening sensors, the odds of the AI hearing the tire sounds are pretty low. The IMU (inertial measurement unit) of the car might be useful to some degree, but whether it is going to register the bumpy ride and be translated into the possibility of a flat tire is something that would need to be explicitly programmed to do.

You might laugh at this next point. One possibility for the AI to become aware of a flat tire would be if there is a passenger inside the self-driving car and the person invokes the AI's Natural Language Processing (NLP) to tell the AI that there seems to be a flat tire. This is somewhat funny because the human is telling the AI, whereas you would likely think that the AI, being the driver, ought to be alerting the human passenger that a tire has gone flat.

Even this aspect of using the NLP to report a flat tire is yet another example of something that needs to be programmed into the AI capabilities. In other words, the AI systems of today do not have any common-sense reasoning or other generalized intelligence, thus, the passenger seeking to warn the AI about a flat tire could fall on deaf ears, as it were. The AI might merely respond that it does not know what the person is trying to convey.

Another angle then is potentially to have the passenger invoke access to a remote agent. Most of the self-driving cars are being equipped with an OnStar-like facility that allows a rider to call up a remote agent. The passenger might explain that there is a flat tire and the remote agent would then potentially be able to take some action. It could be that the remote agent can send signals to the AI to inform it to pull over or might tell the passenger what to say to the AI system about the situation, perhaps using special commands.

Now that you've seen that it is not necessarily straightforward for the AI to realize that a tire is having troubles, there is a simpler solution that might end-up overcoming the detection difficulties. As you likely already know, tires are increasingly becoming "smart tires" in that they contain various electronics. The easiest path toward informing the AI would be if the tire itself told the AI that the tire had gone bad. This is the most likely scenario of how this will ultimately play out, namely, the tire would transmit an electronic signal to the housing of the on-board computer the AI and then the AI would become directly aware of a tire issue.

In that sense, the tire is akin to having cameras, radar, LIDAR, and other sensors attached or associated with the self-driving car. The tires are not just tires, they are also sensors. They sense the status of the tire and can report that status to the AI that's driving the vehicle. One concern is the possibility of false positives, whereby the tire misreports a tire issue when the tire is actually fine. Another qualm is the chances of a false negative, whereby the tire does not report that the tire is having troubles and yet the tire has indeed gotten into trouble. Those problems need to be considered as part of the AI programming to cope with the tire aspects.

All of that touches on the topic of the detection of a flat tire.

What will the AI do once a flat tire or its equivalent has been detected?

Other than the classic pull-over safety regimen, the AI could be explicitly programmed to drive with the same kind of skill that a human driver might have, though only to the degree that the automation can do so (i.e., it is not a human and lacks human thinking). This includes the earlier mentioned recommendations of not taking any sudden action as a driver, no quick turns, etc.

If the tires are run-flats, the AI would need to adjust its route planning to go at slower speeds and figure out where to go. This would potentially involve interacting with the passengers. Why so? If you are a passenger and a driver just suddenly starts slowing down and taking you to a different destination than originally specified, you'd likely freak out, deservedly so. The AI would need to explain the situation to the passenger and then figure out what might be done to accommodate the passenger and meanwhile deal with the tire difficulties.

In the near-term in terms of what AI can accomplish, it would be unlikely that the NLP would be good enough to carry on such a conversation entirely via just between the AI and the human passenger. A remote agent would be invoked and brought into the discussion.

Conclusion

Perhaps an obvious point that I haven't brought up is that the AI is not going to be able to change the tire. If the driver was a human, we might expect that the human driver could get out of the vehicle, and proceed to change the tire, assuming too that a spare existed and was viable. The odds are that self-driving cars are all going to be outfitted with run-flats, which makes sense given the aspect that the AI cannot change the tire. Also, with the run-flat tires, the notion is that the self-driving car will be able to proceed for a while and thus not unduly inconvenience the passengers.

This does not obviate the chances of having a roadside emergency service that gets alerted to come and tend to a self-driving car.

Yes, there are going to be self-driving cars that are sitting on the side of the road, waiting to get towed or have some roadside service performed.

It will be startling to see this, at first. You don't witness this happening today due to the self-driving car tryouts having dedicated service teams that keep those vehicles in top shape. That will not be the same white-glove service that will occur once self-driving cars are prevalent in the millions upon millions of such vehicles (keep in mind that there are about 250 million conventional cars today, and in theory, there will be some equal number of self-driving cars that will ultimately replace those).

Tires, love them, or hate them.

They always seem to become troubling at the worst of times, as though having a mind of their own and wanting to turn a modestly unpleasant situation into a torrent of bad.

For the AI that drives self-driving cars, all I can say is welcome to the club. Eventually, the AI will find itself as troubled about flat tires like the rest of us, and perhaps relish the moments when the tires are working soundly, and be exasperated when they are not (or that might be a bit much on the anthropomorphizing of the AI).

May your ride be smooth and your tires ever round.

CHAPTER 22
WILDFIRE SMOKE
AND
SELF-DRIVING CARS

There has been a recent spate of deadly wildfires throughout the western parts of the country, especially hitting California, Oregon, and Washington. An estimated three million acres of California land alone has burnt in the last month or so, woefully causing fatalities and at times extensive destruction to homes and forests. Most of the fires seemed to be setoff by the nearly 15,000 lightning strikes that had accompanied wandering tropical storms, though some of the fires were initiated by human-led careless or intentional acts.

An especially eerie sight made the news headlines last week when the San Francisco Bay Area and other surrounding locales became thick with smoke and ash, causing the skies to be a menacing orange glow and blotting out any semblance of a normal sky. Pictures of the downtown areas resembled prophetic scenes of the future as depicted in the sci-fi movie *Bladerunner 2049*. During the daylight hours, drivers used their headlights and had to navigate the roadways under a cloak of smoky air.

If driving for humans is difficult during such conditions, this raises an interesting question: *How will self-driving cars handle the roadways during existent and likely adverse aftermaths of widespread wildfires?*

Let's unpack the matter and see.

Self-Driving Cars And Coping With Wildfire Conditions

For Level 4 and Level 5 true self-driving vehicles, there won't be a human driver involved in the driving task.

All occupants will be passengers.

The AI is doing the driving.

For those of you that perchance live in an area where self-driving cars are currently being tried out in California, you might have noticed that many of the companies that are deploying these state-of-the-art vehicles were doing so amid the smoky air conditions.

Your first thought might be that they should close down their operations in those circumstances and not get onto the roadways. If their vehicles were getting in the way of rescue efforts or otherwise obstructing matters, indeed you can expect that the self-driving cars during these tryout periods would most likely be kept off the streets. In this case, it seemed that being on the roadways was not disrupting activities, plus there is a purposeful desire to get the self-driving cars immersed into such smoky air conditions.

Here's why.

Most of the self-driving car development efforts to date have focused on everyday kinds of driving activities. This might involve going from a home to a grocery store or making a quick run on local freeways to exercise the AI driving capabilities on fast-paced byways and navigating amongst normal traffic conditions.

One concern is that the AI is not necessarily ready for extraordinary driving situations, known as edge cases, or sometimes referred to as corner cases.

As we all know, even a newbie teenage driver doesn't begin driving with much experience under their belt. Over time, they end-up driving in a widening variety of circumstances and presumably become familiar with what to do. In a sense, the hope is to do something similar for self-driving cars (do not though misconstrue this point, the AI is not anywhere akin to human intelligence). A wider encountering of unusual driving situations is helpful to the AI in its use of Machine Learning (ML) or Deep Learning (DL) to improve the handling of whatever might happen while on the roads.

Best now to get the AI used to being able to drive in the wildfire aftermath conditions, rather than later on discovering post-implementation that perhaps the AI gets confounded by such circumstances. Imagine that you are using self-driving cars daily, and upon those days or perhaps weeks when a wildfire might cause the air to become blotchy, the self-driving cars were unable to cope and thus were not providing rides. Those self-driving cars would potentially be parked in depots and warehouses, waiting simply for the air to improve, and meanwhile, people needing rides would be potentially stranded.

Let's next consider why the wildfire aftermath conditions would have an impact on the AI and the self-driving cars.

For anyone that has ever parked their car in an area that was filled with smoke and ash, you've undoubtedly come out to your sitting car and noticed a thick layer of soot on the exterior. Besides messing with that nifty paint job, other concerns are related to the driving of the vehicle. As a driver, you likely got into the driver's seat and instantly notice that your windshield is coated with the dust and ash. That's obviously a problem since it can cut down on your ability to see what might be on the roadway ahead of you.

For self-driving cars, they are chockfull of specialized sensors, including cameras, radar, LIDAR, thermal imaging, ultrasonic, and so on. These are how the AI can detect the roadway and the surrounding scene such as traffic signs, pedestrians, bikers, and the like. Without those sensors, the AI would be effectively blind and unable to appropriately drive the self-driving car.

An ongoing problem that has yet to be fully resolved involves assuring that the sensors on the self-driving car are continuously kept free of any obstructions. Sure, you know that for the windshield you can use your wiper blades and spritz windshield wiper fluid to keep the glass clean and clear. In the case of the self-driving car sensors, this is not quite so easy. Different cleaning methods are being tried, including employing tiny windshield wiper blades, specialized chemical dispensers, protective coatings, cages to reduce debris impacts, etc.

Thus, the first and most prominent aspect of driving in the smoke and ash involves making sure that the sensors can function properly. Furthermore, if somehow a sensor is no longer able to adequately function, there must be provisions to consider what they ought to be done.

Let's pursue that line of thinking.

Besides the sensor directly being obscured, another facet is that even if the sensor is working perfectly fine, the air itself is potentially going to present a problem. Human drivers last week in the San Francisco area were reporting that it was like driving through a heavy fog, such that the smoke and ash significantly reduced overall visibility.

Some assume that self-driving cars are immune to such conditions. They seem to think that with all the advanced sensory apparatus, the self-driving car should be able to find its way in any kind of adverse weather or similar foul environments. This is not the case. There are many situations that the sensors will not be able to see or scan sufficiently and therefore those such moments need to be taken into account by the AI driving system.

This brings up an allied topic that is noteworthy.

When a human opts to drive a car, they presumably would judge whether the air is so bad and the visibility so obscured that it would be best to not go for a drive. This is a judgment call and not a hard-and-fast rule that is particularly based on a numeric calculus. The question arises as to how the AI should make such a "judgment" when considering whether to proceed on a driving journey.

You might be tempted to say that the self-driving cars need to be managed by an owner that makes those decisions, such as a fleet of self-driving cars owned by say an automaker or a ride-sharing firm. The humans of those firms need to decide whether to send out the self-driving cars, rather than leaving such decisions to the AI.

Unfortunately, it is not that easy of an answer.

Suppose in the morning the air seems relatively acceptable for the self-driving cars to proceed. Some of the self-driving cars end-up giving rides in places that are suddenly faced with new wildfires, and thus the smoke and ash are especially fierce. The AI, using the sensors, can detect in real-time the conditions, whereas human managers sitting at a headquarters might not be aware of those moment-to-moment circumstances. As such, the AI must be programmed to assess the drivability and ascertain whether it is safe to proceed or not, making such a decision in real-time as needed. From an AI Ethics perspective, there are increasing calls by many that the automakers and self-driving tech firms should make available the nature of the algorithms being used to make these kinds of on-the-spot driving decisions.

An interesting conundrum can also arise in these settings.

You live in a house that at first was untouched by the wildfires and seemed to be safely at a notable distance from the fires.

Keep in mind that these wildfires often get carried by swift winds and move very fast, jumping from place to place, at great distances, without much warning. All of sudden, you realize that the fire is getting close to your home. So, you decide that it is best to get into the car and drive away.

In an era of self-driving cars, here's what could happen. You get into the self-driving car and the AI announces that due to the prevailing wildfire conditions locally, it is not going to proceed.

This comes as quite a shock to you. Imagine that you have loaded the self-driving car with your family, your beloved pet dog, and the family heirlooms, and hurriedly and desperately need to escape. Now, the self-driving car is refusing to drive. If the self-driving car was a conventional human-driven car, you would not be dependent upon the AI and could merely utilize the driving controls. In the overall case of self-driving cars, it is widely assumed and expected that there will not be any driving controls inside the vehicle, thus precluding any human from attempting to manually drive the car.

This makes sense in that if we are going to have fully autonomous self-driving cars, and presumably glean the advantages, we would want to have only the AI doing the driving. If you open the driving to humans, it means that human foibles come back into the picture. Someone that is dreadfully drunk could potentially decide they want to drive, rather than the AI, and summarily grab the driving controls.

Nope, the idea is that an autonomous self-driving car is supposed to be driven by the AI, not by humans.

To clarify, this does not mean that overnight we are going to have all and only self-driving cars on our roadways. For quite some time, likely decades, there will be a mixture of both self-driving cars and human-driven cars. Part of the reason for this mixture is that there are today 250 million conventional cars and they will not readily be replaced by all self-driving cars. Also, debates are raging about whether people ought to be allowed to drive if they wish to do so. There are going to be those human drivers that will insist on never giving up the wheel, and you'll need to pry their dead cold hands from the steering column before they relinquish the privilege of driving.

Returning though to the dilemma, you and your family are anxiously piled into a self-driving car and it refuses to move.

What do you do?

One answer so far is that there will likely be an OnStar-like facility within self-driving cars, for which you can contact a remote agent to tell them if you are having an issue with the self-driving car. In this instance, merely reaching a remote agent, if even possible and maybe the communications linkages in a wildfire area are not functioning, does not necessarily resolve the matter. The remote agent might politely explain that the AI has determined it is not safe to drive.

You meanwhile are screaming at the remote agent to override the AI and tell it to start driving. The remote agent might not have such a capability. But suppose the remote agent can get the AI to proceed, this still does not overcome the assertion that the conditions are so foul that is ill-advised to be on the roads.

If you have not yet been in an area that has wildfires, consider taking a concerted look at the myriad of relevant videos posted online. I say this because the wildfires can do more than filling the skies with smoke and ash. Limbs of trees fall off onto the streets, blocking the path ahead. At times, the debris is on fire, making trying to go around the obstructions highly dangerous. Shrubs and bushes that caught fire can become rolling balls of flame. And so on.

Add to this disarray the aspect that there might be slow-moving bulky bulldozers on the roads, piloted by firefighters that are trying to get to the wildfire hot spots to put out the flames. Animals are oftentimes loose, running in a panic from their homesteads, and darting frantically on the streets. With especially extreme wildfires, there are sometimes aggravated winds created, causing impaling shards from destroyed homes and other manmade objects to fly alarmingly into the streets and strike cars.

So, which is it, allow the AI to make a life-or-death decision about whether it is safe for the self-driving car to proceed, or override the AI and force the self-driving car to get going.

Of course, the AI might move along and get a few blocks from your home, and then reach a point that it is abundantly apparent that nothing can proceed. Perhaps the wildfires have engulfed the roadways and not even human drivers can attempt to drive through the danger. Now what? Maybe you would have been better off to stay at home versus becoming stranded on a roadway while sitting inside a self-driving car, one that is now completely surrounded by the wildfire.

Conclusion

There are tradeoffs as to have AI self-driving cars that will not allow for human driving, and the wildfires help to illuminate that kind of tradeoff.

The response by some self-driving car aficionados is that this is a one in a zillion chance of ever happening. They would argue that the potential for reducing the estimated 40,000 car crash fatalities and 1.3

million car incident injuries in the United States each year via the advent of self-driving cars is worthwhile in comparison to the oddball chances of getting ensnared in a situation that the AI would not drive you out of a dicey situation.

In fact, they would likely further bolster their assertion by pointing out that it is conceivable that the AI will be a safer driver in a setting such as a wildfire than would human drivers. Ergo, it could be that human drivers would drive recklessly and in a panic mode, potentially getting themselves and others into a worse mess than already exists. The AI would presumably not be overcome by emotion, fear, or other panicky afflictions, and thus would drive stably and reliably.

For those of you intrigued by these matters, I've previously analyzed the similar facets of driving in a hurricane, a tornado, snowstorms, and other such calamities.

Though the everyday driving of a car is admittedly done in rather mundane conditions, most of the time, we ought not to overlook the unfortunate fact that there are a slew of "extraordinary" circumstances that can befall large swaths of the country, seasonally and seemingly year-round, and if AI-based true self-driving cars are aiming to become our sole means of car transport, it will ultimately become crucial to figuring out how society wants to handle these AI-driving challenging settings.

Contemplate these matters the next time you see a self-driving car sauntering down your neighborhood street, and consider what would the AI do if there was something other than a nice sunny day with pretty blue skies and nothing at all was afoot. Thinking ahead about adverse driving conditions is not especially pleasant, but it could make all the difference when otherwise jammed-up in a dire moment.

As Benjamin Franklin once said, failing to prepare is akin to preparing to fail).

CHAPTER 23

CRABWALK MODE

AND

SELF-DRIVING CARS

The new GMC Hummer EV truck was showcased in a sneak - peek video teaser that hinted at the use of its Crabwalk mode, a special feature allowing the driver to steer the vehicle diagonally.

Similar to how a crab might weave to-and-fro at dramatic angles, the Crabwalk mode enables all four wheels to be steered in the same diagonal direction and then be driven accordingly. The online video only sparingly demonstrates this capability, being exceedingly brief and obviously intended to whet our appetites for the upcoming October 20 official debut of this potential Cybertruck competitor. As an aside (spoiler alert), the video clip offers some mild amusement by focusing on a darting crab, which luckily avoids becoming roadkill, saved by (of course) the quick activation of the Hummer's special mode and then having the truck steer afield of the scampering decapod crustacean.

There is no word as yet about how far the diagonal driving can be laterally pointed. The odds are that the wheels cannot go a full ninety degrees, a feat that is usually only seen on concept cars or one-off vehicles devised for that purpose. You might have seen grainy footage from the 1930s of cars with a fifth-wheel arranged at a ninety-degree angle, able to lift up the rear wheels when desired and enable a car to essentially be slid over at an obtuse angle. Ever since the initial invention of the car, it seems there has been keen interest in being able to maneuver sideways, one way or another.

The mechanical underpinnings to implement a sideways driving action is a lot harder than it might seem at first glance. Numerous issues arise about the internal mechanisms and shaping of the vehicle to allow such a capacity, plus concerns arise about the tires and how they might fare as a result of such maneuvering. Also, questions immediately come to the forefront about how fast one should be driving, or be allowed to drive, once the vehicle is heading diagonally. All in all, the whole topic generates a lot of headaches and added costs, against which there is a weighing of the benefits of being able to do a crab-like crawl.

Speaking of moving diagonally, when would you use these atypical crossway driving features?

Some assert it is more so a braggart feature than a practical one. You might invoke it to impress your friends or strangers, doing so with much glee upon first driving the vehicle, but after a while, it would seem that the shock-and-awe will inexorably wear off. At that point, you might use the feature from time-to-time, if you perchance remember that it exists. Drivers often forget that they have some extraordinarily amazing capabilities built into their vehicles and therefore fail to activate them, even when it would be prudent and efficacious to do so.

In that sense, some argue that a diagonal driving mode is intended as a marketing ploy more so than a "thank goodness" feature at your fingertips. This notion though of packing exotic or less-used features into a vehicle for purposes of upping the street cred and selling vehicles is nothing to sneeze at. It works. And undoubtedly it still allows the automaker to stand on high ground by emphasizing that these capabilities can and do make a driving difference, some of the time.

The most often cited example of using a diagonal driving mode would involve parking your car or truck. Perhaps you spy a tight parking spot, offering just enough space between two parked cars and you are sure that you can squeeze into it. You could use the mundane and classical parallel parking effort, but it requires muscling back-and-forth versus moving diagonally, a feat that might be rated as exceptionally eloquent and effective. Some would solemnly pledge that if they had such a mode, they would use it all of the time, while others might insist that they've rarely ever experienced a situation that caused them to voraciously clamor for a diagonally devised driving capacity in their vehicle.

Another use would be for close cornering. You find yourself coming upon a tight turn and switch into the diagonal driving mode to hug the road and successfully navigate the curve snugly. Again, one has to wonder how often this is going to happen in any day-to-day type of driving. On the other hand, there is a case to be made than when the moment arises, presumably, you'll decidedly wish you had such a feature, one that you needed readily at your beck and call.

There's another significant viewpoint about the diagonal driving capability that bears crucial consideration, namely off-road driving.

In theory, people buying these super trucks are aiming to drive not just on quiet neighborhood streets and fully paved freeways. With all the muscle built into these trucks, you must have some off-road expeditions in mind. At least that's what the ads portray, though how much of the time that buyers do hit the gravel and mud for true off-road adventures are open for debate.

The good news is that whenever you might decide to go off-road, the diagonal driving feature is bound to come in handy. Furthermore, the capability would undoubtedly be at top-of-mind since this is the time and place that the sideways angling can be a game-changer. Whether doing rock crawling or coping with difficult terrain, the crab-like finessing could spell the difference between getting out of a jam or preventing getting into one. Certainly, if others are driving nearby and you suddenly showoff your diagonal movement, they are apt to burst into applause.

On city streets, rather than getting accolades, you might get some rude commentary. Who so? At this juncture, there are so few vehicles that can shift into a diagonal driving mode that is unfamiliar to most everyone else on the roadway. As such, though it might garner a moment's fascination, the downside is that it entails doing a driving stunt that other drivers are wholly unaccustomed to seeing, confounding other drivers. Also, there is a chance that the capability might baffle pedestrians, causing them to get confused about which way to avoid getting hit by the unexpected surprise of a diagonally moving vehicle.

Shifting gears, consider the future of cars and trucks, and how everyday ground transportation is going to work. The odds are that we'll eventually have self-driving cars and trucks.

This brings up an intriguing question to ponder: *How might a diagonal driving mode impact the advent of AI-based true self-driving cars?*

Let's unpack the matter and see.

Self-Driving Cars And Diagonal Driving

For Level 4 and Level 5 true self-driving vehicles, there won't be a human driver involved in the driving task.

All occupants will be passengers.

The AI is doing the driving.

There are two major facets to consider when assessing the crab-mode diagonal driving capabilities in light of emerging self-driving cars:
1. Self-driving cars needing to anticipate and react to human-driven cars with those features
2. Self-driving cars possessing those features and when to best employ them

First, consider the ramifications of human-driven cars that have the diagonal driving and can use that special feature in everyday driving situations.

As mentioned earlier, other human drivers are bound to be confounded when having to contend with a vehicle that goes into the diagonal mode and begins to drive in that unusual manner. This could irk those drivers that do not have such a feature, believing that the other driver is merely boasting and not genuinely using the capability for a bona fide purpose. Also, if the human driver utilizing the mode gets stuck or somehow takes too long to do a driving maneuver, you can bet that the other human drivers nearby will become exasperated and exhort that the driver should just do things the normal way.

This whole scenario could change if the preponderance of cars and trucks ultimately are loaded standard with the diagonal moving feature. In that case, the world will have completely switched, such that if you aren't using the crab mode when warranted, other drivers will yell at you to get a grip and use the darned feature. It does though seem unlikely that the diagonal mode is going to become so popular and prevalent that this kind of mass switchover is going to occur, at least not for a long time.

What about the AI driving systems that come upon a human driver using a diagonal driving mode?

Most of the AI driving systems for self-driving cars are predicated on observing human drivers that drive in relatively predictable ways. Indeed, oftentimes gobs of driving data and traffic data are collected for use by Machine Learning (ML) and Deep Learning (DL) algorithms to find patterns in how people drive. As a result of those identified patterns, the AI can be established to anticipate how humans will react and undertake the driving task.

One of the biggest hurdles for self-driving cars is the so-called edge or corner cases. Those are instances of oddball or less-frequent driving situations that can potentially arise and yet are so outside the norm that they are rarely seen or otherwise experienced. For example, if a large corpus of traffic data has not ever included a duck that has wandered onto a freeway when the same thing happens in real life, the AI might not have any prior patterns upon which it was able to be set up to cope with this meandering duck edge-case.

If the number of vehicles with a diagonal driving mode are few, and the chances of ever seeing it used are low, this suggests that the AI might be caught off-guard, akin to how other human drivers can be taken aback. A human driver though presumably has common-sense reasoning and general intelligence that can allow them to cope with unusual driving situations. For the AI, please be aware that there is no semblance of common-sense or human intelligence capacity as yet, and so it is unclear how the AI might respond to the diagonal driving circumstances.

That being said, it seems that the diagonal driving could be nonetheless detected by the sensor suite of the self-driving car if it came upon a vehicle using such a feature. In that manner, the AI is informed about where the other vehicle is. And, the usual perfunctory capabilities of seeking to avoid other vehicles and not hit them, nor get hit, would all still readily come to play.

Overall, the odds of the self-driving car getting out of sorts when coming across a diagonally moving vehicle is not especially likely. Eventually, the automaker or self-driving tech firm that is crafting the AI is likely to encompass the appropriate responses into the driving systems, though this is undeniably a low priority in comparison to more pressing aspects such as driving the self-driving safely in everyday scenarios.

Now we can turn to the matter of outfitting a self-driving car with the diagonal driving feature.

Everything else being equal if you merely plunked down the AI into a vehicle that had such a feature and did not adjust the AI driving system accordingly, the bottom line is that the AI would not ever use the feature. Recall that the AI is not sentient, has no common-sense, and lacks overall human reasoning and intelligence. A human placed into a vehicle with the crab mode would likely experiment with it, and reason their way into figuring out how it works. This is extremely unlikely for today's AI (namely, you would need to explicitly set up the AI, rather than having it overtly explore a new feature of its own accord, as it were).

Once the AI was set up for making use of the diagonal moving feature, it would then presumably invoke the feature in those particular settings that it had been programmed to do so. There is a chance that the AI might inadvertently opt to use the mode in situations that it was not necessary to do so (false positives), and fail to use it when the moment to do so was timely (false negatives). In any case, this could be said of human drivers too, though I am not equating human driving and AI driving (this is not an anthropomorphic implication).

We can return to an earlier point about humans that employ the diagonal driving and make a likewise comparison to an AI self-driving car that might do so. If there were say self-driving cars that all had the diagonal feature, and meanwhile most human-driven cars didn't, the use of the feature by the AI would likely spark concern by human drivers. Other nearby human drivers would wonder what in the heck the AI is doing and complain that the use of the feature unsettling.

In case you are thinking that we are going to have only self-driving cars soon on our roadways and no longer have any human-driven cars, you ought to reconsider that leap of logic. Today there are approximately 250 million conventional cars on our roadways in the United States alone. There will not be an overnight replacement of those conventional cars by self-driving cars. In short, there will be many years, seemingly decades, involving both self-driving cars and human-driven cars intermixed on our roadways.

The point being that self-driving cars need to be able to cope with human-driven cars. If we somehow waved a magic wand and had only self-driving cars, the AI of those vehicles could likely use V2V (vehicle-to-vehicle) electronic communications to inform each other about what they are doing. In that case, the moment a self-driving car opted to use a crab mode, it could send an electronic alert to other nearby self-driving cars. This will certainly be taking place, even as there are still human-driven cars on the roadways, though none of that obviates the qualms about how human-driven cars and their human drivers might react to a self-driving car invoking the diagonal driving mode.

Conclusion

Here's an added twist for you.

The earlier indicated levels of self-driving cars do not encompass off-road driving.

Yes, it is somewhat surprising that the existing standard for the autonomous levels of self-driving cars does not include off-road driving. That type of driving is considered beyond the scope of the standard. The main takeaway is that most of the AI efforts to-date are focusing on street and highway on-road driving, rather than off-road driving. This is somewhat of irony because much of the initial research involving self-driving was about doing so off-road, which partially was a safer way to test out the efficacy of self-driving cars. To be clear, the nearer term money to be made by selling the self-driving capabilities is by far in the on-road market rather than the off-road market.

Do not interpret this facet to suggest that there will not eventually be a lucrative and huge market for off-road self-driving. In fact, there already is one developing, doing so for purposes of excavation, working mines, for military purposes, and the like. For those uses, it will be undeniably worthwhile to have a diagonal driving mode, and equally beneficial to make sure that the AI driving systems can accommodate and leverage such a feature.

As a final comment to consider, you might be aware that crabs are invertebrates, meaning they lack a backbone (their exoskeleton protects them). Humans that want to drive diagonally are at times fiercely loyal to the notion and have (one might say) a stout backbone for demanding such a capability.

To some degree, this is opening a can of worms for AI-based true self-driving cars, though, with the right amount of care and attention, it is more of a cornucopia than a Pandora's box.

CHAPTER 24

DANGEROUS MONTH

AND

SELF-DRIVING CARS

Which month of the year is considered the most dangerous for drivers?

Give this question a moment of somber consideration.

There are certainly a lot of factors to take into account. Maybe winter months that involve inclement weather are the most dangerous due to having to contend with rain, snow, and otherwise adverse roadway conditions. Or perhaps the onerous months are when people tend to drink and drive, such as around the holidays.

Get ready for the answer.

Statistics suggest that in the United States the month of September is annually the worst in terms of the number of driving-related fatalities per billion miles driven. So, the answer is September is the most dangerous month for drivers, assuming you are willing to focus on traffic-related deaths versus some other metrics such as the number of car crash injuries or other estimates entailing car accidents.

What makes September snare the highest car-related fatality rate?

Nobody can say for sure, but there is plenty of reasoned speculation involved.

Perhaps the least obvious facet and yet glaringly apparent once you think about it is the celebration of Labor Day during the month of September. I'd wager that you don't necessarily associate September with Labor Day, at least not to the same degree that you align New Year's with January or the celebrating of our nation's independence in

July. Anyway, Labor Day weekend can certainly entail lots of partying and drinking, along with an upsurge in driving to get too celebratory destinations, all of which parlays into the fatalities via automobile driving during September.

Some assert that another key element is that the summer weather usually continues into September and therefore people are willing to go for a drive, more so than once the winter weather starts to appear. Yet another plausible explanation involves the aspect that the days begin to become shorter due to the evening darkness settling in at earlier and earlier hours. People generally drive worse in nighttime conditions, not being able to see the road as clearly and for other associated reasons.

An especially convincing though unproven contention is that people are apt to drive more as a result of schools getting underway, including that there are newly sparked time-based pressures that emerge each September. In brief, the notion is that people get stressed out by having to dovetail their dropping off children at school and picking them up at the end of the school day, which gets intermingled into driving to and from work. This creates heightened pressures to drive fast and meet demanding timetables. All of this then gets stirred into a boiling pot of car traffic and the next thing you know, there are lots of car crashes and related fatalities.

Bottom-line is to please be extra careful when driving during September.

One future aspect to consider involves the gradual advent of AI-based true self-driving cars.

This raises an intriguing question: *Will the emergence of AI-based true self-driving cars eliminate the role of September or essentially any month from being a most dangerous driving time, perhaps due to the safety aspects expected for self-driving car driving?*

Let's unpack the matter and see.

Self-Driving Cars And Most Dangerous Driving Months

For Level 4 and Level 5 true self-driving vehicles, there won't be a human driver involved in the driving task.

All occupants will be passengers.

The AI is doing the driving.

Some pundits are apt to say that once there are self-driving cars on our roadways, you can forget about the per-month fatalities rates about driving because the AI is doing the driving rather than humans. We all know that humans exhibit bad driving behaviors, encompassing driving while intoxicated, driving while distracted, and so on. The AI is not going to drive drunk, it won't be watching the latest cat videos, and generally can be assumed to be fully attentive to the driving task.

As such, in theory, traffic will be much safer overall and the number of car crashes will drop sharply. Some keep saying we will reach a point of zero fatalities. My reaction is that zero fatalities have a zero chance of happening. There are still going to be car crashes, and we have to openly toss aside a utopian fantasy that the number of car fatalities will go to zero.

One reason to expect car crashes to occur will be the realistic perspective that there are going to be human-driven cars intermixing with self-driving cars. Forget about the pie-in-the-sky idea that we will suddenly have only self-driving cars on our roadways and that all human driving will be banned or otherwise expunged off the planet.

There are about 250 million conventional cars in the U.S. alone, and those vehicles are not going to disappear overnight once self-driving cars emerge. Also, many drivers are going to fight tooth-and-nail to keep driving, despite any pleadings to get them to give up the privilege (it is going to be quite an ugly battle over whether humans can still drive or perhaps by government decree no longer be allowed to do so).

This overall discussion is crucial to the question about the fatalities per month aspects.

If you believe that magically there will exclusively be self-driving cars and absolutely no human-driven cars, this would seem to imply that all months will be equal in terms of driving. You might then think that all months would come out to the same number of potential fatalities.

Not quite.

Assuming that self-driving cars will rarely get into car accidents in such a scenario, the number of fatalities is going to logically be at rock bottom, fortunately so. That being the case, there is still the matter of the number of miles driven, namely that assuming there is some relatively consistent rate of fatalities, albeit much less than when only humans were driving, the rate nonetheless would presumably be applied to the number of miles being driven (and, thus, whichever months had the most driving would tend to have a higher raw number of actual fatality incidents).

In that use case, it could be that September remains the most dangerous driving month, but the crucial caveat is that it would be a huge drop in the count of fatalities and thus a lot of lives "saved" (deaths averted) that would otherwise have been lost. Interestingly, the month with the highest number of driven miles historically tends to be July, and using the aforementioned logic, it possibly could be that July would become the most dangerous driving month rather than September.

There is a fly in the ointment on all of this.

Returning to the earlier point that we are going to have an intermixing of human-driven cars and self-driving cars, this is a serious matter worthy of added attention.

As self-driving cars start to become prevalent, how will human drivers react to this phenomenon?

One argument is that human drivers will be inspired to become better drivers, doing so as guided or politely nudged by self-driving cars and AI driving behaviors.

Allow me to elaborate.

Right now, we all tend to react to other human drivers. Someone rudely cuts you off in traffic, and this causes you to get steamed, prodding you to then take out your anger on other drivers. All it takes is one jerk driver to initiate a cascading sense of foul driving in a dominos kind of way. By reducing the number of idiot drivers that provoke road rage reactions, the AI driving systems might indirectly encourage driving civil discourse.

Notice that it isn't as though the AI is telling human drivers nearby to be better drivers. Instead, the absence of doing untoward driving tactics is tantamount to saying something akin to dance with me. The usual tit-for-tat that occurs daily on our streets and highways is turned on its head. Whereas the tit-for-tat is dominated by eye-for-an-eye behaviors today, it could become a contagion of good driving, everyone being courteous and generous toward each other.

Gradually, there will be fewer and fewer human drivers on the roads and the number of self-driving cars will incrementally rise over time. Eventually, the proportion of human drivers in traffic versus the AI driving systems will be reversed such that the self-driving cars are predominant. Thus, in theory, driving safety is getting enhanced by the higher proportion of self-driving cars involved, and simultaneously a lessening of tit-for-tat bad driving takes place.

Some though believe that human drivers might be irked and resort to undesirable driving as a result of all those self-driving cars.

First, human drivers might realize that they can trick the self-driving cars (this is already occurring). If the AI driving systems are programmed to back down from any traffic challenges by other cars, human drivers that are devious will undoubtedly take advantage of this loophole. When you want to cut in traffic, in today's driving you have to play a game of cat-and-mouse with other cars to let you into their lane. Assuming that AI self-driving cars aren't going to play such games, and will immediately allow your car into their lane, the human drivers will be happy to do this all day long.

Second, human drivers might become exasperated at self-driving cars and those darned AI driving systems. Assuming that the AI is programmed to always drive at the legally posted speeds, you can bet that human drivers are not going to like sitting behind a self-driving car going 25 miles per hour down a quiet street that the humans prefer to drive at 35 miles per hour. As such, the human drivers will try to sneak around self-driving cars, undertaking highly dangerous driving stunts to do so.

Third, some human drivers might relish undercutting AI driving systems. In a sense of hating robots and the emerging AI, there will be human drivers that purposely try to shake-up the self-driving cars. These nefarious drivers will veer toward self-driving cars to get the AI to weave or make a sudden maneuver to avoid what appears to be an impending car crash. Human drivers of this ilk will possibly perceive this kind of activity as a means of showing the world that allowing AI to drive is fundamentally wrong and that humanity needs to take back the steering wheel from those infuriating robots, as it were.

What this all adds up to is that the human drivers that are still on the roadways might become more dangerous drivers than we have today, and therefore push up the car crash rates, despite there being less human drivers all told. You could say it is an irrational form of induced demand, consisting of today's otherwise suppressed bad driving that gets unleashed as the advent of self-driving cars arises.

Conclusion

Would the month of September still be the most dangerous driving month?

It is hard to say, and one supposes that it could still hold the sordid title depending upon the other earlier speculated underlying basis for why September is so drivingly wanton.

CHAPTER 25

AI APOLOGIES

AND

SELF-DRIVING CARS

They say that love means never having to say that you are sorry.

When does it make sense though to proffer being sorry and offer someone an apology?

There are AI systems increasingly being designed to emit apologies, doing so when the AI detects that an act of contrition on its part might be suitable or needed.

For example, you apply online for a car loan and the AI system determines that you are not worthy, as it were, and promptly turns you down. The belief is that this would be an ideal moment for the AI to offer you a "heartfelt" apology.

It might go something like this: Dear loan applicant, it is with great sorrow that I must inform you of the unfortunate news that your request to borrow funds to buy a car is hereby denied. Please know that you are not alone in having been spurned and accept this apology for any discomfort that might arise from this outcome. Sincerely, the AI system that reluctantly rebuffed your request.

Do you think this apology will make the person feel any better about the AI-powered decision?

Well, I doubt it would for most people, nonetheless, there is an emerging trend of having AI systems produce these kinds of messages.

We can mull over and debate the tradeoffs involved in having AI that provides these kinds of apologies. There are claimed benefits of having the AI appear to be deferential, while there are criticisms that

221

this is a mockery of humanity and diminishes the potency of apologies all told. Before getting to the overall set of tradeoffs, imagine the myriad of areas that AI is being applied, beyond just adjudicating car loan candidates, and envision how those varied instances might opt to leverage a purposely apologizing AI system.

Here's an intriguing aspect: *Will the advent of AI-based true self-driving cars necessitate the AI being apologetic from time-to-time, and do we really want or expect apologies to be issued by AI driving systems?*

Let's unpack the matter and see.

Self-Driving Cars And Offering Apologies

For Level 4 and Level 5 true self-driving vehicles, there won't be a human driver involved in the driving task.

All occupants will be passengers.

The AI is doing the driving.

Some assert that it makes sense for the AI to render an apology when the situation warrants doing so.

You might be initially baffled that there would ever be any basis for the AI driving system to issue an apology to the passengers of a self-driving car. We certainly do not expect human drivers to particularly offer apologies, and thus there is no well-established tradition of drivers making such utterances. Sure, on a rare occasion a ride-sharing driver might apologize that their car reeks of tuna salad because they just managed to wolf down their lunch on the way to pick you up, but otherwise the number of apologies we receive while riding in cars has got to be pretty low, nearly zero it so seems.

Well, take a step back and ponder the following scenario.

You are nestled in a self-driving car and enjoying some quiet time on the way to work. The seats can fully recline, due to the facet that there aren't any driving controls inside the vehicle (the steering wheel and pedals for true self-driving cars are expected to be excised from the interior and no longer accessible by humans since the AI is doing all the driving).

The AI is dutifully watching the roadway and attempting to provide you with a safe journey from your home to the office. Thankfully, the AI is coping with the darned traffic on the freeways and the equally exasperating jammed traffic on the busy city streets. You can daydream and meanwhile, the AI is observing the surroundings like an alert hawk.

All of a sudden, the AI detects via its sensors, such as by using cameras, radar, LIDAR, and so on, that a pedestrian is weaving erratically on the sidewalk and appears to be nearing the curb of the street. It is hard to discern whether the person is going to actually come into the street. Maybe they will turn back toward the buildings at the last moment and avoid coming into the roadway. Or, in a worst-case possibility, the person might opt to pop into the street, right in front of where the self-driving car is headed.

What to do?

What would you do?

What should the AI do?

For human drivers, we confront these kinds of driving situations all the time. You have to make split-second judgment choices about whether a pedestrian is going to foolishly wander directly into the path of your moving car, and thus calculate in your mind whether to slow down, speed-up, swerve or take no action. Any of those options might be right. Of course, any of those options might be wrong too.

In the case of AI driving systems, to-date the approach has involved setting up the AI to be extraordinarily cautious, more so than perhaps most human drivers might be. If there is even an inkling of an upcoming car crash or similar incident, the AI is going to try and avert the chances by taking the "safest" course of action (more on this in a moment).

Assume that the AI hits the brakes of the self-driving car, doing so to be at a complete stop before reaching where the pedestrian might end-up being. By calculating the intersecting points at which the self-driving car and the pedestrian might have arrived, the AI calculated the stopping distance and figured out that an emergency stop could likely ensure that the self-driving car and the meanderer would not come in contact with each other.

Pedestrian is saved.

Suppose though that the person did not come into the street, and at the last moment veered back onto the sidewalk. This means that the self-driving car needlessly came to a halt. You could presumably give the AI some thankful credit for having avoided a potential accident, but the accident never materialized and so you could equally criticize the AI for being an overly reactive scaredy-cat driver.

Meanwhile, remember that there is a passenger inside the self-driving car (we're still pretending it was you). There you were, comfortably reclining and blissfully inattentive to the roadway conditions, rightfully so, reliant upon the AI to tackle the driving and make the proper decisions thereof.

Upon the sharp braking action utilized by the AI driving system, you are tossed around like a sack of potatoes. Maybe a tad bit of whiplash involved.

What the heck happened, you would likely be wondering, having no clue why the AI made the unexpected and utterly unannounced stop.

At this juncture, at least as a minimum, you would be expecting the AI to explain what occurred. If the AI does not indicate why the roughshod driving action was undertaken, you are beset with doubts and would feel uneasy that the AI can adequately drive the self-driving car. Perhaps the AI has gone nuts, or an electronic power surge made its bits go bad.

We are now at the million-dollar question.

Should the AI apologize to you?

Try this: Dear rider, you undoubtedly sensed that the self-driving car came to a sudden halt, which please accept my apologies for having done so. This was done out of an abundance of caution and potentially might have saved the life of an errant pedestrian. As a driving transgression, it is not what I aspire to do while driving, but hopefully, you understand that such moments have merit and your forgiveness on this matter is welcomed. Sincerely, the AI driving the self-driving car.

Notice that this is a twofer, consisting of an explanation and simultaneously an inserted apology.

The explanation would tend to ease your concerns about the AI having gone off the deep end.

Does the apology also make you feel better?

Let's turn our attention to AI that issues apologies and those earlier alluded to tradeoffs involved in having the AI do so.

AI Apologizing and The Merits Or Demerits

Some insist that any apology by an AI system is completely, unabashedly, a fraudulent and hollow act.

The AI is not sentient. For those of you that might be tricked by the barrage of media postings that suggest that AI is sentient or near-to, do not fall for this hogwash. There isn't any AI today that can be construed as sentient and there is nothing on the horizon that implies or purports to show that sentience can be reached in the near future.

Hence, the point is that the AI generating an apology is not the same as a human that proffers an apology. The AI cannot from-the-heart provide you or anyone with a heartfelt apology. This does not compute. In that overall sense, it can be argued that an apology by AI is nothing but fakery.

Worse still is the notion that by providing an apology there is an insidious insinuation that the AI is indeed sentient. In more formal parlance, this is tantamount to anthropomorphizing the AI. When the AI as a computer-based machine is made to seem like it is human, real humans will begin to think that the machine is a human or an equivalent.

That's a dangerous slippery slope.

People that believe the AI can think and act as a human can are going to become reliant upon the AI to do things that the AI cannot achieve. For example, humans have common-sense reasoning (I realize some might chuckle and note that they know humans that are not able to exercise common-sense, but put that cynicism to the side for the moment), but there aren't AI systems yet that have anything of the same. Thus, the AI is not going to apply common-sense to any instructions you might share with it, and nor should you expect the AI to employ common-sense when performing a task for you.

Speaking of cynics, some people are less heated-up about these AI apologies and claim that any human with a modicum of intelligence knows that the apology emitted by AI is merely a made-up artifact by the humans that programmed the AI. In this viewpoint, there is a hardened belief that everyone already should realize that the AI is just a computer and like any computer that spits out a report or displays a message, the whole thing is just a bunch of 1's and 0's being shoveled to-and-fro.

And, it could be argued that getting an apology, albeit from something that does not "know" what an apology is, provides a nice touch of humanity for the circumstances at hand.

The developers of the AI at least realized that sometimes the AI might go afoul. That alone is important and perhaps a shocker since many times an AI system will make a mistake or a misstep and it doesn't realize what has transpired. Thank goodness that there is an apology, acting as a canary in the cage, showing the light that the AI has been embedded with some kind of error detection and response capabilities.

The words too of an apology can be soothing.

Despite the AI not being human or anything akin, the words alone are being spoken and received.

Returning to reclining in a self-driving car that has come to a jolting halt, perhaps the apology can be the icing on the cake, wherein the cake was the explanation and the delightful icing is the supplemental apologetic words.

How far might this go?

There are stratified levels of apologies being cooked into some AI systems. There is a mild apology that is used when the incident or activity was only modestly disturbing for the human. Waiting to be used is the medium level apology that lays out a lengthier indication of what the AI is sorry about. Then there's the heightened apology, profusely seeking to offer a sorrowfulness befitting a Shakespearean play.

The passenger in a self-driving car that got jostled by the sudden halt might get a mild apology if the stopping action was not especially severe. On the other hand, if the stop was the kind that makes your teeth rattle right out of your skull, the heightened version of the apology would likely be issued.

Skeptics have an entirely different viewpoint on these AI-based apologies.

Give me reparations or something tangible to make me whole and soothed, the skeptics exhort, rather than a bunch of gooey words of an apology.

In the case of a self-driving car, the AI ought to inform you that you will be getting a ten percent discount on the driving fare for the ride, or maybe waive the bill entirely. If there is a loyalty program associated with using the self-driving car, perhaps the AI can add some padded miles into your account, doing so to try and appease your dismay at the sudden stopping action. Etc.

In short, there are the where's the beef critics that eschew the apologies if there isn't a bona fide payoff associated with the words themselves. In this view, any apology from either AI or a human is essentially worthless unless it is backed up by money in their pocket or some other form of compensation that deals with the matter underlying the incident that precipitated the apology, to begin with.

Conclusion

Another concern by some about apologies by AI is that it might open a veritable Pandora's box.

Here's how.

The act of the AI apologizing could be construed as an acknowledgment that the AI did something wrong. This admission can be then utilized for any legal action against the company that made or fielded the AI system.

For the self-driving car, potentially the automaker or self-driving tech maker is shooting their own foot, one might say, due to admitting to being at fault.

The next thing you know, there are zillions of lawsuits launched by people that have received AI-based apologies, and they are all going to use as concrete evidence that the AI apologized, which certainly must mean that the AI was in the wrong and that the maker of the AI knew or could have known that the AI was going to bungle things.

Returning to the skeptics, potentially the AI offering an apology is almost like dollars in their pockets, given that the AI is handing them on a silver platter that the AI was at fault and presumably some compensation should be forthcoming accordingly, perhaps by legal court proceedings.

CHAPTER 26
HAWAII TESTING
OF
SELF-DRIVING CARS

Do you dream of taking a vacation to Hawaii?

If so, you can now bolster those dreamy images in your head by including a new showcase that might not normally seem to go with swaying palm trees and breathtaking sunsets, namely the rolling along of self-driving cars.

Yes, Hawaii became the 29th state to formally approve the testing of self-driving cars, allowing autonomous vehicles onto the streets and highways of this nationally revered wonderous set of islands. Having passed the legislative bill known as HB2590, and subsequently signed into law by Governor David Ige as Act 021, the Hawaiian Department of Transportation (HDOT) is mindfully authorized to forthwith issue permits for the use of self-driving cars.

The legislative process started in January and took over nine months to get settled, partially bumped around due to the pandemic disruption. Meanwhile, for those that have been watching the emerging interest in self-driving cars throughout Hawaii, you might recall that there was a big splash in 2017 when Governor Ige established an executive order to lay the groundwork toward bringing self-driving tech firms and automakers to the islands. There has also been the creation of the Hawaii Automated Vehicle Institute as led by the University of Hawaii Manoa iLab. Recently, it was announced in August that a $6 million federal grant from the FHA (Federal Highway Administration) will enable HDOT to proceed on experimenting with electronic connectivity for traffic aspects on federal highways in the state (a project headed by Professor David Ma at the University of Hawaii).

And so on.

In short, similar to how a long-time struggling actor suddenly gets spirited into the spotlight and miraculously seems to appear out of thin air, the reality about Hawaii and self-driving cars is that this is not an overnight revelation and instead, a statewide ongoing and steadfast pursuit of the matter.

One important point to keep in mind about the regulation is that any approved self-driving cars would only be used on a testing basis and are decidedly not allowed to roam wantonly on their own. Indeed, akin to most other states that have approved self-driving car testing, there must be a back-up human driver, also referred to as a test driver or safety driver, whenever the vehicles are out and about.

An interesting added twist is that in three years the overall program will potentially come to a halt, depending upon a progress report to be prepared and submitted by HDOT, enabling the state authorities and the public to weigh-in on the benefits and downsides of the test trials. At that juncture, presumably, the legislature would extend the regulation or propose something anew, unless things have gone badly, in which case the existing allowances would expire, meaning that the self-driving testing would legally cease to be allowed.

In the executive order that was officially signed on November 22, 2017, this statement emphasized the vital nature of self-driving cars and the role that Hawaii could play therein: "WHEREAS, acknowledging that, today there is something akin to a space race to see who will develop driverless vehicles and advanced wireless technologies (i.e., the Internet of Things)—both of which have the power to influence the future outcomes for the daily lives of all Americans. —Hawaii, with its unique, favorable conditions, has become the ideal locale for testing."

This brings up an intriguing question: *Will automakers and self-driving tech firms flock to Hawaii and promptly proceed to undertake the testing of their AI-based true self-driving cars, or will they be slow to set up shop and perhaps wait to decide whether to inhabit the islands?*

Now that the green light is shining, it does not necessarily mean that self-driving cars are going to be seen right away on Hawaiian roads. There is a business calculus, as it were, involved in choosing to conduct self-driving car testing in Hawaii, indeed the same kind of cost-benefit analyses of doing so in any state that has opened its doors to such an option.

Though you and I might relish going to Hawaii for the holidays, this is not how companies that are crafting self-driving cars and devising the next-generation of self-driving tech are going to similarly view the opportunity on the islands. It might seem shocking that not all firms on the mainland haven't eagerly been champing at the bit to get underway in this tropical paradise.

Undoubtedly, zillions of AI developers and automotive engineers would go there in a heartbeat, likely hoping to get some topnotch surfing into their hectic schedules, but that's not how this decision is going to be made.

Turns out that there are hard tradeoffs involved.

Before jumping into the challenges, it is handy to clarify what I mean when discussing AI-based true self-driving cars.

Time to unpack the matter and see.

Self-Driving Cars And Hawaii

For Level 4 and Level 5 true self-driving vehicles, there won't be a human driver involved in the driving task.

All occupants will be passengers.

The AI is doing the driving.

Now that we've gotten that foundation established about self-driving cars, grab a Mai Tai or a Blue Hawaii drink and consider the question of why it makes sense to have firms opt-in to Hawaii for their self-driving car testing, and also why it might not be quite so prudent.

One aspect that was touted by authorities in Hawaii is that the state is not physically bordered by another state, and therefore offers a rather unique advantage accordingly. You might be at first puzzled why this aspect of being free of bordering states would be of any consequence for self-driving cars.

The answer is quite straightforward.

Each of the states is currently enacting its own proprietary set of regulations overseeing self-driving cars, of which about three-fifths of the states have done so, and the others have not yet enacted such legislation.

There is a possibility that if a self-driving car is being tested in state X, and the self-driving car perchance wanders over the state border into a neighboring state, its presence in that state Y is now either illegal within that state or bound to a differing set of laws as adopted by that state.

Some vehemently are arguing that this is partially the highlighted need to enact federal legislation that would be applicable across all of the states. In theory, a federal enactment would ensure that the laws are consistent and not an oddball patchwork. Readers of my column are aware that I've been covering the federal legislative efforts about self-driving cars, which have recently gotten back underway, but the chances of seeing new legislation getting approved this year, given the other matters grabbing national attention, would seem exceedingly slim.

In any case, for now, and the foreseeable future, Hawaii has the high ground, as it were, by pointing out that there is zero chance of a self-driving car somehow going across the state border and into another adjacent state. About all a self-driving car could do is end up in the ocean, perhaps the AI deciding that it too wants to hit the surf and enjoy those gnarly waves.

Okay, so this no-neighboring state is an actual advantage for being in Hawaii, but does it make a substantive difference?

Not especially.

I mention this with a somewhat heavy heart because, having lived in Hawaii, there is a temptation to aid in spurring self-driving cars to go there, aiming to bolster the state in its pursuits. Nonetheless, it is useful to see the world as it is, not as it is dreamed to be.

Look at it this way.

Most of the self-driving car tryouts are taking place in bustling cities or nestled suburbs, and not at outlier locations that happen to be on the borders with other states. Other than occasional stunts whereby a self-driving car is taken on a cross-country tour, doing so to gain publicity, there is not much testing that requires going from one state to another. Furthermore, unlike perhaps going across country boundaries, there isn't any special driving action typically required when going from state to state, thankfully, and thus nothing unusual or extraordinary for the self-driving car to learn about doing so.

Thus, few of the self-driving car tryouts are being held back because they are not necessarily able to proceed from one state into an adjacent one. Also, for those that suggest this is something that could possibly happen on an unplanned basis, well, that's rather nutty thinking. The testing of self-driving cars is being done on an extremely controlled basis by just about everyone doing such testing. They are not merely letting loose their self-driving cars each day with the fanciful idea that they can go anywhere.

In fact, by-and-large, the self-driving car testing on our public roadways involves extensive preparations for the specific routes to be taken. This includes pre-mapping the routes and anticipating what the roads and the scenery settings consist of. Then, these routes are used over and over again. Be assured that this is not some kind of wild west whereby you just let the horses run free and watch where they trot.

All told, until self-driving cars have mastered a lot more of their activity, the notion of going from state-to-state as part of the testing process is darned low on the list of priorities. Sadly, this pretty much undercuts the border touting exhortations, though they are certainly worth leveraging and maybe it will strike a chord with some.

Given that sentiment about the topic of the neighboring states, we can now proceed into aspects that would be more pronounced at this time.

First, one consideration is whether the state is seriously wanting to have self-driving car testing, or whether it is reluctantly doing so. Some states seem to have jumped on this popular bandwagon, and yet are warily eyeing the mechanizations and perhaps dragging their feet in allowing the testing (they would defend this posture by insisting they are aiming for the highest level of safety for such efforts, which can be argued that not all states are appropriately undertaking).

For Hawaii, it seems reasonable to assert that they are a state that appears to be favorable toward self-driving car testing (more to be known once applicants start submitting for the permits).

It seems fair to render a positive checkmark for Hawaii seriously being interested in the matter.

Of course, until those self-driving cars start to be seen on the roadways, it is difficult to know how the public is going to react. When the abstract idea of self-driving cars being around is simply a conceptual topic, it is easy to romanticize it. The moment that self-driving cars start appearing like bunnies, possibly lots of them on the roadways, the reaction can dramatically change.

Here's something that most people find surprising, perhaps startling, and unimaginable, namely, there are already traffic jams and slow-going driving conditions, bumper to bumper, in some parts of Hawaii.

People that have never been to Hawaii are dumbfounded that this could be the case. They assume that all roads are wide open. Cars zip along, unfettered. Meanwhile, calm breezes and ocean views make any driving into a dream, rather than a chore.

That can be said for much of Hawaii, indeed for most of Hawaii, but not for all of Hawaii.

On Oahu, especially anywhere in or near Honolulu, the traffic can be stifling. Anyone that has been on Nimitz Highway at the wrong hours, which increasingly seems like any hours of the day, knows the equivalent of driving in Los Angeles whereby it is energy diluting and seemingly non-stop soul smashing traffic.

Insiders know why this occurs.

Hawaii happens to be one of the least populated states, approximately 1.4 million residents, and meanwhile, is also one of the most densely populated states in terms of the preponderance of populous being found in predominantly concentrated areas. Oahu alone has about one million of the residents, and Honolulu is both the state capital, the largest city, and a tourist magnet.

In brief, put a lot of people in a given or confined area of geography, and you have yourself an abundance of automobile traffic.

One viewpoint is that adding self-driving cars into that arena is likely to steam the locals. You already have to contend with human drivers, and the next thing that happens is that you'll be trying to weave around those darned self-driving cars.

Though there is a case to be made that perhaps ultimately the adoption of self-driving cars will reduce traffic woes, this is assuredly not the case when doing the testing in the shorter term.

How will public opinion fare if self-driving cars add to the traffic angst?

The counterargument is that the number of self-driving cars that would likely be on those roads is tiny in comparison to the volume of human-driven conventional cars. Thus, it is unfair to point to self-driving cars as potential traffic muddlers. On the other hand, self-driving cars will stand out due to their obvious look-and-feel, which means that though they might be an infinitesimal amount of the traffic, they might nonetheless disproportionately get the blame and attention.

Of course, the self-driving car testing can be adjusted to try and avoid such a public relations calamity. By the self-driving cars being judiciously scheduled by the testers, they can avoid getting into the traffic blaming games.

This does bring up another vital facet to consider.

Where will the self-driving cars be tested in terms of the Hawaiian public roads to be utilized?

In theory, the self-driving cars could be positioned onto any of the islands. If you wanted to do testing that was in areas relatively unpopulated, do not make camp on Oahu, or at least aim for the remote parts of that island (or choose a different island).

Meanwhile, when you do want to mix into the throes of traffic, you know where that exists, and can thoughtfully do testing in those areas when so desired and reasonable to do so.

Oddly enough, the fact that there are places of mired traffic is actually important for the testing of self-driving cars.

Here's why.

If you test self-driving cars in only unpopulated areas, the AI is not likely to "learn" what needs to be known to drive in the populated areas (this advancement is done via the use of Machine Learning and Deep Learning). In the famous old saying, practice what you aim to do in battle, those trying out their self-driving cars realize that merely using roads that have no other drivers and no other traffic is not conducive to advancing their self-driving car capabilities.

This brings us to advantage in using Hawaii for testing. There are a variety of useful testing scenarios that exist, encompassing the classic situation of traffic miseries aplenty, and then lots of opportunities to do testing in areas with little or no prevalent traffic.

Unfortunately, getting your self-driving cars from one island to the other is not going to be easy. The odds are that you would be more prudent to pick one island and stick with it.

Conclusion

There is a slew of additional factors too.

One of them is the weather.

The good news is that the weather in Hawaii is moderate and tropical. This provides a consistency nearly year-round, and one that is easy to work in for the trying out of the self-driving cars. The bad news is that you cannot particularly have your self-driving cars experience the seasonal extremes, such as snow (well, there is snow in some of the highest elevations in parts of Hawaii, but not readily where the self-driving cars are likely to be).

Another aspect is the cost of living in Hawaii, the availability of local AI talent and automotive engineers needed for the testing efforts, the costs to rent the facilities to house and maintain the self-driving cars, etc. On the other hand, living and working in Hawaii can be a blast, and could be used to lure the talent there, along with growing local talent at the same time.

Think too about the advertising bonanza, allowing a self-driving car company to provide video postings of its autonomous vehicles in the splendors of paradise. That's got to put you on the headlines and front pages of the media proclamations that self-driving cars are here and now.

One final aspect, perhaps the 500-pound gorilla of them all, consists of the tourists.

Hawaii attracts about 10.4 million visitors each year, including about 230,000 people each day on average.

The good news is that this adds to the traffic and includes rental car driving, notorious for being unpredictable and erratic (this is good news because it provides more grist for the mill of Machine Learning). The bad news is that if self-driving cars were to irk the tourism trade, and it somehow spoiled the magical glow of the state, this would be akin to the tail wagging the dog, detrimentally.

To make a happy face on this last point, one supposes that perhaps the self-driving car testing could be made into a tourist attraction, as it were. Visitors arriving at Honolulu International Airport might get into a lottery to see which can take a ride in a self-driving car (if permitted), or be told to be on the watch for self-driving cars, spotting them as though they are akin to spotting a rare Hawaiian Monk Seal or a Hawaiian Hoary Bat.

It seems that everyone knows the use of shaka, the popular hand gesture that suggests the Aloha fortitude, and has become popular for indicating a sense of friendship and solidarity. There is an expression "E hele kāua" which generally means let's go, such as let's go party.

For self-driving cars coming to Hawaii, there are tradeoffs involved, but let's hope for the *E hele kāua*, doing so in the grand spirit of the Aloha State.

Mahalo.

CHAPTER 27

TOO MANY OBJECTS

AND

SELF-DRIVING CARS

Have you ever played the game of what-do-you-spy when on a long driving trip that includes a child in the car?

It is a simple and convenient way to pass the time, keeping the youngster preoccupied, and simultaneously entails the possibility of boosting their cognitive skills as a budding toddler.

Here's how the game goes in case you've never utilized it.

While the car is zipping along, the child looks outside the car to try and identify various objects that can be readily seen while the vehicle is underway. For example, perhaps while on a vacation ride through open country areas such as farmlands, you tell the child to spot any cows. This gets the youngster eagerly scanning the surroundings in hopes of spying one.

If the toddler is quite young, it could be that they aren't exactly sure what a cow looks like and might mistakenly call out when they see a horse or a goat. Upon a gentle and definition-providing correction by an adult, the child begins to learn what constitutes a cow versus other animals. This continues for possibly hours upon hours, though the search for cows might become tiresome and repetitive, thus, you might then switch to spotting something else, maybe tractors or plows.

You can up the ante for children that are more advanced in age. While you are driving in a city environment, you might ask the child to spy anyone on a skateboard or possibly find someone that is holding an umbrella. If it perchance is raining, the umbrella search is a bit over-the-top since there are bound to be dozens of them and the game is not particularly taxing (plus, having the youngster continually yelling out that they spotted one can be nerve-wracking for the adults present in the car).

At an extremely young age, a child might not be able to do much in terms of differentiating anything that they see. Asking to look for a cow or an umbrella is beyond their existing comprehension, and so it is usually the case that you might resort to having the youngster find entire buildings or perhaps identify puffy clouds in the sky. Besides the child not being able to identify smaller and distinctive objects, they might also have a difficult time telling one object from another. Asking them to find a particular person in a crowd of pedestrians could exceed their mental acumen and the group of people seems just a blur of many rather than a collection of distinguishable individuals.

Why bring up this popular child's game?

Because it offers some keen insights into an aspect that continues to stymy the advent of AI-based true self-driving cars.

Specifically, one of the greatest challenges for a self-driving car is the AI being able to figure out the various objects surrounding the car and that is within the realm of the driving effort. You might think this is an easy thing to do since, as a human driver, you do this nearly effortlessly. While in the driver's seat, you are constantly scanning back-and-forth to spot the other nearby cars and those pesky pedestrians that might suddenly dart into the street.

You can pat yourself on the back for being quite cognitively astute that you can visually examine the scene, identify the objects that can be seen, and make a myriad of mental judgments about those objects.

Consider what happens as you drive down an everyday neighborhood suburban street.

You look down the street and can see that it is tree-lined and some houses front to the street. There are cars parked on the street and some cars parked in driveways. With a closer look, you can see that there are fire hydrants, telephone poles, light posts, street signs, and so on. If you were to add up all the objects that you can see, the number might surprise you. It is a tremendous cacophony of objects that are within just that one simple and calm street that you are driving on (imagine the torrent of objects when driving down a busy downtown city block).

A newbie driver such as a teenager that is learning to drive can be overwhelmed when undertaking the driving task. For them, the neighborhood street presents a veritable tsunami of objects that each need to be considered. Will that car in the driveway suddenly startup and back down into the street? Are those children playing in the front lawn of a house going to inadvertently dart into the roadway as they chase after a football?

A parent that is teaching their teenager to drive is likely focused on the higher probability concerns and can rapidly assess what is worthwhile for attention and what does not require attention. That pack of kids playing on the grass is far enough from the street that it is unlikely they would reach it in time to get into the path of the car. And those cars on the driveways do not have anyone in them and therefore the odds of any of those cars backing into the street are nearly nil.

That's what happens for seasoned drivers, while newbie drivers have not yet figured out how to optimally size up situations and ascertain what is a potential concern versus what can be given minimal priority.

Switch gears and consider the driving task for an AI driving system.

Via the sensors such as cameras, radar, LIDAR, ultrasound, and other specialized equipment, the AI is collecting data that represents the driving scene. That data has to be examined and interpreted, noting what objects are out there. In addition to identifying the objects, the driving question is whether any of those objects are a potential threat to the car and whether the car is a threat to any of those objects.

One important aspect to realize is that today's AI is not sentient, and it does not have any semblance of common-sense reasoning. In case you are shocked at this revelation, I urge you to take the media exaggerations about AI being superhuman or otherwise close to human cognitive capacities as malarkey and do not fall for the abundant puffery. Perhaps one day we'll have that kind of AI, but not now, and not in the near future.

So, the point is that the AI driving system is churning through numerous computations to try and ferret out the data coming into the sensors and then attempting to discern what the roadway consists of. This is all mathematically taking place and requires extensive computer processing to undertake.

That's why self-driving cars are typically chockful of sensors and lots of computer processors. The computer processing needed is extensive. In the earlier days of self-driving car experimentation, the trunks and oftentimes the backseats of the vehicle were completely occupied with computer processors. Nowadays, given the miniaturization of computers, the devices are generally smaller than they once were, and they thankfully provide faster processing speeds.

We've then established that there is a lot of computational effort needed to examine the sensory data and try to identify what objects exist in the surroundings, along with assessing the nature of those objects, such as whether they are moving or sitting still, whether they are coming toward the self-driving car or going away from it, and other vital particulars.

Here's the rub.

Besides the challenges of doing this kind of object recognition, there is also the time factor that raises its ugly and unrelenting head.

Time is crucial.

Suppose the self-driving car is proceeding down the street at a speed of 15 to 20 miles per hour. As a rule of thumb, a car moving at that speed has a stopping distance of approximately 40 feet or so (this is regardless of human-driven or being AI-driven, it's a physics thing). In that case, if an object enters onto the street and within the existing path of the self-driving car, and that object is less than approximately forty feet ahead, the AI can certainly try to do an emergency stop of the car, but ultimately is likely to hit that object nonetheless.

Meanwhile, realize that the vehicle is already in motion, meaning that it is moving forward at a rate of about 20 to 30 feet per second at the speed of around 15 to 20 miles per hour.

Let's add things up.

The AI receives data from its sensors and attempts to distill the data and assume for sake of discussion that this took the on-board computers around one to two seconds to accomplish. There is the time needed too for figuring out what action to take, so let's add one to two seconds for that computer processing time. The AI then has to invoke the car controls, such as slamming on the brakes, which might take let's pretend around one to two seconds to achieve.

All told, from the instant the sensory data was collected, we have around 3 to 6 seconds of computer processing time that occurred, before taking driving action per se. In that 3 to 6 seconds of processing time, the self-driving car would have proceeded forward at the 20 to 30 feet per second, thus, it has now gone an additional 60 to maybe 180 feet in distance. Add to that the stopping distance once the brakes are engaged, and the distance traveled is about 100 to perhaps 220 feet.

In short, it wasn't just the 40 feet of stopping distance that was involved, but also the fact that the self-driving car was in motion and moving forward during the computer processing time, ultimately leading to a distance of perhaps 100 to 200 feet involved in this scenario.

A child or dog that perchance ran into the street is the kind of "object" that we all certainly hope and expect an AI driving system to avoid hitting, and perhaps it is rather evident that the faster the computer can process the scene, the sooner a needed driving action can be undertaken.

It comes down to this: *Self-driving cars are faced with a very daunting problem, namely that there are in essence way too many objects and way too little time to calculate all the permutations and possibilities, along with then taking the appropriate driving action to ensure safe driving.*

Returning to the discussion about humans, I trust that this depiction of the effort required to drive a car might impress you about how adept humans are at handling the driving of a car.

It is almost a miracle, I assert, that there are about 200 million licensed drivers in the U.S. driving a reported 3.2 trillion miles annually, and yet there aren't even more car crashes than there are now (as emphasis, no car crashes are good, let's be clear about that, but the aspect that it takes a tremendous amount of mental effort to drive safely and avoid getting into car crashes makes what we all do as drivers an astounding feat, I submit).

Okay, the gist is that self-driving cars have a tough job.

This leads to the aspect of what can be done to deal with too many objects in too little time that is the bane of existence for self-driving cars.

Let's unpack the matter and see.

Self-Driving Cars And Time

For Level 4 and Level 5 true self-driving vehicles, there won't be a human driver involved in the driving task.

All occupants will be passengers.

The AI is doing the driving.

What can be done to cope with the too many objects, too little time conundrum?

One obvious factor is to go slower when driving.

A car that is moving at around 20 mph needs 40 feet or so to stop, while a car moving at 60 mph requires about 240 feet to come to a halt (these are all approximations, plus you need to factor the roadway conditions such as the surface of the road, whether it is slick from rain or ice, etc.).

The slower a car goes, the more time there is to make a choice about the driving action and to analyze the potential of hitting something or getting hit.

Most parents have their teenager drive in a parking lot when first learning to drive. This not only keeps the newbie driver away from the hectic antics of being immersed in traffic woes, but it also keeps the speeds low, such as perhaps 5 mph or so. That allows for more reaction time and thinking time.

There are self-driving cars that are being used in retirement communities, offering a ride-sharing service for those that live in the neighborhood and want to get from place to place. These self-driving cars are usually being capped at low speeds, which certainly befits being on such roadways. Also, some delivery oriented self-driving cars take groceries from the store to someone's house, staying on lower speed routes and not venturing onto freeways or highways.

The advantage of being in that kind of driving milieu is that the processing activity does not necessarily need to be as fast. The Operational Design Domain (ODD), a technical term referring to the scope of a self-driving car, entails driving at low speeds in those locales and thus eases somewhat the burden on the AI and the processors.

When you hear about a self-driving car that seems to be operating well while driving, you need to be aware and ask what kinds of speeds are involved. It is somewhat of a trick to have a self-driving car that can readily operate at low speeds since you do not know for sure that it can equally drive as well at higher speeds. That being said, please do not misinterpret this as suggesting that the self-driving cars at the lower speeds are somehow less significant. They deserve as much attention and accolades, but just bear in mind that it is not necessarily the case that they can instantly scale-up to operating at higher speeds (most do, but some do not).

Now that we've covered the notion of moving at slower speeds, it is a facet or restriction that does not especially obviate the issue of too many objects and too little time, plus there is the reality that cars-are-cars and people will expect self-driving cars to be able to go at the full range of everyday speeds.

Okay, consider what else can be done to handle too many objects, too little time difficulties. You can try to reduce the number of objects.

That sounds odd since the number of real-world objects is whatever number there are that happen to be surrounding the self-driving car. You cannot wish away those parked cars on the street or those kids playing on the front lawn. They exist. They are real.

From a processing perspective, you can try to reduce the number of objects, which perhaps humans do, though it is hard to know whether people do so in their minds or not. For example, the fact that there are houses all along the street might not be worthwhile considering per se, since they presumably have almost nothing to do with the objects that might come into the street. In a manner of speaking, you can ignore the houses. You can potentially ignore the trees that line the street. These are all objects that do not require much attention as they are not directly pertinent to the driving scene.

You can try to strip down the volume of objects being given any weight or attention. Fewer objects tend to mean less processing time needed.

Conclusion

Speaking of processing, you can speed-up the processors that are on-board the self-driving car by putting in place faster and faster hardware. The faster the processors, the more processing they can presumably do in any given segment of time.

You can improve the AI software in terms of how it ascertains the potential intersecting of objects and the self-driving car. Mathematically and computationally, the more efficient those algorithms are, the less processing they require, and the less time they tend to consume.

CHAPTER 28

HALLOWEEN ISSUES

AND

SELF-DRIVING CARS

Halloween!

Perhaps you remember as a child going door-to-door in your neighborhood and the excitement at approaching the porch of a house covered with cobwebs and ghosts. Do you dare make your way to the front door? What goblins and other frights might await you? And, upon bravely knocking on the imposing door, recall the absolute delight at being given a chocolate bar or your favorite bubble gum.

Off you would sprint, heading to the next house on the block.

Now, as an adult, hopefully, you either are the one dispensing those candies when impressible youngsters knock at your door, or maybe you will be going outdoors and walking along with your children as they experience the same thrills that you did in your youth.

Anyway, it is fun to relish memories and also look toward future Halloweens too.

Speaking of the future (notice that seamless segue), some readers have asked me to comment on Halloween and self-driving cars.

I realize that your first thought might be that there is no particular connection between Halloween, one of the most revered celebrations each year, and the advent of AI-based true self-driving cars, an amazing technological innovation that is gradually emerging. It might seem odd to consider that there would be any type of connection between these two seemingly disparate facets.

Surprise!

There is indisputably a means to connect the two, very much so.

Note: I hope that my written yelling of "surprise" at you did not startle you, though if you are reading this on Halloween, consider it the equivalent of being frighteningly startled with a spooky but festive boo.

Okay, so the question for today's discussion is this: *What kinds of impacts might the prevalence of AI-based true self-driving cars have upon Halloween and our festivities thereof?*

Great question and I'll get straight to it, but first, let's make sure we all concur on what is meant by referring to AI-based true self-driving cars.

Time to unpack that jargon.

Self-Driving Cars And Halloween

For Level 4 and Level 5 true self-driving vehicles, there won't be a human driver involved in the driving task.

All occupants will be passengers.

The AI is doing the driving.

Let's begin with the important and assuredly upbeat insight that by removing the need for a human driver, there will no longer be any drunk drivers or DUI drivers on our roadways (well, at least with respect to the self-driving cars, though keep in mind that conventional human-driven cars will likely also still be on the highways and byways too).

What does it mean that there won't potentially be intoxicated drivers during Halloween (or, at least a lot fewer ones)?

In short, you can generally cross off your list any of those ghastly car crashes that lead to injuries and fatalities due to those out-of-their-mind human drivers.

This is especially noteworthy on the evening of Halloween since there are zillions of young children at risk that night. Kids love to dart out into the street on Halloween while trick-or-treating. They aren't thinking about cars, they are thinking about the next house that has that inflated menacing ogre and beckons to them via the screeching sounds emanating from the blaring speakers placed in the bushes of the front yard.

Children on Halloween tend to falsely believe that the world has granted them a free pass to run and scamper all around the community.

Though that would be a nice ideal, the reality is that there are today those drivers that insist on driving on the evening of Halloween and getting mired into the realm of where kids think they can go. One has to sympathize with the drivers that are sober and have little choice to drive that evening, perhaps to take their children to a Halloween party or for other needed purposes. Unfortunately, the bad apple drivers can spoil the whole barrel, as it were.

Plus, even a cautious and fully aware driver is bound to find themselves unnerved that evening. You need to drive slowly, really slowly, and this is a hard thing for many drivers to do. They are accustomed to driving at normal speeds and when driving a reduced speed it seems as though their vehicular movement is glacial in nature. Add to this the potential pressure of needing to get to someone's house by a certain time, and you have an adult that can readily misjudge the roadways, leading to a calamity.

Bottom line: The more self-driving cars on the roads, the reduced chances of a human driver in that car that otherwise might have messed-up, one way or another, for whatever reason.

We can stick for the moment with the advantages and benefits side of the self-driving car versus human-driven car equation, and then, once I have covered most of those key points, we'll consider some of the downsides too.

Pretend that you are busy at your home while handing out candy and also hosting your own adult-oriented Halloween party. Turns out that your teenage son or daughter was invited to a Halloween activity at the school grounds, but that is several miles away. Teachers at the school will be watching over the teens and you feel comfortable that your offspring will be safe there on their own.

All you need to do is drive your eager youngster to the school.

Instead of you being the driver, you could use a self-driving car to get your child over there. You would of course first make sure your child gets safely into the self-driving car, perhaps one that you own or that was available via a ride-sharing network, and the AI driving system then proceeds to drive over to the school. Once the event is completed, the self-driving car gives your offspring a ride back to your home.

This frees you from having to make the drive. Also, if you didn't already own a car, or if you didn't have a driver's license, the use of the self-driving car solves several issues when desiring to provide your child with a lift to the Halloween event (and, once again, aids in preventing a potentially tipsy driver from getting behind the wheel).

Admittedly, some people repulsively recoil at the notion of having children riding in a self-driving car without any adult supervision. This will never-ever happen some parents exhort fervently. The idea is rather foreign to us currently and seems unimaginable, but we should be cautious in extending today's cultural norms for what we might accept in the future. For more about the tradeoffs involved in having children riding without adults in a self-driving car.

Let's continue our tour of the ways that self-driving cars will impact Halloween.

Some cities and suburbs have increasingly been setting up areas that allow for a drive-thru Halloween activity (especially due to the pandemic). You and the family pile into your car, and drive over to a park or parking lot that has a kind of haunted mansion or haunted city, as it were, created for providing a fun and spooky experience. Realize that you do not get out of your car. Instead, you remain in the vehicle, as though driving through a fast-food eatery, but in this case, it is an outdoor area set up with Halloween scenery.

If you were driving the car, it would likely be hard to fully relish the festive experience since you would be constantly having to watch where you are driving. Via a self-driving car, you would let the AI do the driving. This means that you and the rest of your family can all enjoy together the Halloween festivities, and nobody needs to be worrying about the driving.

Another somewhat new approach to Halloween that has been getting recent attention consists of *trunk-or-treating*.

Never heard of it?

Yes, it is a rarity but seems to be gaining momentum.

You put Halloween decorations on the trunk of your car. Inside the trunk, you put bags or buckets of candies. When ready, you drive around the community, coming to a stop here and there, allowing kids to obtain their Halloween treats directly from the trunk of the vehicle. As to whether you get out of the car to dispense the candies, this depends (some purposely do not get out of the car as an added pandemic precaution for themselves and the kids that come to the car to retrieve the candies).

Not everyone likes this trunk-or-treating phenomenon.

Some point out that with Halloween candies dispensed from a house, you know where to go if there is something untoward handed to a child. The house is permanently affixed. On the other hand, someone driving a car around could be just about anybody and they might not readily be traceable (for those of you that want to argue this point, it is true that you could copy down the license plate and trace the vehicle, but that's a far cry from the aspect that a house is pinned to one readily known spot).

Anyway, whether you like or hate the idea, it perhaps is apparent that a self-driving car could enable such an approach if desired.

Yet another possibility for Halloween celebrations is the veritable Halloween car parade.

People deck out their cars with Halloween banners and decorations. They put on costumes too if wishing to do so. You and your friends or family then get into the car and drive with other cars in a type of makeshift parade. This conga line of Halloween celebratory cars makes its way throughout the neighborhood. Horns are honked, people inside the cars are making noises befitting Halloween, and kids line the sidewalks, watching as the parade goes past their homes. As you might imagine, this is being spurred partially due to the pandemic, allowing people that already live together to be grouped into their car, and yet going outdoors to celebrate the evening.

One concern that some have about these Halloween parades is the possibility that some drivers will be drinking or have already had a few too many before deciding to join the car procession. Without seeming like a broken record that repeats itself unduly, if those cars were self-driving cars then the parade could meander unabated and without fear of a human driver doing something that could be injuriously unseemly.

Now For Some Scary Twists Too

Having covered the essence of the presumed upbeat or positive aspects of Halloween and self-driving cars, we now turn our gaze toward the less-so elements.

A perhaps obvious aspect about the advent of self-driving cars on Halloween is that it would allow adults to go to bars or parties and get smashed, if they wanted to do so, and not be held back by having to be a designated driver. Actually, this is true for any evening on any day of the week. You cannot fault the self-driving cars for this human behavior, but nonetheless could be a reaction by humans to the ease of having self-driving cars available.

Will self-driving cars spur people to drink or get drunk?

Nobody knows, and we won't likely know until the day arrives of a prevalence of self-driving cars on our roadways. For more about drinking and self-driving cars.

Another aspect is the difficulty of driving on the roadways during Halloween.

Yes, even self-driving cars are going to find this to be a challenging driving task.

Do not falsely assume that merely because the self-driving car is using AI and has a collection of state-of-the-art sensors such as video cameras, LIDAR, radar, ultrasonic, etc., that it will perfectly and unerringly ensure that nobody is every hit or hurt by a collision.

I've stated categorically and repeatedly that the notion of zero fatalities for self-driving cars has a zero chance of occurring. Physics belies such a belief. If a child darts unexpectedly from between two parked cars, and a self-driving car (or even a human-driven car) is cruising down the street, there might be insufficient time to stop the car before striking the suddenly appearing child. That's a fact of physics.

When I mention this point, those in the self-driving industry are apt to instantly object. Therefore, let me be clear, I am not suggesting that self-driving cars will be less safe than human drivers. In fact, the expectation is going to be that self-driving cars have to be safer than human drivers. Thus, in the aggregate, we are presumably going to have many fewer injuries and fewer fatalities once we have a preponderance of self-driving cars. My point is that realistically it won't go to zero. There will still be some non-zero number, though hopefully less than, a lot less, in comparison to the 40,000 annual car crash deaths in the U.S. annually and the approximately 2.5 million injuries.

Anyway, back to the point that on Halloween, especially so, the number of children and adults, perhaps even scampering dogs and cats, upon the roadways can be much higher than what normally is seen on the streets. This means many more objects that the AI needs to detect and discern as to which way the "object" is going and what it will do.

Challenges abound.

Children are small in stature and thus tend to be harder to detect. They might be wearing costumes that make their shape irregular in comparison to the expectations of what a person usually looks like. The kids can be erratic in where they go and whether they are sprinting or walking, or perhaps even crawling on the ground. All of the kids and adults might be quickly stepping off a curb or willing to run amongst the cars that are making their way down the street.

Amidst all of this, it is nighttime and dark out, so the lighting of the scene can be quite problematic. Indeed, children might be carrying flashlights or lasers that they point at the cars, of which the sensors could be hampered by such actions.

In the self-driving car field, there is a well-known dictum that entails dealing with edge problems, also known as corner cases. Essentially, those developing self-driving cars are prioritizing what needs to be accomplished, of which just safely having the AI drive from a house to a grocery store during daylight is a keystone task. Unusual driving scenarios are labeled as being an edge or corner case, meaning that they are oddball or unique situations and presumably can be dealt with at a later time. The rule-of-thumb is to get the core stuff done first, and then worry about the rest later on.

It is safe to say that Halloween is an edge or corner case. How many times a year do we all wander out into the streets, at nighttime, in costumes, with children aplenty? Unless you live in an especially party-vigorous locale, the answer would seem to be that it is a once a year occurrence.

Conclusion

There is no doubt that ultimately self-driving cars will be enhanced to better handle the particulars of a Halloween driving scenario.

CHAPTER 29
AI CHITCHAT
AND
SELF-DRIVING CARS

What usually happens today when you get into a ride-sharing car that you requested as a pick-up for your trip to a local store?

The odds are that an amiable driver will greet you, oftentimes warmly so, and then wait until you get settled and buckled in to then ask if you are ready to proceed on the driving journey. During the drive, some drivers will be relatively quiet and merely act like a silent chauffeur that is intently focused on the roadway and meticulously attuned to the driving task. Other drivers are chattier and will ask you about your day, or potentially tell you a mildly entertaining story about a prior passenger that was an oddball or an eccentric.

It could be that the driver is hoping to have you score them as a five (a topnotch score) on the rating system used by the ride-sharing network and thus will say or do things that are intended to boost your enthusiasm about the ride. The motivation could also be one of boredom or might simply be a driver that relishes interacting with people and ergo is eager to talk your ears off. In some instances, the driver misjudges and talks when a passenger desires silence, while in other cases the rider is hoping for engaging conversation and the driver is a dud in terms of making small talk.

Now that we've covered some of the contexts about what happens when you first get into a ride-sharing vehicle, let's add a bit of a twist to the topic.

What happens when you get into a *self-driving car* that you requested as a pick-up for your trip to a local store or another such itinerary?

Few people have ridden in a self-driving car and therefore I don't

255

expect that many readers would know what to expect and are unsure of the answer to that question. In today's column, we will take a close look at what might, or might not occur, when you get into an AI-based true self-driving car and proceed upon a driving journey.

There are a lot of varied experiences right now when riding in a self-driving car. Each of the companies making and fielding self-driving cars is tackling this matter in different ways and thus there is no singular standardized or across-the-board approach being utilized by all. It is therefore insightful and instructive to consider the various approaches to-date and also weigh the respective strengths and weaknesses involved.

On a related facet, the computer field refers to this generally as the User Experience or UX, entailing the design, coding, and fielding of how a computer system interacts with humans. Some of you might already be more familiar with the longstanding acronym UI (User Interface), which is the terminology that traditionally has dealt with human-computer interactions. The notion of referring to the UX is viewed by some as being wider in scope and can be interpreted as a superset that includes UI, or, depending upon your viewpoint, at a minimum intersects in substantive ways with the UI.

Dovetailing into today's column are some crucial points raised during an excellent session at *TechCrunch TC Sessions: Mobility 2020* on October 6, 2020, that included a presentation and Q&A undertaken by Ryan Powell, Head of UX Research & Design at Waymo.

Self-Driving Cars And The User Experience

For Level 4 and Level 5 true self-driving vehicles, there won't be a human driver involved in the driving task.

All occupants will be passengers.

The AI is doing the driving.

When self-driving cars were first being devised, the attention by those pioneering AI developers was principally toward the driving action and less so attentive to the ride experience per se. In a sense, the dominant view was that the rider is the rider, and they are simply being carried along for the ride. You could almost say that it was though the passenger was little more than cargo, or a sack of potatoes, possibly a slab of meat, meaning that they required no specific attention and ought to be happy to be going along for the astonishing novelty of a self-driving journey.

This admittedly allowed instead for a concentrated focus on the foundations of what a self-driving car is presumably supposed to do. The car has to have sensors that collect data about the roadway and the driving scene. Getting those sensors to work was quite a chore, particularly in the early days. The AI has to examine the collected data from the sensors and interpret what it signifies, doing so in a means that has become commonly known as Multi-Sensor Data Fusion (MSDF). A virtual world model within the AI has to be kept up-to-date and used to figure out where the car can and should be heading. And so on.

Worrying about what a passenger would experience was strictly along the more somber lines of trying to ensure that the self-driving car won't crash or collide with others on the roadway. Also, if possible, the driving by the AI should be relatively smooth and devoid of jerking motions or any kind of driving action that could cause whiplash or similar maladies.

The act of getting into the self-driving car was entirely up to the passenger, and likewise, the notion of getting settled and allowing the AI to proceed was considered perfunctory, often entailing that the user (rider) would press a button inside the vehicle or do so on their smartphone to signal that they were ready for the AI to start driving.

All of that entry and getting underway was typically done in stony silence.

A person opens the automobile door, gets inside, glances around, figures out how to signal that the ride should start, and then the self-driving car whisks along on the driving journey. Simple and straightforward.

But, this is not necessarily an approach that will accommodate a wide range of passengers in terms of communication preferences and modes of human behavior.

Keep in mind that the first crop of riders tended to be techies that were overjoyed to get into a self-driving car and gape in utter wonderment as the vehicle drove along. This type of technologically proficient rider would readily accept the purity of the silence and be inclined to contend that anything else would be annoying or superfluous.

Even more astounding was the general assumption by some of the self-driving tech makers that there would <u>never</u> be a need for any substantive interaction between the AI driving system and the passenger. This viewpoint was that the entire driving trip could and should readily be in silence and without any kind of interactivity. Some assumed that all you needed was the destination, which was usually gotten via the initial request made to use a self-driving car and having it come to pick you up, and therefore the rider didn't need to proffer any additional input or interaction along the way.

Of course, this is a rather narrow view of the world.

People frequently opt to change where they want to go while mid-journey or desire to have intermediate stops along the way to a destination. The retort to this kind of indication of the need for interaction was often met with the assertion that all of those facets could once again be handled by the use of a smartphone or via a display screen mounted inside the vehicle. A rider would be expected to type their driving desires into their smartphone or the mounted display, and the AI would then alter the course accordingly.

Though this might indeed work for some passengers, it is undoubtedly a rather limited perspective on what it means to be a rider inside a moving car. Sure, much of the time that you take a conventional taxi or use a traditional ride-sharing service, the odds are that you can avoid speaking and evade interacting directly with the human driver if you wish to do so, but that is generally not the way that riders prefer to experience day-to-day ordinary driving journeys.

Numerous other interactions often arise, beyond just discussions about driving waypoints or endpoints, encompassing aspects about the local area, concerns about the ride or the interior of the vehicle, and so on.

All told, not much emphasis initially went to the UX regarding the human passengers that would be riding in self-driving cars. The jargon sometimes used is that these were "barren UX" or "desolate UX" and failed to take into account the human factor. Ironically, perhaps, this was based on the presumption that the human passenger was essentially nothing more than some kind of robot or automata that obviate the need for any special care or attention throughout a driving journey.

A modern approach takes quite a contrasting perspective on the UX matter.

Here's why.

There has gradually been a realization that just because you can make a self-driving car does not mean that people will necessarily opt to ride in them. Beyond the novelty of riding in one, after you've done so a few times, the uniqueness wears off rather quickly and the user experience begins to come to the forefront.

In short, why would you choose to ride in a self-driving ride-sharing car versus taking a human-driven ride-sharing car?

Remove momentarily the rapt excitement about not seeing a driver in the seat and the curious telltale clue of the steering wheel turning this way and that way while you are seated inside a self-driving vehicle. That becomes humdrum for anyone that has been in self-driving cars for multiple trips.

I know it seems hard to imagine that the spectacle of a car driving by its own means would seem to be anything other than endlessly fascinating, but if you are using the self-driving car to get from home to the office, day after day, your awareness of the vehicle driving apparatus tends to dissipate. You start to become immune to the AI driving system efforts and more so attuned to what is going on at work and possibly preoccupied with daydreaming about family and friends, etc.

Also, if ultimately there are a multitude of brands of self-driving cars, prospective riders are going to begin to notice the key differences between them, especially in the UX aspects. In other words, assume that the spate of self-driving cars are all driving at about the same safety capacities (which, we don't know will be the case, but assume so for the sake of discussion herein).

Once you've taken safety off the table as a differentiator, what else is next in line?

Availability is paramount, such that if there is only a specific brand of a self-driving car that is being provided for use in your community, you don't have much choice in your selection options. On the other hand, assume that there are going to be several self-driving car networks operating in your area and thus you can choose which one to ride with, and under the notion that they all will be roughly equally available and equally priced.

In that case, now that safety is seen as equivalent among your choices, and availability and price are about the same amongst the choices, it would undoubtedly seem that your user experience would become notable and a significant determiner of your selection. You could even argue that the UX could potentially surmount some of those other top priority factors, such that you might be willing to pay a bit more for the ride if the user experience was demonstratively better than a lower-priced possibility.

Now that we are considering the UX, a human-driven car could surpass a self-driving car in terms of the user experience due to the interactivity with the human driver. Self-driving cars then are said to be competing in two major ways, namely amongst each other, and also competing against the rides that could be had via a human-driver.

The Customer Journey Is Vital

What then are the self-driving tech makers doing about the UX?

One important aspect involves understanding the customer journey as it relates to using a self-driving car.

As a side note, you could certainly make the case that knowing the customer journey for even a human-driving ride-sharing car is important too, though by-and-large this is not given as much focus since the assumption is that the human driver will take care of the UX facets. I dare say, that is a somewhat faulty assumption in that there are abundantly human drivers that do a rotten job of the user experience for passengers. For contemporary ride-sharing, this translates into low scores by riders, and then a ride-sharing network tends to cast aside those drivers. In short, rather than necessarily prodding human drivers to be better at serving up a robust user experience, the ride-sharing firms can just rely upon an outcomes-oriented Darwinian process. Those drivers that get high scores can remain as drivers in the network, while drivers that get lower scores are dumped. Inevitably, the assumption is that the network will principally contain just the higher scored drivers and therefore presumably have an underlying sufficient level of user experience.

Compare this type of business model to self-driving cars.

In theory, there isn't any variability among your "drivers" since the driving is being done by the AI system that was devised for your brand of self-driving cars. You aren't any longer going to weed out the bad drivers and nor reward or keep intact the good drivers within your fleet of ride-sharing cars. The driver is the driver, albeit whatever the AI has been developed to do, and based upon periodic updates and refinements that will be pushed out to the self-driving cars via the OTA (Over-the-Air) electronic updating capabilities.

The UX capability has to be directly incorporated into the AI driver (a one-and-done aspect).

Consider then the typical elements of a customer journey for the first stages of seeking to use a self-driving car:

- Approach the self-driving car

- Open the door to the self-driving car

- Get into the self-driving car

- Become settled inside the self-driving car

- Indicate readiness to commence the driving journey

First, realize that the self-driving car has the potential of leveraging several modes or mediums of communication with a rider. This is worthwhile to point out because some assume that the only means of communication with a human passenger would be via their smartphone or by the use of a display screen and perhaps a keyboard or buttons within the self-driving car.

Voice is a key aspect of interacting with human drivers, and the expectation by riders is that they ought to be able to do likewise with the AI. Voice interaction has become almost commonplace due to the advent of Alexa and Siri, thus, increasingly we all have become expectant that anything using advanced technology should also be able to speak to us.

One interesting question about self-driving cars is whether the AI should speak to you only once you are inside the self-driving car, or also speak with you while you are outside the vehicle.

In essence, as you approach the self-driving car, the AI could call out to you, perhaps saying your name (this might be a privacy concern), or possibly indicating something else about the vehicle (I am car number twenty-two). The advantage is that if you are unsure whether the self-driving car is there to pick you up since you might be at say a concert and there are lots of self-driving car milling around, you might then know which ones is for you.

Some believe that AI talking to those outside the vehicle could be construed as creepy and unnerving.

Also, some worry that this might go overboard, such that the ride-sharing services might have the AI be aggressive trying to troll for a rider, yelling out to those on the sidewalk that the person in the blue hat or wearing a green shirt ought to go for a ride, offering a special discount for those desirous of heading over to the grocery store or a destination paying for getting consumers to come to its location.

An open question is how to adapt Natural Language Processing (NLP) voice capabilities to be attuned to the context of conversational dialogue for car riding passengers.

Besides voice, the self-driving car can use music. As they say, nothing soothes the soul as much as music can, and therefore it might be clever to have a soft layer of music playing in the background as the AI drives the car (possibly calming the passenger, plus distracting the passenger from being overly watchful of how the driving is being undertaken).

Sounds can also be used to indicate key moments of the driving journey, such as when the vehicle gets underway, when it reaches the destination, and so on.

The self-driving car could also be outfitted with special equipment and automation to partake in aspects of the customer journey. For example, opening the door automatically for a rider, though even this has downsides since the door could be opened at the wrong moment or otherwise create added issues. Etc.

Conclusion

Pundits that take a dim view of the UX considerations are apt to argue that there is a slippery slope involved.

Those that prefer a slimmed-down and streamlined UX are prone to saying that we are heading toward the other end of the extremes, going from a scant UX to perhaps an exorbitant or overly extravagant UX.

Maybe the AI will become an annoying chitchat buddy, though, unlike a human that might be somewhat grating on your nerves, presumably you can sternly tell the AI to tone things down, doing so without worrying about hurting anyone's feelings.

It is said that beauty is in the eye of the beholder. There are facets of the UX for passengers of self-driving cars that are readily labeled as fundamental, along with capabilities that are differentiators, and though it is perhaps early on to be worrying about how to competitively make a self-driving car brand stand out from the others, the day will come, sooner rather than later.

CHAPTER 30

GAME OF GO

AND

SELF-DRIVING CARS

We already know and expect that humans will exhibit novelty or flashes of brilliance.

That's a given.

It might not happen all the time, and indeed could be considered a rarity, but nonetheless, the act itself is welcomed and not altogether unimaginable or otherworldly disturbing when it perchance occurs.

What about when Artificial Intelligence (AI) seems to display an act of novelty?

Any such instance is bound to get our attention.

Questions arise right away.

How did the AI come up with the apparent out-of-the-blue insight or novel indication? Was it a mistake or did it fit within the parameters of what the AI was expected to produce? There is also the immediate consideration of whether the AI somehow is slipping toward the precipice of becoming sentient.

Please be aware that there isn't any AI system as yet that is anywhere close to reaching sentience, despite the at times feverish pitch claims and falsehoods tossed around in the media. As such, if today's AI seems to do something that appears to be a novel act, you should not leap to the conclusion that this is a sign of human insight within technology or the emergence of human ingenuity among AI.

That's an anthropomorphic bridge too far.

The reality is that any such AI "insightful" novelties are based on various concrete computational algorithms and tangible data-based pattern matching.

In today's column, we'll be taking a close look at an example of an AI-powered novel act, illustrated via the game of Go, and relate these facets to the advent of AI-based true self-driving cars as a means of understanding the AI-versus-human related ramifications.

Realize that the capacity to spot or suggest a novelty is being done methodically by an AI system, while, in contrast, no one can say for sure how humans can devise novel thoughts or intuitions.

Perhaps we too are bound by some internal mechanistic-like facets, or maybe there is something else going on. Someday, hopefully, we will crack open the secret inner workings of the mind and finally know how we think. I suppose it might undercut the mystery and magical aura that oftentimes goes along with those of us that have moments of outside-the-box visions, though I'd trade that enigma to know how the cups-and-balls trickery truly functions (going behind the curtain, as it were).

Speaking of novelty, there is a famous game match involving the playing of Go that can provide useful illumination on this overall topic.

You might be vaguely aware that Go is a popular board game that is typically situated in the same complexity category as say chess. There are arguments to be made about which is tougher, chess or Go, but I'm not going to get mired into that morass. For sake of civil discussion, the key salient point is that Go is highly complex and requires intense mental concentration when especially played at the most topnotch of tournament levels.

Generally, Go consists of trying to capture territory on a standard Go board, consisting customarily of a 19 by 19 grid of intersecting lines. For those of you that have never tried playing Go, the closest similar kind of game might be the connect-the-dots that you played in childhood, which involves grabbing up territory, though Go is considered magnitudes more involved. If you are an avid Go player, do not get your dander up that a comparison was made to connect-the-dots, it was just a quick and simplistic means of denoting the territorial elements that are involved.

There is no need for you to know anything in particular about Go to get the gist of what will be discussed next regarding the act of human novelty and the act of AI novelty.

A famous Go competition took place about four years ago that pitted one of the world's top professional Go players, Lee Sedol, against an AI program that had been crafted to play Go, coined as AlphaGo. There is a riveting documentary about the contest and plenty of write-ups and online videos that have in detail covered the match, including post-game analyses.

Put yourself back in time to 2016 and relive what happened (even if you weren't aware of the match at that time).

Most AI developers did not anticipate that the AI of that time would be proficient enough to beat a top Go player. Sure, AI to play chess and already been able to best some top chess players, and thus offered a glimmer of expectation that Go would eventually be equally undertaken, but there weren't any Go programs that had heretofore been able to compete at the pinnacle levels of human Go players. The rule-of-thumb was that it would probably be around the year 2020 or so before the capabilities of AI would be sufficient to compete in world-class Go tournaments.

A small-sized tech company named DeepMind Technologies devised the AlphaGo AI playing system (the firm was later acquired by Google). Using techniques from Machine Learning and Deep Learning, the AlphaGo program was being revamped and adjusted right up to the actual tournament, a typical kind of last-ditch developer contortions that many of us have done when trying to get the last bit of added edge into something that is about to be demonstrated.

This was a monumental competition that had garnered global interest.

Human players of Go were doubtful that the AlphaGo program would win. Many AI techies were doubtful that AlphaGo would win. Even the AlphaGo developers were unsure of how well the program would do, including the stay-awake-at-night fears that the AlphaGo program would hit a bug or go into a kind of delusional mode and make outright mistakes and play foolishly.

A million dollars in prize money was put into the pot for the competition. There would be five Go games played, one per day, along with associated rules about taking breaks, etc. Some predicted that Sedol would handily win all five games, doing so without cracking a sweat. AI pundits were clinging to the hope that AlphaGo would at least one of the five games, and otherwise, present itself as a respectable level of Go player throughout the contest.

Spoiler alert, I am about to tell you what happened.

In the first match, AlphaGo won.

This was pretty much a worldwide shocker. Sedol was taken aback. Lots of Go players were surprised that a computer program could compete and beat someone at Sedol's level of play. Everyone began to give some street cred to the AlphaGo program and the efforts by the AI developers.

Tension grew for the next match.

For the second game, it was anticipated that Sedol might significantly change his approach to the contest. Perhaps he had been overconfident coming into the competition, some harshly asserted, and the loss of the first game would awaken him to the importance of putting all his concentration into the tournament. Or, possibly he had played as though he was competing with a lesser capable player and thus was not pulling out all the stops to try and win the match.

What happened in the second game?

Turns out that AlphaGo prevailed, again, and also did something that was seemingly remarkable for those that avidly play Go. On the 37th move of the match, the AlphaGo program opted to make placement onto the Go board in a spot that nobody especially anticipated. It was a surprise move, coming partway through a match that otherwise was relatively conventional in the nature of the moves being made by both parties (i.e., by Sedol and by AlphaGo).

At the time, in real-time, rampant speculation was that the move was an utter gaffe on the part of the AlphaGo program.

Instead, it became famous as a novel move, known memorably now as "Move 37" and heralded in Go and used colloquially overall to suggest any instance when AI perchance does something of a novel or unexpected manner.

We'll come back to this aspect in a moment.

In the third match, AlphaGo won again, now having successfully beaten Sedol in a 3-out-of-5 winner competition. They continued though to play a fourth and a fifth game.

During the fourth game, things were tight as usual and the match play was going head-to-head (well, head versus AI). Put yourself into the shoes of Sedol. In one sense, he wasn't just a Go player, he was somehow representing all of humanity (an unfair and misguided viewpoint, but pervasive anyway), and the pressure was on him to win at least one game. Just even one game would be something to hang your hat on, and bolster faith in mankind (again, a nonsensical way to look at it).

At the seventy-eighth move of the fourth game, Sedol made a so-called "wedge" play that was not conventional and surprised onlookers. The next move by AlphaGo was rotten and diminished the likelihood of a win by the AI system. After additional play, ultimately AlphaGo tossed in the towel and resigned from the match, thus Sedol finally had a win against the AI in his belt (he ended-up losing the fifth game, so AlphaGo won four games, Sedol won one). His move also became famous, generally known as "Move 78" in the lore of Go playing.

Something else that is worthwhile to know about involves the overarching strategy that AlphaGo was crafted to utilize.

When you play a game, let's say connect-the-dots (using this to readily indicate the essence of the matter), you can aim to grab as many squares at each moment of play, doing so under the belief that inevitably you will then win by the accumulation of those tactically oriented successes. Human players of Go are often apt to play that way, as it can be said too of chess players, and nearly any kind of game playing altogether.

Another approach involves playing to win even if only by the thinnest of margins, as long as you win. In that case, you might not be motivated at each tactical move to gain near-term territory or score immediate points and be willing instead to play a larger scope game per se. The proverbial mantra is that if you are shortsighted, you might win some of the battles, but could eventually lose the war. Therefore, it might be a better strategy to keep your eye on the prize, winning the war, albeit if it means that there are battles and skirmishes to be lost along the way.

The AI developers devised AlphaGo with that kind of macro-perspective underlying how the AI system functioned.

Humans can have an especially hard time choosing at the moment to make a move that might look bad or ill-advised, such as giving up territory, finding themselves to be unable to grit their teeth, and take a lump or two during play. The embarrassment at the instant is difficult to offset by betting that it is going to ultimately be okay and you will prevail in the end.

For an AI system, there is no semblance of that kind of sentiment involved and it is all about calculated odds and probabilities.

Now that we've covered the legendary Go match, let's consider some lessons learned about novelty.

The "Move 38" made by the AI system was not magical or mystical. It was an interesting move, for sure, and the AI developers later indicated that the move was one that the AI had calculated would rarely be undertaken by a human player.

This can be interpreted in two ways (at least).

One interpretation is that a human player would not make that move because humans are right and know that it would be a lousy move.

Another interpretation is that humans would not make that move due to a belief that the move is unwise, but this could be a result of the humans insufficiently assessing the ultimate value of the move, in the long-run, and getting caught up in a shorter timeframe semblance of play.

In this instance, it turned out to be a good move, said by many to be a brilliant move, and turned the course of the game to the advantage of the AI. Thus, what looked like brilliance was in fact a calculated move that few humans would have imagined as valuable and for which jostled humans to rethink how they think about such matters.

Some useful recap lessons:

- **Showcasing Human Self-Limited Insight.** When the AI does something seemingly novel, it might be viewed as novel simply because humans have already pre-determined what is customary and anything beyond that is blunted by the assumption that it is unworthy or mistaken. You could say that we are mentally trapped by our own drawing of the lines of what is considered as inside versus outside the box.

- **Humans Exploiting AI For Added Insight.** Humans can gainfully assess an AI-powered novelty to potentially re-calibrate human thinking on a given topic, enlarging our understanding via leveraging something that the AI, via its vast calculative capacity, might detect or spot that we have not yet so ascertained. Thus, besides admiring the novelty, we ought to seek to improve our mental prowess by whatever source shines brightly including an AI system.

- **AI Novelty Is A Dual-Edged Sword.** We need to be mindful of all AI systems and their possibility of acting in a novel way, which could be good or could be bad. In the Go game, it worked out well. In other circumstances, the AI exploiting the novelty route might go off the tracks, as it were.

Let's see how this can be made tangible via exploring the advent of AI-based true self-driving cars.

Self-Driving Cars And Acts Of Novelty

For Level 4 and Level 5 true self-driving vehicles, there won't be a human driver involved in the driving task.

All occupants will be passengers.

The AI is doing the driving.

You could say that the AI is playing a game, a driving game, requiring tactical decision making and strategic planning, akin to when playing Go or chess, though in this case involving life-or-death matters driving a multi-ton car on our public roadways.

Our base assumption is that the AI driving system is going to always take a tried-and-true approach to any driving decisions. This assumption is somewhat shaped around a notion that AI is a type of robot or automata that is bereft of any human biases or human foibles.

In reality, there is no axiomatic reason to make this kind of assumption. Yes, we can generally rule out the aspect that the AI is not going to display the emotion of a human ilk, and we also know that the AI will not be drunk or DUI in its driving efforts. Nonetheless, if the AI has been trained using Machine Learning (ML) and Deep Learning (DL), it can pick up subtleties of human behavioral patterns in the data about human driving, out of which it will likewise utilize or mimic in choosing its driving actions (for example, see my analysis of potential racial biases in the AI and the possibility of gender biases.

Turning back to the topic of novelty, let's ponder a specific use case.

A few years ago, I was driving on an open highway, going at the prevailing speed of around 65 miles per hour and something nearly unimaginable occurred. A car coming toward me in the opposing lane, and likely traveling at around 60 to 70 miles per hour, suddenly and unexpectedly veered into my lane. It was one of those moments that you cannot particularly anticipate.

There did not appear to be any reason for the other driver to be headed toward me, in my lane of traffic, and coming at me for an imminent and bone-chillingly terrifying head-on collision. If there had been debris on the other lane, it might have been a clue that perhaps this other driver was simply trying to swing around the obstruction. No debris. If there was a slower moving car, the driver might have wanted to do a fast end-around to get past it. Nope, there was absolutely no discernible basis for this radical and life-threatening maneuver.

What would you do?

Come on, hurry, the clock is ticking, and you have just a handful of split seconds to make a life-or-death driving decision.

You could stay in your lane and hope that the other driver realizes the err of their ways, opting to veer back into their lane at the last moment. Or, you could proactively go into the opposing lane, giving the other driver a clear path in your lane, but this could be a chancy game of chicken whereby the other driver chooses to go back into their lane (plus, there was other traffic further behind that driver, so going into the opposing lane was quite dicey).

Okay, so do you stay in your lane or veer away into the opposing lane?

I dare say that most people would be torn between those two options. Neither one is palatable.

Suppose the AI of a self-driving car was faced with the same circumstance.

What would the AI do?

The odds are that even if the AI had been fed with thousands upon thousands of miles of driving via a database about human driving while undergoing the ML/DL training, there might not be any instances of a head-to-head nature and thus no prior pattern to utilize for making this onerous decision.

Anyway, here's a twist.

Imagine that the AI calculated the probabilities involving which way to go, and in some computational manner came to the conclusion that the self-driving car should go into the ditch that was at the right of the roadway.

This was intended to avoid entirely a collision with the other car (the AI estimated that a head-on collision would be near-certain death for the occupants). The AI estimated that going into the ditch at such high speed would indisputably wreck the car and cause great bodily injury to the occupants, but the odds of assured death were (let's say) calculated as lower than the head-on option possibilities.

I'm betting that you would likely concede that most humans would be relatively unwilling to aim purposely to go into that ditch, which they know for sure is going to be a wreck and potential death, while instead willing (reluctantly) to take a hoped-for chance of either veering into the other lane or staying on course and wishing for the best.

In some sense, the AI might seem to have made a novel choice. It is one that (we'll assume) few humans would have given any explicit thought toward.

Returning to the earlier recap of the points about AI novelty, you could suggest that in this example, the AI has exceeded a human self-imposed limitation by the AI having considered otherwise "unthinkable" options. From this, perhaps we can learn to broaden our view for options that otherwise don't seem apparent.

The other recap element was that the AI novelty can be a dual-edged sword.

If the AI did react by driving into the ditch, and you were inside the self-driving car, and you got badly injured, would you later believe that the AI acted in a novel manner or that it acted mistakenly or adversely?

Some might say that if you lived to ask that question, apparently the AI made the right choice. The counter-argument is that if the AI had gone with one of the other choices, perhaps you would have sailed right past the other car and have not gotten a single scratch.

Conclusion

For those of you wondering what actually did happen, my lucky stars were looking over me that day, and I survived with nothing more than a close call. I decided to remain in my lane, though it was tempting to veer into the opposing lane, and by some miracle, the other driver suddenly went back into the opposing lane.

When I tell the story, my heart still gets pumping and I begin to sweat.

Overall, AI that appears to engage in novel approaches to problems can be advantageous and in some circumstances such as playing a board game can be right or wrong, for which being wrong does not especially put human lives at stake.

For AI-based true self-driving cars, lives are at stake.

We'll need to proceed mindfully and with our eyes wide open about how we want AI driving systems to operate, including calculating odds and deriving choices while at the wheel of the vehicle

APPENDIX

APPENDIX A
TEACHING WITH THIS MATERIAL

The material in this book can be readily used either as a supplemental to other content for a class, or it can also be used as a core set of textbook material for a specialized class. Classes where this material is most likely used include any classes at the college or university level that want to augment the class by offering thought provoking and educational essays about AI and self-driving cars.

In particular, here are some aspects for class use:

o Computer Science. Studying AI, autonomous vehicles, etc.

o Business. Exploring technology and it adoption for business.

o Sociology. Sociological views on the adoption and advancement of technology.

Specialized classes at the undergraduate and graduate level can also make use of this material.

For each chapter, consider whether you think the chapter provides material relevant to your course topic. There is plenty of opportunity to get the students thinking about the topic and force them to decide whether they agree or disagree with the points offered and positions taken. I would also encourage you to have the students do additional research beyond the chapter material presented (I provide next some suggested assignments they can do).

RESEARCH ASSIGNMENTS ON THESE TOPICS

Your students can find background material on these topics, doing so in various business and technical publications. I list below the top ranked AI related journals. For business publications, I would suggest the usual culprits such as the Harvard Business Review, Forbes, Fortune, WSJ, and the like.

Here are some suggestions of homework or projects that you could assign to students:

a) <u>Assignment for foundational AI research topic</u>: Research and prepare a paper and a presentation on a specific aspect of Deep AI, Machine Learning, ANN, etc. The paper should cite at least 3 reputable sources. Compare and contrast to what has been stated in this book.

b) <u>Assignment for the Self-Driving Car topic</u>: Research and prepare a paper and Self-Driving Cars. Cite at least 3 reputable sources and analyze the characterizations. Compare and contrast to what has been stated in this book.

c) <u>Assignment for a Business topic</u>: Research and prepare a paper and a presentation on businesses and advanced technology. What is hot, and what is not? Cite at least 3 reputable sources. Compare and contrast to the depictions in this book.

d) <u>Assignment to do a Startup:</u> Have the students prepare a paper about how they might startup a business in this realm. They must submit a sound Business Plan for the startup. They could also be asked to present their Business Plan and so should also have a presentation deck to coincide with it.

You can certainly adjust the aforementioned assignments to fit to your particular needs and the class structure. You'll notice that I ask for 3 reputable cited sources for the paper writing based assignments. I usually steer students toward "reputable" publications, since otherwise they will cite some oddball source that has no credentials other than that they happened to write something and post it onto the Internet. You can define "reputable" in whatever way you prefer, for example some faculty think Wikipedia is not reputable while others believe it is reputable and allow students to cite it.

The reason that I usually ask for at least 3 citations is that if the student only does one or two citations they usually settle on whatever they happened to find the fastest. By requiring three citations, it usually seems to force them to look around, explore, and end-up probably finding five or more, and then whittling it down to 3 that they will actually use.

I have not specified the length of their papers, and leave that to you to tell the students what you prefer. For each of those assignments, you could end-up with a short one to two pager, or you could do a dissertation length paper. Base the length on whatever best fits for your class, and the credit amount of the assignment within the context of the other grading metrics you'll be using for the class.

I mention in the assignments that they are to do a paper and prepare a presentation. I usually try to get students to present their work. This is a good practice for what they will do in the business world. Most of the time, they will be required to prepare an analysis and present it. If you don't have the class time or inclination to have the students present, then you can of course cut out the aspect of them putting together a presentation.

If you want to point students toward highly ranked journals in AI, here's a list of the top journals as reported by *various citation counts sources* (this list changes year to year):

- o Communications of the ACM
- o Artificial Intelligence
- o Cognitive Science
- o IEEE Transactions on Pattern Analysis and Machine Intelligence
- o Foundations and Trends in Machine Learning
- o Journal of Memory and Language
- o Cognitive Psychology
- o Neural Networks
- o IEEE Transactions on Neural Networks and Learning Systems
- o IEEE Intelligent Systems
- o Knowledge-based Systems

GUIDE TO USING THE CHAPTERS

For each of the chapters, I provide next some various ways to use the chapter material. You can assign the tasks as individual homework assignments, or the tasks can be used with team projects for the class. You can easily layout a series of assignments, such as indicating that the students are to do item "a" below for say Chapter 1, then "b" for the next chapter of the book, and so on.

a) What is the main point of the chapter and describe in your own words the significance of the topic,

b) Identify at least two aspects in the chapter that you agree with, and support your concurrence by providing at least one other outside researched item as support; make sure to explain your basis for disagreeing with the aspects,

c) Identify at least two aspects in the chapter that you disagree with, and support your disagreement by providing at least one other outside researched item as support; make sure to explain your basis for disagreeing with the aspects,

d) Find an aspect that was not covered in the chapter, doing so by conducting outside research, and then explain how that aspect ties into the chapter and what significance it brings to the topic,

e) Interview a specialist in industry about the topic of the chapter, collect from them their thoughts and opinions, and readdress the chapter by citing your source and how they compared and contrasted to the material,

f) Interview a relevant academic professor or researcher in a college or university about the topic of the chapter, collect from them their thoughts and opinions, and readdress the chapter by citing your source and how they compared and contrasted to the material,

g) Try to update a chapter by finding out the latest on the topic, and ascertain whether the issue or topic has now been solved or whether it is still being addressed, explain what you come up with.

The above are all ways in which you can get the students of your class involved in considering the material of a given chapter. You could mix things up by having one of those above assignments per each week, covering the chapters over the course of the semester or quarter.

As a reminder, here are the chapters of the book and you can select whichever chapters you find most valued for your particular class:

Chapter Title
1 Eliot Framework for AI Self-Driving Cars
2 Congestion-Free Pipedream of Self-Driving Cars
3 Demolition Derby of Self-Driving Cars
4 AI Intelligence Explosion and Self-Driving Cars
5 AI Truthteller and Self-Driving Cars
6 Drive-In Theatres and Self-Driving Cars
7 AI Mind-Copying and Self-Driving Cars
8 Mental Wayfinding and Self-Driving Cars
9 Automated Machine Learning and Self-Driving Cars
10 Fast AI Ethics and Self-Driving Cars
11 I Think Therefore I Am and Self-Driving Cars
12 AI Politeness and Self-Driving Cars
13 Income by Sharing Self-Driving Cars
14 Mand on Hood and Self-Driving Cars
15 Puddles and Self-Driving Cars
16 Unhinged and Self-Driving Cars
17 Reversibility and Self-Driving Cars
18 Driving Nude and Self-Driving Cars
19 Towing of Self-Driving Cars
20 Consumer Reports and Full Self-Driving
21 Tire Blowouts and Self-Driving Cars
22 Wildfire Smoke and Self-Driving Cars
23 Crabwalk Mode and Self-Driving Cars
24 Dangerous Month and Self-Driving Cars
25 AI Apologies and Self-Driving Cars
26 Hawaii Testing and Self-Driving Cars
27 Too Many Objects and Self-Driving Cars
28 Halloween Issues and Self-Driving Cars
29 AI Chitchat and Self-Driving Cars
30 Game of Go and Self-Driving Cars

This title is available via Amazon and other book sellers

Companion Book By This Author
Self-Driving Cars:
"The Mother of All AI Projects"
by Dr. Lance B. Eliot, MBA, PhD

This title is available via Amazon and other book seller

Companion Book By This Author

Innovation and Thought Leadership on Self-Driving Driverless Cars

by Dr. Lance B. Eliot, MBA, PhD

This title is available via Amazon and other book sellers

This title is available via Amazon and other book sellers

Companion Book By This Author

Introduction to Driverless Self-Driving Cars

by Dr. Lance B. Eliot, MBA, PhD

Chapter Title

This title is available via Amazon and other book sellers

Companion Book By This Author

***Autonomous Vehicle Driverless
Self-Driving Cars and Artificial Intelligence***

by Dr. Lance B. Eliot, MBA, PhD

This title is available via Amazon and other book sellers

Transformative Artificial Intelligence Driverless Self-Driving Cars

by Dr. Lance B. Eliot, MBA, PhD

This title is available via Amazon and other book sellers

Companion Book By This Author

Disruptive Artificial Intelligence and Driverless Self-Driving Cars

by Dr. Lance B. Eliot, MBA, PhD

<u>Chapter Title</u>

This title is available via Amazon and other book sellers

Companion Book By This Author

State-of-the-Art
AI Driverless Self-Driving Cars

by Dr. Lance B. Eliot, MBA, PhD

This title is available via Amazon and other book sellers

Companion Book By This Author

Top Trends in
AI Self-Driving Cars

by Dr. Lance B. Eliot, MBA, PhD

Chapter Title

This title is available via Amazon and other book sellers

<u>Companion Book By This Author</u>

AI Innovations and Self-Driving Cars

by Dr. Lance B. Eliot, MBA, PhD

This title is available via Amazon and other book sellers

Companion Book By This Author

Crucial Advances for AI Self-Driving Cars

by Dr. Lance B. Eliot, MBA, PhD

Chapter Title

This title is available via Amazon and other book sellers

Companion Book By This Author

Sociotechnical Insights and AI Driverless Cars

by Dr. Lance B. Eliot, MBA, PhD

Chapter Title

This title is available via Amazon and other book sellers

Companion Book By This Author

Pioneering Advances for AI Driverless Cars

by Dr. Lance B. Eliot, MBA, PhD

This title is available via Amazon and other book sellers

Companion Book By This Author

Leading Edge Trends for AI Driverless Cars

by Dr. Lance B. Eliot, MBA, PhD

This title is available via Amazon and other book sellers

Companion Book By This Author

The Cutting Edge of AI Autonomous Cars

by Dr. Lance B. Eliot, MBA, PhD

Chapter Title

This title is available via Amazon and other book sellers

Companion Book By This Author

The Next Wave of
AI Self-Driving Cars

by Dr. Lance B. Eliot, MBA, PhD

Chapter Title

This title is available via Amazon and other book sellers

Companion Book By This Author

Revolutionary Innovations of AI Self-Driving Cars

by Dr. Lance B. Eliot, MBA, PhD

Chapter Title

1 Eliot Framework for AI Self-Driving Cars

2 Exascale Supercomputer and AI Self-Driving Cars

3 Superhuman AI and AI Self-Driving Cars

4 Olfactory e-Nose Sensors and AI Self-Driving Cars

5 Perpetual Computing and AI Self-Driving Cars

6 Byzantine Generals Problem and AI Self-Driving Cars

7 Driver Traffic Guardians and AI Self-Driving Cars

8 Anti-Gridlock Laws and AI Self-Driving Cars

9 Arguing Machines and AI Self-Driving Cars

This title is available via Amazon and other book sellers

AI Self-Driving Cars
Breakthroughs

by Dr. Lance B. Eliot, MBA, PhD

This title is available via Amazon and other book sellers

<u>Companion Book By This Author</u>

Trailblazing Trends for
AI Self-Driving Cars

by Dr. Lance B. Eliot, MBA, PhD

<u>Chapter Title</u>

This title is available via Amazon and other book sellers

This title is available via Amazon and other book sellers

Companion Book By This Author

AI Self-Driving Cars
Inventiveness

by Dr. Lance B. Eliot, MBA, PhD

This title is available via Amazon and other book sellers

Companion Book By This Author

Visionary Secrets of AI Driverless Cars

by Dr. Lance B. Eliot, MBA, PhD

Chapter Title

This title is available via Amazon and other book sellers

Companion Book By This Author

Spearheading AI Self-Driving Cars

by Dr. Lance B. Eliot, MBA, PhD

Chapter Title

This title is available via Amazon and other book sellers

Spurring
AI Self-Driving Cars

by Dr. Lance B. Eliot, MBA, PhD

Chapter Title

This title is available via Amazon and other book sellers

Companion Book By This Author

Avant-Garde
AI Driverless Cars

by Dr. Lance B. Eliot, MBA, PhD

Chapter Title

This title is available via Amazon and other book sellers

Companion Book By This Author

AI Self-Driving Cars Evolvement

by Dr. Lance B. Eliot, MBA, PhD

This title is available via Amazon and other book sellers

<u>Companion Book By This Author</u>

Boosting
AI Autonomous Cars

by Dr. Lance B. Eliot, MBA, PhD

This title is available via Amazon and other book sellers

Companion Book By This Author

AI Self-Driving Cars
Trendsetting

by Dr. Lance B. Eliot, MBA, PhD

This title is available via Amazon and other book sellers

Companion Book By This Author

AI Autonomous Cars
Forefront

by Dr. Lance B. Eliot, MBA, PhD

This title is available via Amazon and other book sellers

Companion Book By This Author

AI Autonomous Cars Emergence

by Dr. Lance B. Eliot, MBA, PhD

This title is available via Amazon and other book sellers

Companion Book By This Author

AI Autonomous Cars
Progress

by Dr. Lance B. Eliot, MBA, PhD

This title is available via Amazon and other book sellers

Companion Book By This Author

AI Self-Driving Cars Prognosis

by Dr. Lance B. Eliot, MBA, PhD

This title is available via Amazon and other book sellers

Companion Book By This Author

AI Self-Driving Cars
Momentum

by Dr. Lance B. Eliot, MBA, PhD

This title is available via Amazon and other book sellers

Companion Book By This Author

AI Self-Driving Cars
Headway

by Dr. Lance B. Eliot, MBA, PhD

This title is available via Amazon and other book sellers

<u>Companion Book By This Author</u>

AI Self-Driving Cars
Vicissitude

by Dr. Lance B. Eliot, MBA, PhD

<u>Chapter Title</u>

This title is available via Amazon and other book sellers

Companion Book By This Author

AI Self-Driving Cars
Autonomy

by Dr. Lance B. Eliot, MBA, PhD

This title is available via Amazon and other book sellers

Companion Book By This Author

AI Driverless Cars Transmutation

by Dr. Lance B. Eliot, MBA, PhD

This title is available via Amazon and other book sellers

Companion Book By This Author

AI Driverless Cars
Potentiality

by Dr. Lance B. Eliot, MBA, PhD

This title is available via Amazon and other book sellers

Companion Book By This Author

AI Driverless Cars
Realities
by Dr. Lance B. Eliot, MBA, PhD

Chapter Title

This title is available via Amazon and other book sellers

Companion Book By This Author

AI Self-Driving Cars
Materiality

by Dr. Lance B. Eliot, MBA, PhD

This title is available via Amazon and other book sellers

Companion Book By This Author

AI Self-Driving Cars
Accordance

by Dr. Lance B. Eliot, MBA, PhD

This title is available via Amazon and other book sellers

Companion Book By This Author

AI Self-Driving Cars
Equanimity

by Dr. Lance B. Eliot, MBA, PhD

This title is available via Amazon and other book sellers

Companion Book By This Author

AI Self-Driving Cars
Divulgement

by Dr. Lance B. Eliot, MBA, PhD

Chapter Title

This title is available via Amazon and other book sellers

AI Self-Driving Cars
Consonance

by Dr. Lance B. Eliot, MBA, PhD

This title is available via Amazon and other book sellers

Companion Book By This Author

Revelatory AI Self-Driving Cars

by Dr. Lance B. Eliot, MBA, PhD

Chapter Title
1 Eliot Framework for AI Self-Driving Cars
2 Congestion-Free Pipedream of Self-Driving Cars
3 Demolition Derby of Self-Driving Cars
4 AI Intelligence Explosion and Self-Driving Cars
5 AI Truthteller and Self-Driving Cars
6 Drive-In Theatres and Self-Driving Cars
7 AI Mind-Copying and Self-Driving Cars
8 Mental Wayfinding and Self-Driving Cars
9 Automated Machine Learning and Self-Driving Cars
10 Fast AI Ethics and Self-Driving Cars
11 I Think Therefore I Am and Self-Driving Cars
12 AI Politeness and Self-Driving Cars
13 Income by Sharing Self-Driving Cars
14 Mand on Hood and Self-Driving Cars
15 Puddles and Self-Driving Cars
16 Unhinged and Self-Driving Cars
17 Reversibility and Self-Driving Cars
18 Driving Nude and Self-Driving Cars
19 Towing of Self-Driving Cars
20 Consumer Reports and Full Self-Driving
21 Tire Blowouts and Self-Driving Cars
22 Wildfire Smoke and Self-Driving Cars
23 Crabwalk Mode and Self-Driving Cars
24 Dangerous Month and Self-Driving Cars
25 AI Apologies and Self-Driving Cars
26 Hawaii Testing and Self-Driving Cars
27 Too Many Objects and Self-Driving Cars
28 Halloween Issues and Self-Driving Cars
29 AI Chitchat and Self-Driving Cars
30 Game of Go and Self-Driving Cars

This title is available via Amazon and other book sellers

ABOUT THE AUTHOR

Dr. Lance B. Eliot, Ph.D., MBA is a globally recognized AI expert and thought leader, an experienced executive and leader, a successful serial entrepreneur, and a noted scholar on AI, including that his Forbes and AI Trends columns have amassed over 2.8+ million views, his books on AI are frequently ranked in the Top 10 of all-time AI books, his journal articles are widely cited, and he has developed and fielded dozens of AI systems.

He currently serves as the CEO of Techbruim, Inc. and has over twenty years of industry experience including serving as a corporate officer in billion-dollar sized firms and was a partner in a major consulting firm. He is also a successful entrepreneur having founded, ran, and sold several high-tech related businesses.

Dr. Eliot previously hosted the popular radio show *Technotrends* that was also available on American Airlines flights via their in-flight audio program, he has made appearances on CNN, has been a frequent speaker at industry conferences, and his podcasts have been downloaded over 100,000 times.

A former professor at the University of Southern California (USC), he founded and led an innovative research lab on Artificial Intelligence. He also previously served on the faculty of the University of California Los Angeles (UCLA) and was a visiting professor at other major universities. He was elected to the International Board of the Society for Information Management (SIM), a prestigious association of over 3,000 high-tech executives worldwide.

He has performed extensive community service, including serving as Senior Science Adviser to the Congressional Vice-Chair of the Congressional Committee on Science & Technology. He has served on the Board of the OC Science & Engineering Fair (OCSEF), where he is also has been a Grand Sweepstakes judge, and likewise served as a judge for the Intel International SEF (ISEF). He served as the Vice-Chair of the Association for Computing Machinery (ACM) Chapter, a prestigious association of computer scientists. Dr. Eliot has been a shark tank judge for the USC Mark Stevens Center for Innovation on start-up pitch competitions and served as a mentor for several incubators and accelerators in Silicon Valley and in Silicon Beach.

Dr. Eliot holds a Ph.D. from USC, MBA, and Bachelor's in Computer Science, and earned the CDP, CCP, CSP, CDE, and CISA certifications.

ADDENDUM

Revelatory
AI Self-Driving Cars

Practical Advances in Artificial Intelligence (AI)
and Machine Learning

By
Dr. Lance B. Eliot, MBA, PhD

———

For supplemental materials of this book, visit:
www.ai-selfdriving-cars.guru

For special orders of this book, contact:
LBE Press Publishing
Email: LBE.Press.Publishing@gmail.com

www.ingramcontent.com/pod-product-compliance
Lightning Source LLC
Chambersburg PA
CBHW071103050326
40690CB00008B/1092